D1570885

People and Predicaments

People and Predicaments

Milton Mazer

Harvard University Press
Cambridge, Massachusetts, and
London, England   1976

Library of Congress Cataloging in Publication Data

Mazer, Milton
  People and Predicaments.
  Bibliography: p.
  Includes index.
  1. Social psychiatry—Massachusetts—Martha's
Vineyard. 2. Community mental health services—
Massachusetts—Martha's Vineyard. 3. Martha's
Vineyard, Mass. I. Title. [DNLM: 1. Community
mental health services—Massachusetts. WM30 M474p]
RC455.M35   362.2'2'0974494   75-45364
ISBN 0-674-66075-7

For Virginia

ON THE PEOPLE OF MARTHA'S VINEYARD

All was peace here, and a general decency prevailed
throughout . . . here I found without gloom, a decorum
and reserve, so natural to them, that I thought myself in
Philadelphia . . . Wherever I went, I found a simplicity of
diction and manners, rather more primitive and rigid
than I expected; and I soon perceived that it proceeded
from their secluded situation . . . everyone in the town
follows some particular occupation with great diligence
but without the servility of labour which I am informed
prevails in Europe.
                    J. Hector St. John deCrèvecoeur, 1782

The islanders are quick in their sensibilities, easily excited and easily depressed . . . With this the climate has
much to do, operating as it does, powerfully upon the
nervous system. Other causes . . . are the free use of
strong tea and coffee . . . the nature of sea life, which
carries the men far away from their homes and exposes
them to great hazards, thus depriving their families of
their counsel and encouragement and keeping these in a
continual state of anxiety—their out-of-the-way-of-the-
world situation . . . and hence they are more liable to
turns of excitement and depression than the dwellers
upon the continent.
                         Samuel Adams Devens, 1838

Preface

It has been nearly twenty years since I came for the first time with my wife and two young children to vacation on Martha's Vineyard. We rented a small house in a small village in the geographic heart of the island, a village with a church, a two-room schoolhouse, a library, an agricultural hall, a general store and post office, a mill pond, and three hundred and fifty people. For the next five summers we returned to the same place, eventually building our own salt-box house in a field back of the school. What drew us was a sense of community which we felt was rapidly disappearing from American life. We wanted to be a part of it and contribute to it. So, when a group of local physicians and clergymen came to me with a proposal that I move to the island and start a psychiatric service for its six thousand inhabitants, I decided to leave my psychoanalytic practice in New York and venture into the newly emerging field of community psychiatry.

This book is based on my clinical work on the island, the findings of the formal research studies, and what I have learned about the nature of community from my fellow islanders. It owes much to the subtle intimations that came to me day by day as I became more and more a part of the community, joining in its everydayness, sharing its joys and sorrows, knowing of each birth, each death, reacting to its tensions and changes, and participating in its social and political life. For in addition to my job as director of the Martha's Vineyard Mental Health Center I have for nine years been moderator of the

West Tisbury town meetings. I have come to believe that the second
job is of equal importance to and complements the first.

The observations described in this book were made while I functioned in a number of roles, as clinical psychiatrist, researcher,
citizen, and others. The claims of confidentiality require that what I
learned from my fellow islanders as a physician remain inviolate,
and this I have scrupulously adhered to. The brief descriptions of
the lives of islanders with which the book begins and those that
follow in the text do not, therefore, describe actual islanders, and it
would be an error to attach identities to them.

Contrary to standard practice, I have used the actual name of the
community whose life is described. I have done so to guard against
the illusion that the place could remain anonymous and thus to help
me keep in mind the sensibilities of my fellow islanders and the
inexorable claims of my profession.

In attempting to be clear, I have tried to avoid the use of technical
terms wherever possible. I have also adhered to the generic usage
in referring to human beings. The word *he* may refer to persons of
either sex, and the word *human* to all members of *Homo sapiens.*

An effort of as long duration as this bears a great indebtedness to
many people. My chief debt is to the people of Martha's Vineyard,
who in a period briefer than I anticipated admitted me into their
community and shared their knowledge of island life with me. To
Robert W. Nevin, native island physician, I owe much for his guidance in my adaptation to a community unlike any I had known.

For their help in acquiring the data on which the epidemiological
studies were based, I am especially indebted to the island's town
clerks, the clerks of its district and probate courts, the past judges
of those courts, to officials and teachers of its school system, and to
its public welfare workers. I am grateful to the five general practitioners who let me intrude into their busy schedules for three
general practice studies, the late Joseph Frisch, Russell S. Hoxsie,
Donald R. Mills, Robert W. Nevin, and David Rappaport.

Nancy H. Whiting, who participated in the project from the outset
and was the study's epidemiological research worker, made notable
contributions to many aspects of the work. Margaret Drolette and
Carol Leonard helped in designing the data-recording and retrieval

procedures. Edward E. Handy made available his own skills as well as the data-processing facilities of the National Marine Fisheries Service at Woods Hole, Massachusetts, and Paul Breer performed the statistical analyses for the data on which Chapter 12 is based. Jo-Ann Ewing gave her skillful care to the manuscript through its various renderings. Her patience far outstripped my own, and without her help these pages would not have become a book.

I was fortunate in having from the outset the encouragement of the late Erich Lindemann. Alexander H. Leighton, whose Stirling County studies clearly influenced the point of view taken here, read a substantial part of the manuscript and made a number of helpful comments. William K. Bruff, Robert M. Eisendrath, and Robert W. Nevin also gave me the benefit of critical readings of parts of the manuscript.

The epidemiological studies reported in a number of published papers and reviewed here were supported by contract PH 43-64-493 and research grants MH 01860, MH 14900, and MH 21811 from the National Institute of Mental Health. That organization and my co-workers in the clinic made it possible for me to be relieved of my clinical duties for the time necessary to make a start on writing this book. I am also indebted to the publishers of the *Archives of General Psychiatry* 27:270-273 (American Medical Association, copyright 1972), *Community Mental Health Journal* 5:320-330 (Behavioral Publications, copyright 1969), *Medical Care* 7:372-378 (Lippincott, copyright 1969), and *Social Psychiatry* 9:85-90 (Springer Verlag, copyright 1974) for permission to use material first published in those journals. A substantial portion of Chapter 19 first appeared in *The Practice of Community Mental Health*, edited by Henry Grunebaum (Little, Brown and Co., copyright 1970).

Finally, I owe much to the representatives of the community, to the past and present directors of Martha's Vineyard Community Services, Inc., to the staffs of its agencies, and to its president, Marian Angell McAlpin, for their responsiveness to what was for all of us a new and uncertain departure in the development of a network of human services.

Contents

xii
CONTENTS

TABLES

FIGURES

1

The People

1

People in Predicament

The place is an island off the coast of Massachusetts. The people are the more than 7,800 men, women, and children who make their homes there. The problems and predicaments they experience are similar to those of other Americans in the 60s and 70s of this century. But since they live in a unique setting, a rural island in the midst of megalopolis, the stresses to which they are exposed and the predicaments they experience have their own character.

Here are five episodes in the lives of islanders. The people described do not exist: they are not known, they have not been interviewed, there are no clinical studies of them. But the predicaments illustrated are real and recur in the lives of islanders. In this sense only, the accounts that follow are true.

Samuel Arey

On a clear evening in February, after five days of a northeaster, but with winds yet up to ten to fifteen miles per hour, Samuel Arey of Edgartown and his wife began one of their frequent arguments. Edna Arey, far more skilled in verbal encounter than was her husband, began to get the better of it, so Samuel stopped yelling and began to break the legs off each of the kitchen chairs. When he turned to attack the table legs, the first one resisted him, so he swung around and punched his fist through the glass of the kitchen door. A neighbor called by Edna took him to the hospital where his family doctor met him, as he had on three or four similar occasions.

Forty minutes later, his lacerations neatly sutured, Samuel was on his way home, ashamed of his violence but unable to recall its cause.

Sophia Barden

While Samuel Arey was being driven home, Sophia Barden of Chilmark had just gotten the last of her children to bed. Insufferably lonely, her husband having left her for a woman in Vineyard Haven just six months before, she decided to drive down the lighthouse road. Bathed in despair, she felt the car slip off the road and scratch its way through the tall underbrush of vines and bush until brought to a stop by a tree. She was dazed, but recovered before John Cargon, a police officer and her first cousin, checking a reported break-in at a summer house nearby, arrived. She told him she had swerved to avoid a deer crossing the road ahead of her, though this was hardly terrain for deer. The officer shook his head, unbelieving, backed her car out into the road, and followed her until she had safely entered her driveway. He remembered that this was the third single car accident she had had within the year.

John Castaldo

He had come home later than usual, and Brenda Castaldo knew that he had stopped for a drink or two at the Belleview Cafe. Refusing his dinner, he spent the evening before the television set methodically drinking can after can of beer, the sound set to a deafening volume, oblivious of his children trying to do their homework at the nearby kitchen table. When all were up in bed, John staggered to the rear door, opened it, urinated, then moved to the stove, where he made himself a hamburger. He soon fell heavily to the couch and was asleep in minutes, still there the next morning as his children prepared to get off to school. They hardly noticed; the pattern had become part of their lives.

Daniel Benedict

The next morning dawned bright and clear, the wind having

stilled. Daniel Benedict of Oak Bluffs, thirty-two years of age, of an old Vineyard family, and married to an energetic girl of Portuguese ancestry, waited for her to leave for work so that he might make his breakfast alone, free of the ever-present concern at what she might put into it. He was convinced that his impotence was of his wife's doing. He believed that she put saltpeter into his food to make him less of a man so that she could go to her lover during the day while saying she was at work. As soon as she had left, he got his own salt cellar from a hiding place and had his breakfast. At 10 o'clock he washed his sheets and underwear by hand, though a clothes washer sat in the laundry room, and made up his narrow bed in the basement. This had been his routine for the past six years, during which time he had never once left his home.

Tommy Starbuck

It was his twelfth birthday that day and the 22 rifle he had been promised was not among his presents. Only some clothes and a pair of sneakers that he would have gotten anyway. Unlucky to be born in February, the worst month of the year for jobs. He quickly left the house after supper and headed for North Water Street, avoiding Main Street and the police cruiser. At North Water and Village Streets, he stopped at the biggest house in town, the Starbuck house, now owned by summer people named Dearing. The street lights illuminated the front room, the furniture covered with ghostly sheets. He could see the gun case in the corner and tried to count the guns in it. Leaning against the case were Timmy Dearing's water skis. He remembered the summer's day he had carried ten five-gallon cans of gas to the dock to fill the Dearing power boat and watched as Tim and his father chugged away for Cape Pogue. Startled by a raccoon getting into a garbage can, he ran around the corner, tripping over a pile of bricks left by a mason for the next morning's work. Not knowing why, he began to throw the bricks at the windows of the Dearing house, hitting one after another of the panes. By the time the police cruiser arrived, he had broken some of the handmade lights in seventeen of the twenty-four windows on the south side of the house. Leaning against Jim Buckley in the police cruiser, he cried all the way home.

These are all people in predicament, expressing in one way or another psychological distress. Yet in the ordinary course of events, they are quite unlikely to reach a source of effective help. Samuel Arey's family physician suspected the cause of the extensive laceration of Samuel's hand, but he had learned that an inquiry would be met with evasion. The police officer who appeared at Sophia Barden's accident knew that her husband had left her, vaguely perceived that she was lonely, and knew, too, of her two previous accidents. He had more than a suspicion that her life situation was related to the three accidents, but he was late for his own dinner and feared that a suggestion that she see her family doctor would earn him more than a sample of her sharp tongue.

Brenda Castaldo wanted her husband, John, to do something about his drinking, see the family doctor, or go to Alcoholics Anonymous, but she had learned that it was easier to suffer and even to cherish the anesthetizing effect alcohol had upon him than to speak of the problem and risk a torrent of abuse or a beating. She had considered divorce, in spite of her Catholic faith, but had never been able to save enough out of her weekly allowance for a lawyer's retainer. Further, she feared physical assault should divorce papers be served on him. Finally, with four children yet in school, she knew that she would have to depend on funds doled out by public welfare, with all of the humiliation that might involve, and her pride would not permit her to make her misery so public.

Daniel Benedict's problem came to no one's attention, yet was most pathological of all. His wife rationalized his oddness because she was afraid to face the fact of his disorder. At times she hoped that an acute illness would bring him to the family doctor who might give him medication that would be of help, and at other times she prayed that he would remain well so that the secret could be kept. But of course, the secret was not kept. The villagers knew of Daniel Benedict's self-imprisonment. Because they recalled him as a child, they maintained that kind silence which those who live out their lives together develop in the interests of civility. Only the children of the village, excited by the mystery of him, speculated how to lure him from his house, but walked by it a bit faster than usual.

These five people who are among the psychologically disordered got no help for a number of reasons. The main reason was that their distress was out of effective awareness and revealed only in acts that were soon rationalized. Samuel Arey did not know that his problem lay in the fact that he could not express anger in words, and possessing a strong sense of the fatedness of all things found in the value system of his heritage and class position, both he and Edna thought that he was simply "that way," a man destined by fate to break things when angry. Daniel Benedict got no help because he was paranoid and believed intently in his delusions. His wife denied his disorder, as is common in the families of people in psychosis, because her belief that a psychosis is incurable made its recognition intolerable. The family doctor who sewed up Samuel Arey's hand knew that his problem was psychological in origin, but he did not quite know how to translate the act into the idea, and he had little time to spare for psychotherapeutic sessions. The police officer who followed Sophia Barden home after she had run her car into a tree could do little for her aside from not booking her for "driving to endanger." Even the public welfare worker who saw Sophia occasionally and who might have served as her first acceptable psychotherapist spent most of her time dispensing or withholding funds or seeking houses for her clients. Domestic discord, problem drinking, the violent acting out of anger, are rarely thought of as problems that one takes to one's family doctor.

Tommy Starbuck, heir of a disappearing and once proud Vineyard name, was a child of poverty and frustration. One of seven children of a seasonally employed father, he contrasted his life not only with those of his island friends but with those of the summer children he painfully encountered each year. He was aware of their possessions, their freedom, their calm assurance, and he resented the fact that he was one instrument of their summer adventures. Not only was he an instrument, but his own father was as well. Though his father was six feet tall and a bass derby winner, Tommy had once seen him standing mute while berated by an Edgartown yachtsman to whom he delivered supplies. Worst of all, like his father, Tommy had no words for his anger. There was no one at home to hear in a family where language was used for prohibition and abuse, never for reflection or communication.

This has been a cursory look at five people in predicament. The purpose of this book is to describe and to analyze the number and variety of predicaments that occur in the lives of the other few thousand islanders. It also shows how, starting literally from scratch, a network of human services has been developed and is still developing on the island to meet the needs of those with such predicaments. The term *predicament* here indicates both the difficulty of the individual's situation and his relative helplessness to extricate himself from it on his own. The term is used in essentially its dictionary definition—"a difficult situation bringing perplexity about the best procedure for extrication, sometimes with lack of freedom to do what one would prefer (*WTI* 1961)." A predicament always involves personal distress, either in awareness or out of awareness. It almost always affects others within the sufferer's interpersonal field. Almost invariably it eventually comes to public notice. The ways it becomes public are many and varied. It may be revealed in the family doctor's office, if the doctor is not too harried or the patient not too reticent. If there is a psychiatrist in the community, he may be the first to know. But as often as not the predicament comes to light through the school, the law, the church, the welfare office, or even through the observation of a sensitive relative or neighbor. What happens next to the person in predicament may depend on the kind of community in which he lives, the services it has to offer, and the caringness with which they are administered.

Five or six decades ago the urban settlement house, such as Hull House or the Henry Street Settlement, was the common point of entry into the then more limited human services system. Even as recently as a decade and a half ago the clergyman was the most frequently sought source of help for those in predicament (Gurin et al 1960). But now, with the rapid development of mental health clinics in the United States, the initial contact of the person in predicament is more and more often with a mental health worker.

The language used in this book is frequently psychiatric, because the community where the studies were made and the resources were developed first perceived its major human problems as psychiatric in nature. At another point in history it might well have begun with a different sort of effort, such as a religious revival or the establishment of community centers with wholesome recreational activities for young people. Indeed, no predicament is ever exclusively psychiatric, religious, social, economic, or in the terms of another time, dependent on the wickedness or goodness of the sufferer. Every human predicament is the consequence of many factors and usually requires a variety of efforts for its resolution, if that resolution is within human capacities.

The Start of the Venture

The venture to provide human services for the island was begun in 1960 by a small group of island physicians and clergymen. Their almost daily experience with the many islanders overwhelmed by human predicaments had led them to look for remedies, and a psychiatric service seemed a good place to begin. By the summer of 1961 they had persuaded a psychiatrist who regularly summered on the island to commit himself to living on the island year round in order to establish such a service for its then six thousand people.

There was no precedent for so small, so unaffluent, so isolated a community to start its own community mental health clinic. The difficulties of the proposal argued loudly for themselves. Would a traditional, rural New England community accept the presence of a psychiatric clinic in its midst? Would people be willing to consult a psychiatrist in numbers sufficient to justify his presence? What sorts of therapy would be feasible where anonymity is absent and a knowledge of the lives of one's neighbors is a part of the gruel of life? And above all, how could such a service be supported in a county with the lowest median income and the highest rate of poverty in its state?

In the face of these hard questions psychiatric service for the island was begun. On July 1, 1961, the psychiatrist began to see island patients. On November 15 the Martha's Vineyard Guidance Center, now the Martha's Vineyard Mental Health Center, was officially opened in half of the ground floor of a house in Edgartown built in 1703, the floors of which, because of either a shipwright's design or the ravages of time, listed precariously.

This report of that venture, almost fifteen years after its beginning, is based on several kinds of data. The observations of life in the community outline the coherent and stressful elements in the lives of islanders, the resources they lack, and the nurturing they find when experiencing disorder. The formal research studies of the human predicaments of islanders give information on the burden of psychiatric disorder they bear, show how their predicaments come to the attention of others, and indicate which segments of the population are at high risk of developing psychiatric and psychosocial disorder. Finally, the account shows how, starting with a community mental health clinic, a small traditional community went about establishing a responsive network of human services, so that its people now have a richness of resources rarely available save to larger, affluent populations.

Stress, Loss, and Transition

At the time when the project was begun, the belief that psychiatric disorder was essentially an intrapersonal problem which had its origins within the first decade of life was waning. The importance of crucial life experiences in the occurrence of psychiatric disorder had been emphasized by Meyer (1948). Neo-Freudian revisionists had noted the role of social factors in psychological disorder (Horney 1939; Sullivan 1953; Fromm 1941, 1955; Thompson 1950). The sociologists had laid the groundwork for a consideration of man as a social being (Durkheim 1951; Cooley 1956; Mead 1934), and the theologians had shown increasing concern with man in being (Buber 1965; Maritan 1966; Tillich 1952). The realm of psychiatry had also been extended by a few important studies in psychosocial epidemiology (Rosanoff 1917; Mangus and Seeley 1955; Carstairs and Brown 1958).

The belief that social stress might precipitate psychological crises had received some clinical support (Lindemann 1944; Grinker and Spiegel 1945; Parkes 1964), while epidemiological studies in New

Haven, Midtown Manhattan, and Stirling County, Nova Scotia had given evidence that sociocultural experiences might be crucial for the development of significant psychiatric impairment (Hollingshead and Redlich 1958; Srole et al 1962; D. C. Leighton et al 1963).

More than two thousand years ago Theophrastus, the heir of Aristotle's Lyceum, posed an important question that continues to engage attention today. "Why is it," he asked, "that while all Greece lies under the same sun and all Greeks are educated alike, it has befallen us to have characters variously constituted?" There is in Theophrastus' question a note of dismay. Speaking both of nature and of nurture, he expresses surprise that men vary. This was a source of wonder in his time, since Greeks of the period generally believed that men were essentially alike, as though stamped from the same mold. In fact, the Greek word *character* refers to the identifying marks stamped on a coin (Hamilton 1957). There is, however, another note in his question. When he asks "why . . . it has befallen us," he is expressing the Greek belief, particularly in the Homeric period, that fate is what determines character and that the character a man has is simply the instrument used by the gods to drive him to his destiny.

We know now to a greater extent than did Theophrastus that while the characteristics of a man's dwelling place and his education affect him, there are other factors which help determine his make-up. Many have speculated about the effect that living on the vast unmarked stretches of the desert has upon the characteristics of its nomadic inhabitants. The Danish physician Panum (1940), studying an epidemic of measles on the Faroe Islands in 1846, related what he believed to be a high rate of mental illness to the environment. "If I have described the Faroese landscape in unusual detail," he wrote, "it is because I feel almost certain that the impress made upon the mind by the character of the landscape, supplemented by the frequent fogs, is the most potent predisposing cause of the frequency of mental disease in the Faroe Islands." Similar observations have been recorded about the effect of the wind known as the mistral upon the people of southern France, of the williwaw wind upon Alaskans, and of the long Arctic darkness upon the prevalence of depression in the Arctic town of Tromsoe in Norway. A psychiatrist studying the mental illness that had appeared on Cape Cod, Nantucket, and Martha's Vineyard in the nineteenth century was moved to comment, "when I think of the bleakness of shifting sand, dunes, stunted vegetation and limited interests, I marvel that the whole population did not storm the hospital doors!" (Briggs 1928).

But for most human beings, the social environment is far more crucial for the development of character and for the occurrence of mental disorder than is the physical environment. Generally human beings develop their characters, their beliefs, their values, and their propensity for mental well-being or mental disorder during the course of interactions with others within a larger social environment.

A basic, if a frugal, premise is that each of us faces each day with a psychic organism of some degree of resiliency and adaptability. Had we none, the first experience of stress would bowl us over. We can assume with confidence that the adaptive capacity of each of us has been developed, or limited, by the vicissitudes of our lives. A genetic fault may cause one man to make his way through life with only a fraction of the intellectual capacity of another. Infectious diseases, dietary deficiencies, hormonal deficiencies may all produce psychological disorder or mental retardation. The nature of one's rearing as determined by locale, by climate, by the economic resources of one's parents, or by custom may have profound effects upon human personality. Still more significant for the development of the adaptive capacity of the individual is the psychological atmosphere provided by his parents and later by his peers, teachers, and all of the others in the ever-changing interpersonal field in which he spends his life (Sullivan 1953).

Experience shows that life changes from day to day and week to week. We grow, we learn, we are praised or humiliated, loved or not loved. We strive and succeed or strive and fail. We leave the comforting presence of nurturing parents for the unknown experiences of a schoolroom, or depart the hostile deforming atmosphere of a home to find validation of ourselves in that same school. We experience the stresses of bodily change in adolescence, the striving for identity, the separation of self from family, and the new ventures of work, marriage, parenthood. We move from one place to another, give up significant people and meet soon-to-be significant others. We experience the loss of those close to us by divorce or death and acquire intimacy with others as yet unknown. We move up the ladder of occupational success or slip back a rung.

Each of these experiences—whether they are developmental events, losses, or transitional states, whether they are experienced as pleasant or unpleasant—requires an adaptation, an effort of personality to give up the old and integrate the new. If our attempts to cope with the crises experienced are handled effectively, we have polished a useful tool and will no doubt be more competent in handling the next transition. If our adaptive resources prove inadequate or if the stressors are too intense or too manifold, the adaptive mechanism fails, and we experience symptoms, depression, anxiety, phobias, or one of the psychophysiological disorders (Scott and Howard 1970). But whether the failure to adapt and move on is seen as due primarily to the incapacity of the adaptive mechanism, or to the heavy load of stress experienced over too short a time, is a matter of great practical importance.

If the clinical focus is on the first premise, that the individual possesses a defective adaptational system with insufficient coping techniques, the effort at helping him must be individual, historic, and deeply searching. It must be no less than an attempt at a revision of his adaptational system so that he will be better able to cope with the stressors to which life has already and will surely continue to subject him. This means, too, that the procedures will be long, will demand uncommon characteristics of the patient, and will be time-consuming for the mental health worker. While some persons no doubt require such intensive therapy, it is not a technique that can be applied to the great number of those in distress. In contrast, if the focus is on not a revision of character structure but the predicaments of the moment and the handling of stress, the mental health worker's task, though more limited in intent, is much wider in scope. Because this approach is economical in time, it spreads the mental health resources more widely. Because it does not demand the long training and apprenticeship required by psychoanalysis, it is applicable to a greater proportion of the population. And because it does not limit the mental health worker's services to one or two dozen patients over a three-year period, it gives him the self-regenerating joy of working for the common weal.

The shift in approach from an attempt to revise character structure in a few to the more democratic thrust of the community mental health movement demands the use of methods that may serve to prevent disorder. For the extremely high rates of notable psychological disorder among the population make impossible under any foreseeable circumstances the intensive individual treatment of all who might benefit from it. Aside from the inadaptability of many people for exploratory psychotherapy, it is certain that the task is far beyond present or potential capacities. If all of the psychoanalysts and psychotherapists in the country were to begin at the northern tip of Maine, working their way down while treating the "primary" basis of mental disorder, they would no doubt all be dead before reaching Boston, and if not, the people of Boston would certainly do them in. But if the mental health worker starts with the premise that it is possible to diminish the intensity of episodes of psychological disorder or to eliminate the life stressors that precipitate them, much can be done for individuals in distress and perhaps even for communities.

Starting with the assumption that all people have more or less of an adaptive capacity, the public mental health worker asks a number of questions. What aspects of life within the community produce so much stress as to tax human adaptive capacities? What may be done to diminish the stress? How can people best be helped in coping with the stresses that they inevitably encounter? What resources are available in the community to help in these tasks? What can be done to make the community more responsive to the needs of its members? These are some of the issues raised by a community approach to human predicaments.

2

The Island and Its People

Who are the people who live on the island of Martha's Vineyard the year round? What makes up the fabric of their lives? How do they differ from the great mass of other Americans? What characteristics of their lives make for stress which, if not adequately handled, results in psychological disorder? What elements in community life make for the neighborly nurturing of those in difficulty? What formal social supports does island life offer? What are its resources and how responsive is the community to the needs of its members?

The lives of islanders are shaped by their geographic setting, their relationships to each other, and the institutions that give structure to those relationships. Of great import are the characteristics of island life that make for both social coherence and social stress, since most human interactions and institutions have elements of each. The difficulty in defining *coherence* is the same as that in defining *mental health* (Jahoda 1958). But its dictionary definition, the "integration of social and cultural elements based on a consistent pattern of values and a congruous set of ideological principles," will do (*WTI* 1961).

Another Nation

Although the United States is now an urban nation, its institutions were designed for a country of towns and villages, and a significant proportion of native-born Americans began life in small towns. A

15

sign of the country's rural origin is the fact that the Bureau of the
Census defines a rural place as one with fewer than 2,500 people,
though in the common culture even a town of 10,000 or 15,000 is
considered quite small. As the United States becomes more and
more urbanized, a large number of Americans continue to live in
rural communities. Despite the notable migration from rural to urban areas over the past few decades, the rural population today is
larger than it was fifty years ago. In four of the New England states
the rural population grew faster than the urban in the 1960-1970
decade (U.S. Bureau of the Census 1961, 1971). In 1970 approximately 54 million people or one-quarter of the population lived in
communities of less than 2,500 people, making up "another nation"
as large as the United Kingdom. Since the census definition is functionally arbitrary, evidence for the country's small town aspect also
comes from the fact that in 1970 33 percent of Americans lived in
places of 10,000 or less, and 44 percent in places of 25,000 or less
(U.S. Bureau of the Census 1973).

The lives of the Vineyarders are summed up in the terms *island*
and *rural*, which distinguish them from the urban and suburban life
lived by most Americans. It is probable that much of what is described as elemental to life on the island applies to many, if not
most, rural communities in North America, and thus the observations made and the mental health resources developed for Vineyarders should be relevant to similar enterprises in other rural communities.

Now, let us look at our community.

The Land and the Seasons

The people of Martha's Vineyard live on almost 100 square miles
of soil deposited by two great glacial lobes which covered the northeastern United States until about ten thousand years ago. Receding,
they left behind a land of rolling hills, a band of terminal moraine
along its northern edges and a large area of fertile outwash plains
gently sloping to its southern shore. Though the island is five times
the size of Manhattan, its inhabitants are nowhere far from water.
Its shoreline on sound and ocean extends for 95 miles, its land is dot-

ted by circular kettle ponds, and a string of fresh water ponds edge its southern shore.

Despite the size of the island, most islanders live near the sea. They are aware of the sea as they make their daily rounds, noting the lean of the buoys that mark the strength and direction of the current at Vineyard Haven, the force of the surf against the sea wall on stormy days at Oak Bluffs, or the course taken by the three-car ferry on its brief run from Edgartown to the satellite island of Chappaquiddick.

The larger boats that carry the islander, his car, and all of his sustenance to and from the mainland, a distance of three miles at its closest point but seven by the course required for a vessel, mark his lifeline. On the three or four days of the year when the ferry cannot make the run because of high winds, he is reminded that he is island bound. On such days he does not get his off-island mail, his metropolitan newspaper, or the building materials for which he may be waiting.

Because it is surrounded by water, the island's climate is milder and more even than that of nearby inland places. Its autumns are warmer and last longer and its springs are later and cooler than those of the mainland. It rarely has the great disrupting snow storms of the northeastern United States. Characteristic of its climate are its winds, which in summer come from the west and southwest, shifting as the season advances to the cold, wet, dreary "northeasters" of winter.

The island is not isolated from the great populations of its region, since it lies within what has been called megalopolis, a concentration of cities, towns, and suburban networks that stretches almost uninterruptedly from southern New Hampshire to northern Virginia (Gottman 1961). Its population is small, now about 7,800 during the winter, with an average of about nine acres of land for every year-round inhabitant. In summer its population doubles, triples, quadruples, and by mid-August reaches five times its winter population. Its summer houses, which outnumber its year-round dwellings, become full. Then, within a few weeks of Labor Day, the summer visitors are almost gone, save for the few who linger to savor the delights of its mild and quiet autumns. The summer shops close, most restaurants stack their chairs on their tables, movie boardings announcing the "Coming Attractions" become almost bare, and the people of the island resume their normal patterns of life during the "off-season" of their summer visitors.

But the cycle of the year moves on. Longtime relationships interrupted by the work and confusion of summer are resumed. School buses begin their daily round. Fishing gear is gotten out and put into order. Boats and drags are readied for the opening of the ponds to scalloping. Guns are cleaned for the deer and fowl seasons. Hobbies, digging for old bottles, searching for fossils and arrowheads, genealogical research, caning, weaving, local archeology, and many others are taken up again. Scores of organizations resume their meetings. The school system's program of adult education returns hundreds of islanders to school for one or two nights a week studying auto mechanics or the Elizabethan poets.

For most islanders, January to March are the difficult months. There are periods when day after day, heavy low clouds oppress the island, the sun gone, the night sky moonless and starless. The early thaws in March or April make quagmires of unpaved country roads, and cars that easily traversed the light snows of winter dig themselves in hubcap deep. The opportunities for outdoor recreation become minimal, and most stressful of all, rates of unemployment are at their highest. During these months, unemployment rates of 14 to 15 percent in the occupations covered by the employment security laws are common; in the uncovered occupations they are likely to be significantly higher. In addition to those who are totally unemployed, a significant percentage of those who work in the largest occupational group at this time, the building trades, often have spells when they cannot work, perhaps due to bad weather or the failure of needed supplies to arrive.

The period tends to be one of isolation, when people remain in their houses and unemployed men spend the day before the television set. Once evening falls, it is unusual for people to leave their homes save on weekends. It is a time when alcoholism becomes a more important problem than ever, even in those who are not perennial alcoholics. With the advent of April, the unemployment rate begins to drop. The weather makes easier the repainting of summer houses, the digging of foundations for new ones, the brick work and masonry for pavements and homes. By mid-April a few restaurants have begun to open and the unemployment rate falls further. There is a lift to the spirits with the premonitory signs of summer; gardens get planted, work becomes more plentiful, summer visitors begin to open their houses on long weekends, and then the three months of summer from mid-June to mid-September begin. Unemployment rates are lowest at this time. The stresses of winter are over, but new stresses appear.

Employed islanders work long hours in the summer under great pressure, often with anxiety about their children, who are left to make it on their own. During this period, they give up their normal social life, and islanders have been known to say good-by to their friends as June approaches, knowing that the relationships will not be resumed until September. The problem of alcohol decreases, but another problem is revealed. Because many of the summer employment force are young women, often hired because of their attractiveness, many island women in new marriages become anxious. Summer liaisons between island men and single summer girls are common, and there are island women who, anxious about the possibility of such an occurence, refuse well-paying jobs that would keep them busy in the evening.

The Population

The Vineyard and the neighboring Elizabeth Islands make up Dukes County. Since the latter islands are inhabited by only one percent of the county's population, the data for Dukes County in the census reports approximate those for Martha's Vineyard with only negligible error. The census data and that acquired locally add up to a detailed demographic picture of the island's population (Appendices 1-6). In 1960, the population of Martha's Vineyard was 5,763; in 1965, 5,959; in 1970, 6,117; and in 1975, 7,812 (U.S. Bureau of Census 1961, 1971; Mass. Census 1965, 1975). Thus, the population of Dukes County has been remarkably stable in numbers until the last five years. Between 1970 and 1975, almost entirely as a result of in-migration, the number of islanders increased by 28 percent, a change which, along with the rapid growth of the summer population, will no doubt have notable effects on island life.

Approximately three-quarters of the inhabitants live in the three unincorporated coastal villages of Vineyard Haven, Oak Bluffs, and Edgartown, with the remaining one-quarter sparsely scattered over the remainder of the island. Only one in seven islanders lives in the three up-island towns, West Tisbury, Chilmark and Gay Head. The name "Vineyard," once descriptive, is now legendary. Formerly there were many working farms. Today there are few farmers, and they must supplement their income by other work. Their average nonfarm income is greater than their farm income. Ironically, one of the most successful of the extant farmers calls his place Barely-Make-It Farm and every few years sells off a few more acres to summer people. What is true of farming also holds for fishing, which today supports only a small percentage of the population, though many more supplement their income by scalloping. Come the cold months of the scallop season, whole families take to the icy waters in their blunt-nosed boats, and even school children know the price of a bushel of scallops. Today the major occupation of the majority of islanders depends on the island's chief industry: summer people. What began in the 1890s with a few hotels and a cluster of cottages around the Methodist Tabernacle in Oak Bluffs has proliferated into an industry on which the livelihood of most islanders—like it or not—depends. This includes carpenters, masons, electricians, and realtors, as well as doctors, lawyers, and merchants.

The two largest groups are "old American" and Portuguese. The old Americans are mostly of northern European ancestry. The segment of the population that is of Portuguese origin, largely descendants of fishermen and whalemen, began to come to the island from the Portuguese islands, the Azores, Madeiras, and Cape Verdes, in the thirties of the last century. The second largest non-native-born group comes from the maritime provinces of Canada. The original native population, the Indians of Gay Head, once members of the Algonquin Federation, estimated at 3000 in 1642 (Devens 1838), now number only a few score.

Only three percent of the island's population is black. Of the 207 black people living on the island in 1970, more than half lived in Oak Bluffs and almost one-third lived in Vineyard Haven (U.S. Census 1971). Many were first drawn to the island, particularly to Oak Bluffs, because of its reputation as a resort congenial to blacks; for many decades of this century, the island's beaches were among the very few along the eastern seaboard that were not segregated. This also explains the island's sizable black population during the summer.

Life on the island for black people has many of the same problems it does elsewhere in the United States though probably of lesser degree. Because the population is small, prejudicial stereotypes are more difficult to maintain than elsewhere. Since most encounters are frequent and in various roles, individual qualities soon determine the nature of relationships. Self-segregation, so common in many urban schools, is unknown, and dating across color lines is not uncommon.

The age of the population leans heavily toward the higher end of the age scale. In 1970, 19 percent of the population was 65 years of age or over, as compared with 11 percent for the state. Thus, almost one in every five islanders has passed the usual retirement age. In contrast, there is a relative deficiency in the immediate post-high-school age group. In the recent past, approximately 80 percent of graduating high-school students left the island for employment, trade school, college, or military service. Fewer are now leaving than were a decade ago. Those in the 20-34 year age group made up 15 percent of the population in 1970, a reversal of a long-term downward trend. In the 1960-1970 decade this group accounted for 45 percent of the total population growth (U.S. Bureau of the Census 1961, 1971). The significance of this change cannot be doubted. With the rapid growth of the retired population, requiring goods and services, and the past decrease in size of the most vigorous age group, the discrepancy between need and supply threatened the availability of services. The recent increase of the 20-34 year age group, which has probably accelerated since the 1970 census, may soon redress the balance.

The island's population is distributed unevenly. There are approximately 16 or 17 people per square mile up-island, while Tisbury, with its village of Vineyard Haven, has a density approximating 300 per square mile. Because of the low population density in the up-island towns, there may be a scarcity of local services, and the Gay Header often has to make a round trip of 44 miles to satisfy his everyday needs.

The small size of the age groups in which marriage is most frequent makes for a severe limitation in marital choice. While the numbers themselves may seem adequate, the other factors that enter consciously or covertly into these decisions, such as height, complexion, personality, ethnic group, race, social or economic position, and those imponderables involved in the term *love*, may sharply restrict the actual number of possible mates. This limitation may well result in unsuitable marital choices and thus in marriages that begin as, or soon become, predicaments.

Community and the Common Destiny

The word *community* suggests a group of people holding something in common. The notion of a community of scholars transcends geographic lines and includes those whose common interest is in the acquisition of learning. But most communities occupy delimited geographic areas and include those who hold many things, including economic interests, in common.

A sense of community implies a knowledge of one's fellows and a commoness of interest, which makes it easier to achieve in a small than in a large place. Islanders hold many things in common, one being the 64,000 acres of land that is their domain. Another is their propinquity, which allows them to see each other frequently. They share family names, even when the blood relationships are too dilute to be remembered. They are daily reminded of their heritage by the street signs, for in 1969 more than 10 percent of islanders bore old family names that were also street names.

A limit to the number of people one knows and encounters is important to the sense of community, for the larger the number of people in a community, the fewer the interests they can hold in common. The islander living in the center of Edgartown could, in ten minutes' walk, encounter at most the entire population of his village, 1,200 persons. In midtown Manhattan, it would be possible for him to encounter fifty times as many people in the same amount of time.

The islander who visits a city for the first time often experiences a sense of incomprehensible disturbance. He has not yet learned to screen out the great variety of sensations to which he exposes himself. Walking down the street, he looks into each face as he is accustomed to do in his own village and soon finds himself experiencing psychological nystagmus. Finding no face he recognizes, he may be swept by a feeling of dread and isolation so intense that he returns home forthwith. It is not uncommon for island children beginning college to find separation from their social network too stressful and to return home within a few days. For on the island no resident is perceived as a stranger, and he is assumed to share the common values and the common trials of life.

The urban detachment that ensures a tolerable degree of social privacy is not found on the island. For better or worse, people either know each other or know much about each other. This does not mean that encounters are always friendly and cooperative. Although people generally meet "face to face," they often find themselves "back to back" (Frankenburg 1966). Conflict is in fact as necessary as consensus to the solution of the community's problems, and indifference stifles both. Important to the sense of community on the island is the feeling of sharing a "common destiny," signifying a shared past and an anticipated sharing of the future (Howe 1964). Often the newcomer first knows he has become an islander when a native refers to experiences they have shared in the past, or occasionally to events that actually occurred before his arrival.

Each of the towns of the island has more elements of community than does the population as a whole. People living close to each other naturally develop a greater sense of relationship, whether positive or negative. Because the opportunities for interaction are greater, they cannot be indifferent to one another. A resident of the village of Edgartown, for example, encounters many of his townspeople every day. A woman sees her neighbors as she shops. They drop in for coffee. They babysit for each other. They bring their children to one another's houses for play or meet each other at any one of the great number of clubs. The importance of the post office as a meeting place is illustrated in Vineyard Haven. Because the town is large enough to have a first-class post office, it could, if it desired, have its mail delivered by carrier, and this would provide a number of sorely needed year-round jobs. The town chooses, however, to retain its present system because the post office provides a meeting place which enlivens its sense of community. In the up-island town of West Tisbury a considerable part of the population lives within a mile from its center. The general store, which also houses the post office, is the daily meeting place. Friends and neighbors meet there as they go about their business. Older children wait for the school bus on its porch in poor weather and are let off there at the end of the school day. If one is in need of conversation, the purchase of a cake of soap can serve as an excuse for visiting the store to chat with neighbors, to hear the gossip, or to discuss town affairs, and there is always a group of people with time on their hands sharing in its neighborliness.

All of this is not to say that the Jeffersonian belief in the superiority of rural life is a totally valid one, for community satisfaction has many dimensions. Indeed, some studies assessing such satisfaction in overall terms have found it to be directly related to community size, so that the larger the community, the greater the degree of overall satisfaction (Davies 1945; Jesser 1963). However, when the factors that determine satisfaction with community life are treated individually, significant differences are found. A study of seven urban and fourteen rural townships in North Dakota analyzed the factors that contribute to community satisfaction or dissatisfaction (Johnson and Knop 1970). Urban residents gained satisfaction from shopping and medical facilities, teacher competence, employment opportunities, and resources for entertainment and recreation, while rural people enjoyed the spirit of cooperation they found among themselves, took pride in their community, cherished the opportunity for participation in community decision making, and held fast to their belief that individual merit has a greater chance of recognition in smaller than in larger places. In brief, urban people valued services and opportunities, while rural people cherished relationships and participation.

The study suggests that urban satisfaction is based on those dimensions that best fill the striving values of middle class American life, while rural satisfaction is concerned with the more traditional values. Such values are again beginning to seem attractive to an increasing number of Americans, and rural areas and small towns are where most Americans say they would like to live (NYT 1973; Duane et al 1974). Such a search for the sense of community has been part of the Vineyard experience during the past six years, with a growing in-migration of young adults disaffected with the anonymity and turmoil of the city and frustrated with their powerlessness to influence an oversized, distant government.

It is not enough that people live close to each other in order to be members of a community. To partake in one of the essentials of community, they must interact with each other, both in amity and in conflict. In short, important to community is communication, so that people who may not see each other every day remain informed about the lives of their friends and neighbors. One of the most important means of communication in a small community is by word of mouth. Gossip transmits the good as well as the bad. It is faster and usually more vivid than the weekly newspaper. It is often practiced face to face at community meeting places, the post office, the general store, the supermarket, even the library. Though the telephone plays an important role, its role was even more important before the island acquired a dial system in April 1966, for the telephone operators were an essential part of the island's communication network. They not only operated the telephone system but transmitted messages, and a repeated attempt to reach Mrs. Gwathmey might finally be ended by the operator's informing one that Mrs. Gwathmey was visiting her sister in Falmouth.

The local weeklies, the *Vineyard Gazette* and the *Grapevine*, as well as the off-island *New Bedford Standard-Times*, play an important role in the interpersonal communication network, particularly the *Gazette*. If news is defined as events of public concern, then certainly most of what happens on the island—in the courts, in government, in weather or the tides—is of general interest, for people are always affected. Each of the six towns of the island has a local reporter, who in a town column in the *Gazette* reports on events in the lives of its citizens, meetings attended, entertaining done, trips taken, illnesses experienced. It is not unusual for the participants in a dinner party or the off-island visitors to one's home to be mentioned by name. The content of the town columns is addressed to the citizens of the town, and events are often so described that outsiders are unable to interpret them. A few years ago one town reporter's column carried as a complete item, "Edgar Amherst came home from Providence to dig the grave." There is little doubt that she was understood by the people of her town. When a private quarrel has not reached public attention or is felt to have been distorted in the telling, a paid advertisement may give one or both of the parties an opportunity to state his case. A recently published paid notice in one island weekly read:

NOTICE

I, Joshua Vinson, am no longer associated with Central Electrical Company, contrary to what has been said. I had reason to leave and gave due notice to all affected by my decision.

The importance of such information to islanders is confirmed by its magnitude. During the month of April 1970 the names of 404 individual islanders were mentioned in the *Gazette*, or approximately one in every eighteen. Those whose activities are restricted, the very young and the very old, were mentioned least frequently. Men were mentioned slightly more frequently than women. There was a clear relationship between the number of mentions and age. Twelve percent of the men between 25 and 54 years of age, or one man in eight, had their names mentioned in the *Gazette*, and approximately the same rate prevailed for each of the three age decades. The rate of mentions for women reached its peak in the 45-54 age group, more than 10 percent of the island women in that age group having had their names noted in the *Gazette* during the month. Being mentioned in the *Gazette* was also related to one's social class position as measured by occupation. For both men and women, the higher the social class position, the more frequently the name appeared. While a few of the mentions were due to appearances in court, most of them were for participation in the social life of the community.

Although the data do not tell whether or not the actual volume of social activities was related to social class, which is probable, they at least suggest that access to this source of the communication system is more available to those in the upper classes.

Kinship and Class

Human beings everywhere identify themselves with groups. Those who live in simple societies, with little differentiation between what one person does and another, place themselves in and are considered by others to belong to kinship groups. In industrial societies with sharp divisions of skill, people become more differentiated; kinship ties become less important and individuals are ranked in social classes (Susser and Watson 1971).

The position of the islander is somewhere in between this sharp division. He lives in the midst of an industrial society and uses its products, but he is not yet part of it. Labor is not yet highly differentiated, and many islanders earn their living in a variety of activities over the course of a year, shifting from one occupation to another as the seasons change. The job a man holds does not as readily place him in a fixed class as in technically advanced communities. When the weather gets too cold for the easy use of mortar or cement, the mason may be seen in the uniform of a police officer directing traffic for a road-building operation. As fall and the scallop season approach, a taxi operator may put up his cab and tidy up his scalloping gear. Since it remains a preindustrial enclave, the island holds to the old mix of occupations. Members of the old professions—medicine, law, and religion—far outnumber members of the new ones—engineering, architecture, and science—as they do not in technological societies.

Kinship on the island often remains as important as class. The possession of an old family name which has not been tarnished by either sloth or personal disaster adds luster to a man's position. Current relationships with those in positions of influence or power—the president of a bank, a chief of police, the manager of a public utility—may give one special privileges.

Since people know each other as individuals, personal characteristics have an influence in placing a man, which may compensate for financial reverses and downward occupational mobility. In brief, the criteria by which people are usually classified into socioeconomic groups by occupation, education, and housing are less critical for the island population, and the techniques of status evaluation that use the ranking by others in the community probably come closer to the actualities of one's position in the island community (Warner 1960). In addition, there yet remains in many islanders the belief in "good blood" and "bad blood" which was found among Irish peasants (Arensberg 1937). A number of very old families of distinguished ancestry have experienced misfortunes over the past few generations which have earned them a stigma of being thought of as "lazy" or "no-good" or "always on welfare."

Modes of Relationship

One of the essential differences between relationships in large and small places is that those in small communities are almost entirely relational, while those in large populations are both legal and relational. The term *relational* is used here to indicate that the transactions between islanders do not depend solely on the business at hand, as they do in legal relations. The individuals concerned know each other as human beings, have had prior connections, and because they both live in the same small community, are certain to continue to have a need for transactions long after the current business is over. In friendship, we do not fight for every advantage. We know each other's past, that there will be a future, and that human relationships cannot be based on the legal rules of equity alone.

Since islanders operate largely within a set of common assumptions and values, they find the techniques of accommodation readily at hand. The small town resident engaged in a conflict with his neighbor counts the possible loss in amity before he presses too hard for equity, for relationships are as precious as anything else available to him, and they are limited in number. If a man should find himself overcharged by a small amount, he might well decide that it would be uneconomic in a larger sense to press for the return of so small a sum, since the cost in mutual dependence might be greater than the return in money.

An important result of this accommodation is that the islander often represses anger. He cannot charge the shopkeeper with cheating him and leave confident that he need never see him again. Indeed, it is likely that they will meet again in other roles, perhaps that very evening as members of a committee of their town's government. The problem is often handled by sidling up to it, at a chance meeting and with a touch of humor. The islander charged $20 for filling his water pump motor with a half-quart of oil may wait until he next encounters his plumber and then archly comment that he wished he had known the price in advance, because then he could have called in Dr. Cathcart for $15 and had his chest "sounded" as an extra. This might well result in a credit on the next bill, whereas confrontation might have put excessive strains upon the relationship.

Privacy in Public

Much is reported about the anonymity of the city dweller, of his indifference to the plight of his neighbors, and of his loss of a sense of community. The islander, in contrast, often finds himself wishing for a brief period of anonymity, a time for repair and renewal, for exploring a relationship away from the public eye, or for indulging in a secret vice, his privacy protected by the size or newness of the place.

If a husband has a divisive argument with his wife and leaves for a walk, the meaning of his walk remains no secret to his neighbors, for islanders simply do not walk the roads at night. If he drives aimlessly about, his movements are noted by the police and quite likely understood. The police who respond to a family quarrel are not the unknown representatives of the government but acquaintances or relatives whom one must confront the next day.

Some islanders find in a trip to Boston a welcome respite from the constant exposure to scrutiny. They describe the delights of drinking in a bar where they are not known or conducting an affair in relative privacy. But this anonymity is often breached in a city as close as Boston because a sufficient number of islanders regularly visit it on town, county, and personal business. One islander, a man with a drinking problem, made annual visits alone to Puerto Rico for gambling and other adventures, but his behavior a thousand miles away was not unnoticed. When a series of checks for sizable sums cleared his local bank, a bank official advised his wife that she might do well to send for him.

True privacy is difficult to achieve in the small community. The limitation of privacy fosters an interest in the lives of one's neighbors. Even one's automobile is easily identified, and if a doctor's car is parked in front of a particular house over a prolonged period of time, it may raise either anxiety or eyebrows. The network among people is close-knit; persons one knows are also likely to know each other, and the relationships of individuals are best visualized not as the branches of a tree or of a genealogical table, but rather as a fishnet. This closeness results in either tolerance or the muting of personal criticism of others, since few persons are strangers. A woman at a cocktail party once began to speak critically of someone to a native islander. Smiling, he stopped her quickly. "You'd better not go on," he said, "she might be some sort of cousin of mine." At the same time, the fact that the network is close-knit gives each person a great store of knowledge about the lives of others. For this and other reasons, rural people have a keen curiosity about each other, which may even be satisfied at times by institutional means. The town in which the island hospital is located often publishes in its annual town report a list of deaths during the year, including the causes of death. Thus occasionally there will be a note to the effect that John Secum died of a "self-inflicted gunshot wound." First-born children have been known to look up their parents' marriage date and their own date of birth in the town reports when they suspect that they were conceived premaritally.

Locals and Cosmopolitans

Martha's Vineyard differs from most mainland rural communities in that its human traffic flows in two directions. While rural areas

that depend on farming as a major source of income have been losing population rapidly in the last few decades, the island replaces
by in-migration the population it loses by out-migration. As a result,
it has a significant non-native population. Of those who migrate to
the island, an increasing proportion come from the great cities of
the eastern seaboard, which for the first time have been decreasing
in population.

Such influences divide islanders into two groups, which have been
called locals and cosmopolitans (Merton 1957) or traditionalists and
nontraditionalists (Stacey 1960). Locals are those whose ties are
almost exlusively to the local community, whose interests and hobbies remain island bound. If they travel, it often is to someplace
where friends and relatives are already living. When their children
go to college, they are likely to remain close to home and enroll in
schools or colleges that islanders have attended for a long time. If
they read any but the island weeklies, they read the *New Bedford
Standard-Times*, which reports island news in addition to providing
a summary of state, national, and international news in decreasing
order of depth.

Cosmopolitans, on the contrary, have many ties off island. They
may be island born or mainland born, but they retain their contacts
with the world outside. They read metropolitan dailies, the *New
York Times*, or the Boston papers. They travel to see the world and
have friends beyond the confines of a few hour's drive from the
mainland port at Woods Hole. If specialized medical or other services are required, they go to Boston or New York. When Alfred
Antone, storekeeper, needed a major operation he had it at the local
hospital, while his son Bill, now a cosmopolitan, went to a medical
center in Boston for a simpler procedure. Indeed, Alfred Antone at
the time of his death had not been off the island for more than thirty-
five years.

The difference in roles played by locals and cosmopolitans in island life is seen in community activity and organization. Locals,
when they desire change, try to achieve it by internal means
through an intimate knowledge of their fellows. They know where
the sources of power are and the positions of the levers. Cosmopolitans are more formal and legal in their operations. They know the

tested techniques for getting things done. In community innovations, each group plays a significant role. Innovation is often initiated by the cosmopolitans. They know how such things have been done elsewhere and can call upon expertise outside of the community. The locals often behave as though the innovation under discussion has no previous history and is being born for the first time on the island. This belief often leads to false and ineffective starts and to what appears to be antiprofessionalism. Hence the island saying that "An expert is someone who comes from off-island."

Justice and Law

Many of the characteristics of life in a small place are seen in bold relief in the operation of its legal system. The dramas that occur in the courtroom are of interest to all, and they are reported extensively in the local newspapers. The knowledge that the court has of the case at hand is almost never limited to the facts presented. If, as is usual, the judge is a resident in the community, he may know a great deal about the person on trial, his family background, and some of the exigencies of life to which he has been subjected. He is often aware of the feelings of his fellow citizens concerning the point at issue.

The red brick courthouse on the Main Street of Edgartown is the visible sign of the legal power of the Commonwealth, for here regularly sit its district and probate courts and twice yearly the traveling superior court. Despite this visible symbol of the state's legal authority, which is generally believed to run with equal force and equity from Williamstown in the northwest through the municipal courts of Boston and down to Cape Cod and the islands, there is in fact another set of actors who temper the statutes written into the General Laws of the Commonwealth. The other actors who complete the cast are local: the police who bring charges against the defendant, the clerk of the court who exercises many judicial functions, the district attorney, and the local lawyers who defend most of those charged with offenses against the state or others. The local members of the cast take and exercise important roles, for they reflect the values and morals of the community and convey a sense of where it now stands on the issues that come before it.

The judge of the district court, by statute and in practice, shares many of his powers with the clerk of the court, a local citizen appointed to a life term. The power of the clerk of the court, particularly where the judge may be present for only a day or two a week, is substantial. He takes evidence as to probable cause that a crime has been committed and may issue complaints and warrants for arrest. He has the power to set bail and to summon witnesses in criminal trials. In misdemeanors, he may hold hearings to determine whether a complaint should be issued. Important though these duties are, his major role is to inform the judge of the prevailing state of mind of the community. For the attitude of the community on an offense may change with time, and a sentence of one year in a correctional institution may seem proper at one time, yet outrage the community at another.

An example of such rapid change in local attitudes occurred over a few years in respect to arrests for the possession of marijuana, in part because of a growing recognition of the widespread use of the substance and its relative lack of toxicity. The use of paid informants of questionable character and in some cases with criminal records, in order to secure evidence of drug use or sale against local young people, was at first acceptable to the community. It fitted the attitudes prevalent at the time, and the first arrests generally involved the least favored and weakest social classes as well as long-haired young people from off-island. As drug use increased and large-scale raids began to involve young people of higher social class families, there was a strong community reaction against rigidly enforcing the marijuana laws. In one town, a petition was circulated seeking to discharge the chief of police of that town after the child of a town official had been arrested. As the police became aware of the changing climate of opinion and of the hazards of involving the sons and daughters of the more substantial members of the community, the use of the informers decreased.

Justice on the island, as in other places, is not entirely even-handed, and this makes for stress. The influence of social class position on attitudes toward one's fellows affects the police as it does other human beings. The prestige and power that go with high social position have their effects, and the lawyer or merchant who staggers down the main street under the influence of alcohol is likely to be escorted home in the police cruiser, while the laborer of marginal reputation may be taken to the county jail to sober up. To some extent this distinction between the rich and the poor, the lower and the middle and upper classes, is smoothed out in small communities such as the island, where the offender's qualities as a human being are likely to be known to the police so that the effect of his social position is modified by their knowledge of his personal history.

Because personal idiosyncracies and deviant behavior are publicly known, the litigants in a legal action may not come before the court on equal terms. In 1972 a known alcoholic in a suit against a number of islanders was able to persuade the judge to have the case heard in a mainland town, one of the grounds being that his known alcoholic problem might prejudice any island jury against him. Of importance in the treatment of alleged offenders is their ability to purchase legal skill, which favors the financially able over the poor. While Massachusetts has a public defender system, its lawyers are overworked, with an average of 360 cases per year for each in the district courts alone (Bing and Roosevelt 1970). The public defender who until 1973 came to the island to defend the indigent often first saw his client a half-hour before the trial and, unable to prepare an adequate defense or summon witnesses, was more likely to bargain with the prosecution for a guilty plea to a lower offense than would have one's private attorney. At present, attorneys appointed by the court defend the poor. They often do so reluctantly. Some by choice have had little prior trial experience, and the established fees are very low.

The fact is that the poor do not have high expectations of receiving justice. They are well aware of the class differences in their treatment, and they occasionally verbalize it, as did Mrs. Allemand, whose son had just been arrested for petty larceny. "I know they'll give it to him," she said, "but if he was Mr. Gart's son"—naming a public official—"he'd get off or maybe he wouldn't have been arrested at all." As a result of the belief that they can expect relatively little from the court, the poor often use the courtroom proceeding not as an arena in which to assert their rights but as a stage in which to express their anger against the community for its biased treatment of them. It is common for those in the lowest socioeconomic position on the Vineyard to hire not the most competent lawyers, who attempt to persuade the court by the weight of evidence on their side, but at no lesser fees the one or two lawyers who can be depended on to conduct what the newspapers often call "a spirited and vigorous defense." Instead of making a case for his client, the lawyer attacks the prosecution vigorously and attacks the rulings of the judge repeatedly, as though to make a case for retrial in a higher court when a new trial can be had for the asking in Massachusetts district courts. His function is not to get his client off but to perform the public ritual by means of which his client and his client's family can release their sense of outrage.

The actual decisions of the island court, as in other rural communities, reflect not only the customs of the community but also the fact that those who come before it, along with their families, share a common destiny. The decisions of the court, therefore, are rarely punitive; the search is always for ways and means, not of extruding the individual, but of controlling and containing his behavior. As in the early New England communities (Smith 1968) and more recently in Plainville (West 1945), the means of redemption within the community are offered and readily accepted. The fact is that a small community can hardly afford to extrude all of those who are "different." The cost in family and social coherence is too great, and since the agents of such extrustion must continue to live in the same community with the families of the deviant, there is an added stake in local rehabilitative efforts.

Access to Power

Whatever else he lacks, the dweller in a small community has the chance of influencing those who affect his life. On the Vineyard no avenue of access to his government is effectively shut, save by the citizen's own inhibitions, which among the disadvantaged may be major. By custom and statute, each citizen may take the floor in his town meeting and seek to persuade his fellow citizens to vote for or against an article on its warrant. Should he himself wish to introduce legislation, he requires only the additional signatures of nine other voters to put such legislation on the agenda of the annual meeting. Between town meetings he may by a petition of 20 percent of the town's voters require that a special meeting be held. Through an ancient but still retained element of Massachusetts law, any seven citizens may by petition introduce a bill into the Massachusetts legislature, though without the support of their representatives and a larger consensus such a bill has little chance of being reported out of committee.

Between town meetings, the islander has access to the deliberations of a whole series of functioning town committees. Owing to the open meeting law of Massachusetts, the weekly meetings of the board of selectmen are open to him, as are the meetings of the school committee, the planning board, the zoning board, the board of appeals, and any ad hoc committees appointed for special purposes. It is not suggested that his access to such committees is enough. He must also have the self-assurance required to present his case and the competence to present it effectively. He must know something of parliamentary procedure, how to get the floor, to make a motion, to present an argument, but these he can begin to learn from early adulthood simply by participating in the multiple activities of his town.

In addition to the formal ways by which the islander can affect his own destiny, he can also have an effect in more personal ways. The selectmen with whom he deals are frequently neighbors or friends, and they may have shared the same duck blind as young men. He is likely to know and have access to his representative to the Massachusetts legislature, and much as in the government of ancient Greece, a complaint or other initiative at town meeting may earn him a place on an appropriate committee (Hamilton 1957).

This is not meant to suggest that every citizen in a small community has equal access to the sources of power. His position in the class system, his heritage, his reputation, his sobriety, whether psychological or chemical, and his personality will all be factors in determining the degree to which he is heard. And his own sense of worth may determine the extent to which he demands to be heard. But at least the opportunity to be heard exists for him in far greater degree than in larger places, and if he feels particularly helpless he may, as some do, use the town meeting to express his general and diffuse anger about life as a whole.

The Summer Season

As spring moves toward summer, the pace of island life quickens. Summer shops begin their annual refurbishing, shop signs stored all winter reappear. The builder finds his weekends occupied by visits from summer people to see the state of construction of the house he had so readily promised last summer for this summer's occupancy. Young people arrive looking for work, an effort begun as early as January through advertisements in the local newspapers. The weekend traffic on the ferry gets heavier. Real estate agents are busy showing houses to renters.

In the weeks following Memorial Day, the exact date often being determined by school closings in the cities and suburbs, each boat disgorges its cargo of cars, heavily laden with family possessions, cats and dogs commingled with children, an occasional parakeet in a cage, small boats car-topped and, almost always, bicycles fastened to rear bumpers. The stream continues until almost every one of the island's 6,500 dwellings is filled.

What begins as a trickle in early June becomes a flood by its end, the number of cars and people increasing through July and August, until a few days after Labor Day when, with the rapid inevitability of a receding tide, they are gone. A few continue to return on weekends in September, the finest month of the island year. A smaller invasion occurs between September 15 and October 15 when the Bass and Bluefish Derby, a Chamber of Commerce enterprise, brings another group of visitors, though fewer than those of summer.

Most of the summer visitors to the island come from the eastern seaboard, but there are some from almost every state and always a few from abroad. Most are affluent perennials, owning their summer houses or renting the same house year after year. They enter their individual summer enclaves and rejoin their summer friends. By day they sport on the beaches, the ponds, and the surrounding waters, while a good proportion of their evenings are spent at cocktail, dinner, or yacht club parties, often seeing the same people day after day and night after night.

For the islander, the coming of the summer season is a time of both pleasure and pain. His pride in being an islander and his belief that he possesses something of value is confirmed by the presence of the summer people. Life becomes more exciting as bars and restaurants reopen, first-run films appear in his movie theaters, often closed all winter, and he may enjoy, though with some tension, being the guest at a cocktail party in a house that he himself has built.

But the islander is constantly reminded that he and his visitors belong to different economic worlds. He sees wealth beyond any dreams he has ever had and consumption so conspicuous as to earn his envious disdain. Above all, and this is most painful of all, he is reminded again and again by the presence of his summer visitors that his conviction of being his own man, barely maintained during the rest of the year, rests on shaky ground. Each demand, each day, calls his attention to the fact that he is a hired hand of others.

The differences between summer people and islanders are perhaps felt most keenly by children, who have not yet accepted the fact that life is unfair and justice never pure. As he grows older, the young islander becomes more and more aware of the differences between him and the summer children. They have strange accents and wear strange clothing. They are both wise and ignorant, full of assurance and knowledge he does not have, yet unwise in the ways of nature. He finds it odd that they search for jobs without needing money and that they live in fine houses which are left empty all winter.

The distance maintained by summer children from their island age mates is often quite clear and painful. This occurs most frequently in the down-island towns of Vineyard Haven and Edgartown, where the yacht clubs as social and recreational centers serve to keep island and summer children apart. The occasional island family that belongs to a yacht club may find its children unwilling to take part in the club's activities as a matter of loyalty to their year-round friends.

The early pain produced by these differences is well remembered by Edgartown adults. An Edgartown man recalls carrying five-gallon cans of gasoline from his father's filling station to the tanks of yachts at the pier, while impeccably dressed children of his own age watched him patiently as he struggled to manage two at once. He recalls at sixteen being refused a date by a lovely fair-haired summer girl on the grounds that she was not allowed to date "town boys." Many years later, when called to her bedside as a physician, he observed her surprised chagrin as she said, "Why didn't you tell me you were going to be a doctor?"

The yearly coming of the summer visitors has another effect on islanders, which is often disruptive of the comity they enjoy the rest of the year. The upwardly mobile islanders sometimes enjoy the temporary rise in station conferred on them by their acceptance, often patronizing, by their summer visitors, and this is usually resented by their friends and neighbors. Such islanders can often be identified by the transformations in their dress during the summer, when they mimic that affected by the yacht club set even to the color of the men's trousers.

While islanders and their summer visitors may have an equal affection for the island, their interests differ in many respects. Summer visitors think of it as another Eden. Some of them appear to believe that its people go into hibernation when summer is over, coming to life again as summer approaches. They occasionally ask, "What do you do here all winter?" forgetting that once they leave the island, its real life, active and meaningful to its inhabitants, is taken up again.

Many summer visitors who appreciate the island and its year-round residents would like to believe that all of their interests are in common. But the economic situation of the island as the lowest income county in its state makes this impossible. For many summer visitors, ecological conservation means keeping the island unchanged. From the moment the lease is signed for the property they have just acquired, they wage a constant battle against the coming of the summer "day trippers" and any activity that might increase the island's population. The working class islander, on the contrary, has no such luxurious position; he has a more important item on his agenda, feeding his family, and for him "the economy" must be more important than "the ecology." At the same time, the trends of the last few decades often convince him that he is fighting a losing battle, and he experiences the stresses of those who are powerless to affect their own destiny.

3

The Values of Islanders

What is most important about a person or a community often exists neither visibly nor in awareness, for much of what moves individuals or groups to behave in one way or another is long buried among the assumptions by which they live. As Louis Wirth put it, "the most important thing, therefore, that we can know about a man is what he takes for granted and the most elemental and important facts about a society are those that are seldom debated and generally regarded as settled" (Mannheim 1936). Because assumptions are regarded as settled and out of everyday awareness, they are spared from critical scrutiny while they exert a powerful effect on human lives.

One of the major sources of stress for islanders arises from the fact that their values are often in conflict with those of the larger society of which they are a part. The assumptions which guide their lives are challenged daily by what they see on television or read in the newspapers that reach the island. Perhaps more important, their assumptions about life are challenged massively each summer when their values come into conflict with those of their summer visitors, who are many times their number.

The islander has not yet accepted many of the dominant values of his country. He is only beginning to be troubled by the fact that fewer of his children go to college than is customary on the mainland. The island's high school, in its annual reports to the towns in the recent past, noted not the number of students going off to college but the number enrolled under a vague rubric called "post-second-ary education," which included college, beauty culture, barbering, cooking and automobile mechanics. The failure to distinguish be-tween college education and education for the trades reflected an attitude not only within the school system but within the community at large.

The islander refuses to be hobbled by the values of the Protestant ethic: thrift, piety, work for work's sake. He is willing to earn less as the price of freedom. He shows little interest in the unionization that would increase his wages, because he fears it would limit the range of his occupation and curtail his free time. When the deer season comes, he expects to be able to take the week off because he is often paid only when he works. If he cannot afford to, he expects to be able to have his gun at hand if the job is out of doors and near a wood. If he has inherited land, he values it more than the things its sale might permit him to have, for the possession of land gives him prestige and deference from his neighbors, and its sale is felt as a betrayal of his past. Many islanders who are rich in land live quite poorly, selling bits of land in crises when illness strikes or when a child wants to go to college. The term *land poor*, though archaic in many places, has real meaning on the island. Planning for the future is of no great concern; the now seems more important than the mor-row. When Samuel Covell, electrician, was asked to have a drink with a summer visitor while at work in his home, he accepted read-ily, though it was mid-afternoon and he had a long list of promised calls in his pocket. When the summer visitor, knowing that Samuel had once tried working in Providence, asked why he had come back to the island, Samuel raised his glass, grinned, and asked, "Where else would I be doing this in the middle of the day?"

There are many ways in which the values of a group or individual may be classified. One of the most useful, because it gets at the main issues which confront all societies, is that devised by Florence Kluckholn (1950). She suggested that all human beings are con-fronted by five crucial problems and that the major attitudes taken toward these problems by a group represent its dominant values. The five problems may be put in the form of questions. First, is hu-man nature evil, good, or a mixture of both? Second, is man in subjugation to nature, in harmony with her, or master over her? Third, is the focus of human life generally upon the past, the present, or the future? Fourth, is being or doing more important? And fifth, are the individuals in a society concerned mainly with their lineal relationships, with their collateral relationships, or with individualism? The answers people give to these questions are called their human nature, man-nature, time, activity, and relational orientations.

While the members of each human group may embrace different values, one set of values is usually dominant for any group. Those in the group who hold values not dominant for the group are of two sorts: some preserve values that are relics of the group's past, while others maintain values that are in the process of fighting for the future. The values held by individual members of a group, though hidden and taken for granted, have a great effect on their lives. To live by values not dominant in one's group, and thus to listen to a "different drummer," often makes that person feel out of step with his fellows. Yet while the possession of variant values may cause one discomfort and a sense of alienation from the group, the ability to cast aside the common assumptions may free one for uncommon adventures. It is much as Albert Einstein once said when asked what had permitted him to discover the theory of relativity, "I never believed an axiom."

In order to study the values of the islanders, two methods were used. The first was to record the choices they made when presented with twelve different human situations common to rural life, three for each of four of the orientations: relational, time, man-nature, and activity (Appendix 7). The situations were selected from twenty-two situations covering four orientations used in a study of five small communities in the Southwest (Kluckholn and Strodtbeck 1961). With this method the values of groups of island high-school students and of island teachers were determined.

By the second method, the values of adult islanders were estimated by a group of eighteen knowledgeable observers—sixteen teachers, a nurse, and a psychiatrist—and their consensus was recorded as the value choices of islanders for all five orientations. This procedure was based on the finding of Kluckholn and Strodtbeck that observers familiar with the communities they studied were able to predict with accuracy how each community tested on the orientations. While estimates cannot be treated with the same confidence as the results of tests, the high degree of agreement by the eighteen island observers gives assurance that the estimates are reasonably valid.

The values of young and adult islanders, of young male and female islanders, and of island teachers and other adult islanders were compared for the following orientations: relational, time, man-nature, and activity. In addition, the values of island adults and American middle class adult values from another study (GAP 1970) were compared for all five orientations. The five orientations and the possible choices for each are:

Relational: individual, linear, or collateral
Time: future, present, or past
Man-Nature: control over, subjugation to, or living in harmony with nature
Activity: doing or being
Human Nature: evil, good, or a mixture of both

Adult Islanders

In their relationships people in the modern era have shown a gradual development from the lineal to the collateral to the individual. Increasingly, children are trained and allowed to make their own decisions rather than to consult their elders. The "I" gains increasing acceptance over the "we." The recently popular retort of the young, "Don't bug me," is a statement of the demand for individuality. By and large, American lineal relationships are gone, preserved only in recollection and on nostalgic covers of the old *Saturday Evening Post*.

Modern corporate enterprise also rewards those who embrace individualism. The transfer of an executive from one office to another requires the sacrifice of the collateral relationships that are so sustaining and which continue to exist in confined and peasant societies. But Americans, driven by the Protestant ethic and by the need for economic security, have increasingly given up the protection of the close-knit kinship system into which many of them were born.

To a greater extent than in contemporary America, the adult islander lives a less individual and a more collateral life (Appendix 8). His dominant preference in the relational orientation is for collateralism, with individualism a second choice. For those who are native to the island, extended families are large, and they are often called upon for collateral support in times of trouble. A man building a house seeks out his brothers and other collaterals for help, for within one family there are usually men of many skills.

In their attitude to time, middle class Americans are primarily oriented to the future, whereas the adult islander's dominant orientation is to the present, with the future a third choice. He is more concerned than are most Americans with the pains and pleasures of the present. *Planning* and *zoning* were until recently troublesome words, dangerous to use in public meetings. The islander's primary interest is in what he will do today and, after that, his recollections about the past. Until recently, when the very nature of his life was threatened by the unrestrained plans of "land developers" and speculators, he rarely concerned himself with what might be; he was more interested in what is and what had been.

In the man-nature context, one of the values dominant in contemporary America is that man can acquire power over nature. We dam our streams to harness their waters, we transplant organs from one man to another, and we confidently expect to be able to modify if not control the weather. The islander, on the contrary, is more inclined to accept, and enjoy, his subjugation to nature or at least to hope to live in harmony with her. Even today island fishermen boast that they cannot swim, an activity derisively considered an amusement for summer folk. They recognize that the sea is great, that their boats are small, and that if they chance into a great storm, they will simply be meeting their inexorable fate. Even illness is often approached as a part of life, and the effort to maintain life for a few more days or weeks in the presence of a terminal illness is not pursued as relentlessly as it is in some of the great hospitals of the cities. Suicide, which the islander's religious values teach him is immoral, is treated by him with the same fateful stoicism rather than with the guilt of those who feel that all human problems are capable of human solution. When high winds and tides cause the ferry to remain in the harbor at Woods Hole, cutting the islander off from the mainland, he does not rail either against the sea or at the men who man the ships, as his summer visitors often do, for he has long been persuaded that in such a struggle, nature always wins.

In the activity orientation of Americans, doing rather than being is a preoccupation. A child seen observing nature makes us anxious. We want him to do something with it, to collect its shells or its butterflies, or in some way to rearrange it closer to his desires. Adult islanders have a greater inclination to being than do most Americans. They walk down the street at what was once called a saunter; they greet friends and neighbors, sniff the air, and comment on the weather. They are aware of the moods of the day and the feelings of the hour. A purchase at a shop is not simply a commercial transaction; it must begin with a social encounter between buyer and seller.

Middle class Americans prefer activity that is goal directed in tangible terms. Education is seen not as a way to self-enrichment but as a means to success in life, measured by position, money, or power. The contrast between islander and visitor shows in bold relief each summer at the agricultural fair. The island child seems eager to savor what he has produced, the cake he has baked, the vegetables he has grown, or the exhibit he has fabricated. The summer child often appears to work for the reward, the varicolored rosetted ribbons indicative of first, second, and third prizes, and he often requires consolation if no prize is won.

The islander's view of human nature departs from the generally optimistic, liberal belief that man is innately good and is corrupted by the evil in society. Human nature is usually seen by the islander as innately evil, in comparison to his middle class summer visitors who see it as a mixture of good and evil. This orientation often shapes the islander's attitude toward his children, particularly in the lower social class positions. Instead of being viewed as collections of potentialities to be brought to fulfillment by careful guidance and education, fertilized by loving concern, the islander's children are often viewed as creatures of inordinate drives with a proclivity for sin. The anticipated danger grows as the child grows. Since the parent thus becomes more and more powerless in relation to his children, his anxiety increases. He becomes most anxious as his children approach adolescence, and his concerns are generally negative. He fears that his children will "get into trouble," the girls by becoming pregnant and the boys by breaking the law.

Young Islanders

When the Kluckholn-Strodtbeck test of value orientations designed for rural and folk communities was given to an unselected group of high school seniors on the island, they were found to have values closer to those dominant for contemporary American culture than did their elders (Appendix 9). To some degree the values of female students were more traditional than those of males.

Though island young people have less traditional values than do their elders, they possess some of the values of folk peoples. In failing to be dominantly oriented toward doing, toward individualism, and toward the future, the young people do not on the average possess those value orientations that are generally held necessary to the drive for success which has long been a part of the American urban and suburban outlook.

At the completion of high school, young islanders are confronted with a crucial choice, whether to remain on the island or leave it. Those who wish to go to college or for special technical training have no choice but to leave. Others may leave for jobs elsewhere. Since the choice of leaving or remaining on the island involves a high degree of self-selection, the orientation data were analyzed in respect to those who remained and those who left. There were significant differences between the two groups in two of the orientations. Those who left the island were notably more future-oriented than those who remained and also believed to a greater degree that man could prevail over nature rather than exist subordinate to her or in harmony with her. It is likely that the group which left the island also contained a higher proportion of non-natives, but the consequence for the community would be the same. The implication of this self-selection process is important because of its effect on the composition of the island population. In brief, the island retains young people with more traditional values, while those whose values are more consistent with the demands of the American dream tend to leave. Such a selective out-migration cannot but be a factor in the maintenance of traditional island values. Further, it is likely that the significant number of young people who have come to live on the island during the past five or six years have largely repudiated American middle class values.

Adults and Young People in Conflict

There were two significant differences between the adults of the island and their children with respect to their value orientations (Appendix 10). While control over nature was a dominant value for young people, subordination to nature was a dominant value for adults. In the time orientation, while young people appeared to have an equal preference for present and future, adults clearly were present oriented.

Such differences in values between parents and children no doubt lead to conflict, for holding different values, they operate from different premises. Since we are generally unconscious of the values that motivate us, parents and children are rarely aware of the nature of the conflict in which they are engaged.

The second most important adults with whom high school students interact are their teachers. The value orientations of fifteen island teachers, all but one of them in-migrants, were determined on the basis of the same test given to the students. The fifteen teachers had essentially the same dominant value orientations as were found in middle class Americans. They differed from their students in preferring individualism over collateralism, were more future oriented, and to a greater degree chose doing over being. Such differences in values between teachers and students probably exist in most publc school systems, except those in upper middle class suburban communities, and they cannot help but affect the attitudes of teachers toward their students, of students toward their teachers, and in consequence, the entire educational process. The teacher who is oriented toward doing, the future, and individualism—values that he does not find to be dominant in his students—may find his efforts frustrated. If his students do not respond to his efforts, which are clothed in middle class values, there is a danger that he will come to believe that they are either stubborn or stupid, for one thing of which each of us is certain, is that his values are preferable to those held by others, and often the perception of a difference in values results in an effort to "reform" the other person. Yet the educational process may benefit from the experience of the psychotherapeutic process that an appreciation of the difference in values between patient and therapist, and a modification of psychotherapeutic techniques in the light of these differences, may be salutory (Spiegel 1959).

Ethnic Groups

Since the island population has a significant ethnic structure, the data on value orientations were analyzed by ethnic group. Those bearing old American names, generally Anglo-Saxon in origin, were classified as "old Americans." Those bearing Portuguese names, American variants of Portuguese names, and in five cases French Canadian names were classified as "new Americans." The only orientation in which there was a statistically significant difference, and in that one it was highly significant, was the activity orientation. Whereas 62 percent of the old American group gave doing as a dominant value, more than 76 percent of the new American group gave being as their dominant value. This finding suggests that old Americans find it easier to adapt to the demands of off-island urban and suburban life than do newer Americans.

The Implications for Island Life

A number of inferences flow from these findings. The difference in values between those leaving the island and those remaining tends to preserve the old values on the island. This may explain why whenever there is a movement in the direction of economic venturesomeness, it does not take the form of seeking manufacturing enterprises but hearkens back to the possibilities of increasing the value of the shellfish industry, developing the cottage craft and beef industries, or more nostalgically, making the island again a vineyard in order that it may produce wine for the market.

One of the difficulties which comes with having a value system other than that prevalent in one's society is that it makes more difficult the achievement of conventional desires. Take, for example, the value system of the island's high school students. One of the requirements for success in the modern industrial system is a belief that man has power over nature. Modern industrial enterprise grows and develops upon this premise, and the significant proportion of business enterprises that invest in research is testimony to this belief. In addition, such enterprise requires a value of individualism rather than of collateralism. Modern industrial enterprise rewards those who are adaptable, who are willing to move from place to place, who can give up one social network and enter another. Island young people with a dominant value of collateralism find this requirement difficult and are therefore handicapped. Those young people studying or working away from home suffer greatly from the loss of their collateral network. They return at every opportunity, often met at the dock by a cohort of friends, and frequently quit altogether.

The implications of these findings for mental health or mental disorder are governed by the fact that islanders are composed of two groups, those who were born and have lived on the island all of their lives and those who have come to the island. Whether the in-migrants possess the dominant values of contemporary American culture to a greater degree than do the natives, or whether their choice of the community represents a deviance from those values, is not certain. What is known is that the native islander and perhaps too the incomer lives with a system of values which are not shared by the world outside or by the large number of people he encounters each summer. He experiences the contrast between his values and those of the American culture through his access to newspapers and television and, more important, by his interactions with and observations of the large number of people who descend upon his island each summer. Since his dominant values are a mixture of those of peasant societies and of the contemporary middle class, he may be said to suffer from value inconsistency in the same way that he frequently suffers from the stress of status inconsistency.

Such conflict between values and desires must certainly be stressful. The island farmer, even though his farm loses money each year, often strongly feels that the land bequeathed to him over the generations is a trust held by him in the name of the past for the future. If his daily work brings him a modest living, if he does not yearn for other places or other climes, he may be content as the custodian of his acres, and he enjoys the status that goes with being a large landowner. Such a status is frequently reaffirmed each summer when his summer visitors make the inevitable inquiry as to whether he will sell some of his land.

But then as his children grow, the financial demands upon him may increase. If one of them desires to go to college, an enterprise that may be beyond his regular income but quite possible if he sells his land, he is thrown into a conflict, for to sell any bit of land is to be faithless to the past, to engage in wickedness.. To deny his child the help that he is forced to realize he can afford is equally disturbing, and from this conflict between two belief systems which cannot be harmonized much stress arises.

4

The Stresses of Island Life

The life of the Vineyarder is defined not only by the island's physical geography, its insularity, its rural character, and the values of its people. The circumstances of his life also possess characteristics that have been suggested as presumptive or proven factors in the occurrence of psychological disorder (Hughes et al 1960; D. C. Leighton et al 1963; Langner and Michael 1963; Susser 1968). Specific events or social circumstances that are likely to produce stress in individuals may also, when they occur with notable frequency in a community, be used as indices of sociocultural disintegration, for eventually the sociocultural life of a community has an impact on the individual to the degree that its noxious or coherent elements affect him directly or indirectly (A. H. Leighton 1959). For example, a high frequency of broken homes in a community produces a climate that is disadvantageous even to those whose homes are not broken, although certainly the effect is far greater and more noticeable on members of the broken homes. While stress disrupts existing states of balance or adaptation, those elements in the structure of a community that fit together and enhance life are countervailing forces. In any consideration of the stresses to which Vineyarders are exposed, therefore, the coherent elements in island life should be kept in mind.

Needing and Having

Many studies have described the effects of poverty. The poor live

52

less long than the better off, are sick more often, receive inferior care, are more often mentally ill, and have the most severe disorders for which they receive the least adequate treatment (Anderson and Feldman 1956; Hollingshead and Redlich 1958). But poverty rarely causes mental illness directly, save in those illnesses due to dietary deficiency or poor prenatal care. It operates through interfering with human needs, such as the acquisition of food, shelter, clothing, and sleep, the securing of adequate medical care and equal justice before the law, the development of self-esteem, respect from one's fellows, and a sense of belonging to a coherent social and moral order.

If, for example, the ability to express anger verbally and therefore effectively prevents to some degree the development of psychological disorder, it can easily be seen that the poor are comparatively handicapped, for they cannot often afford to express anger or to demand justice. Much of what they receive, they receive because of their compliance. When an attempt was made to organize a consumer council on the island, it was discovered that low income people felt they could not participate. Although the result might eventually be lower prices for the things that they bought, they were afraid that the local merchants who carried their accounts over the winter would retaliate by demanding cash payment for all purchases. A man employed by the only establishment on the island that can use his skill cannot voice his grievances if his next week's food supply is dependent on this week's salary. He may avoid a dispute with the registrar of motor vehicles if he fears that the registrar as a consequence of the dispute may decide that he is in terms of the Massachusetts law an "improper" or "incompetent" person to drive a motor vehicle, a circumstance which might seriously impair his ability to earn a living.

The island has been a low income community for a long time. Over decades it has been the lowest income county in Massachusetts, both because it lacks a wage-paying industry and because its economy is based on the annual low wage scales of a seasonal tourist economy. Unemployment rates are high during the winter, and the job market during the summer is severely competitive, when the islander must compete with a large number of visiting young people who are willing to work for substandard wages in order to spend the summer on the island. To complicate the islander's economic problem, the island's cost of living is one of the highest in the country (DCPEDC 1972). Some of the islander's high cost of living is due to the need to transport virtually everything across the water, but this too is often taken advantage of. He pays higher prices for many of the essentials, since he does not buy in a truly competitive market. His banks charge significantly higher interest rates than do Cape Cod banks, a fact which adds thousands of dollars to the paying-off of his mortgage. In heating his home, he finds that the fuel oil he buys is higher in price than on the Cape and varies little or not at all among retailers (DCPEDC 1972). Although the Steamship Authority can buy its fuel cheaper on the island than on the mainland because it is brought there by water, the individual citizen pays more for gasoline for his car than does his neighbor on Cape Cod.

Even while living on a low income, the islander got less help than the citizens of the other thirteen counties of Massachusetts in 1969 (U.S. Census 1972). The four hundred island families receiving social security payments that year received an average of $1,337 yearly, substantially less than that in any other county. For persons on public assistance or public welfare, the average amount given to island families that year was significantly lower than in the other twelve counties for which data were available. Finally, the 6.5 percent of islander families living below the poverty level had a yearly mean family income of $1,229, 26 percent below that of nearby Cape Cod and 31 percent below that of the island of Nantucket.

It has become trite to say that poverty is relative, that the poorest of our citizens commands commodities, powers and opportunities denied to the kings of centuries ago. But if the presence or absence of poverty cannot be measured by what we possess in property or in power, how do we perceive it? What makes a man feel poor? What makes a man in fact poor?

For the islander at the lower end of the American economic and social scale, and this includes most islanders, such questions give rise to much confusion. If he thinks in conventional terms, he knows he is poor. He knows absolutely, because during the winter after the work-filled days of summer and the brief but heady windfall of the scalloping season, he finds his income meager, his bills mounting, and the advent of Christmas with its demands for extra purchases a serious problem.

When summer arrives, he sees the contrast between his possessions and those of the visitor to his island. The island, during most of the year a repository of old automobiles called "Vineyard cars" because no one dares to drive them off the island, is suddenly flooded with the latest models of domestic cars and a large variety of foreign vehicles. He sees yachts anchored in the harbors whose upkeep takes more than he earns all year, and at the end of summer he searches for and finds in the town dumps household objects discarded by summer visitors that later grace his own house. While his wife and children work long hours, he sees those they serve engaged in a kind of consumption that he can only identify as thoughtlessly conspicuous.

But the very coming of the summer people confirms his belief that he already possesses something of great value. Through them he reappraises his possession of the island. He realizes that he has taken for granted what they prize. As spring matures and inquiries come in for rentals, one island woman yearly announces to her family, "Just think, all over the United States, people are getting ready to come to the Vineyard," and then, after a dramatic pause, "and we are already here!"

To counterbalance his poverty, the islander in fact has a number of assets. Perhaps most important, he is part of a community. What Simone Weill (1955) described as "the need for roots" is readily satisfied. He is part of a town or village with a network of relationships that touch on kinship, friendship, occupation, club membership, religious affiliation, and his role in the civic affairs of his town. Beyond his town he is an islander, but this loyalty is perhaps less important than town loyalty. As one islander put it, "on the other side, we're all Vineyarders, but once we cross the Sound, we become Chilmarkers or Edgartonians or Gay Headers." It is a Vineyard custom when driving along the roads for each driver to wave to the driver of any approaching car long before he can recognize him. The point of the custom is that the odds are he knows the other driver anyway and there is no point in taking a chance. Further, by making the greeting automatic, the problem of conflict between persons is avoided. Finally, it is a recognition that there are a limited number of islanders and that they are all on the same island.

With the coming of Labor Day, the great mass of summer folk leave and again the islander can walk his pavements, arms swinging, and again he can recognize the faces of his friends. He may express his delight in the return of his living space and remark to acquaintances, "Well, it's ours again."

The Loss of Power

Islanders were once people who owned their land, had free access to its beaches, and used the sea and the land as their larder. With time they have increasingly lost access to their beaches, their land is rapidly finding its way into the hands of summer visitors and land speculators, and the technologies available to other countries have left them unable to compete successfully in their own fishing grounds. Increasingly they must ask permission to hunt on land which once they roamed at will, now in the hands of rich landowners. Beaches from which they fished as children are now blocked to them by the warning signs of absentee owners. Access to the ocean, which they once thought of as theirs by right though they recognized that its title was held by either God or the Commonwealth of Massachusetts, they now find effectively owned by off-islanders whose caretakers are busy tacking up "No Trespassing" signs, while their own police enforce, often reluctantly to be sure, the new order against them. A large part of their island is state forest, once theirs, but they may now use it legally only under conditions made by legislators in "far off" Boston.

Once dependent only on their own skill and effort, they are now subject to decisions made by nameless people, the fish broker in New York, the legislature in Boston, and even closer at hand and therefore more painful, the tastes and wishes of the summer people. In the employer-employee relationship with summer people, the overt power is on one side. The summer visitors who require houses to be built and land to be cleared and landscaped have the money which islanders require for their livelihood. The power of the islander is covert. He rarely can indulge in the luxury of open defiance.

Often latent in the islander's relationship with summer employers is his resentment at being dependent on them for his livelihood. Consciously or unconsciously, he can express this resentment in ways that will discomfit his employer but avoid open defiance. He may promise to finish a house by a certain date and not comply. Having dug the foundation and done part of the work, he moves his crew to another job, leaving his employer fuming in impotence 250 miles away. Not all employer-employee relationships are of this nature, but the occurrence is sufficiently frequent to be of consequence. In brief, the meaning of the islander's apparent disinclination to live up to his work promise is not that he is indolent, incompetent, or defective in character. Rather it represents one way in which he tries to maintain some internal sense of freedom in a world that increasingly forces him to become the hired help of others.

There are a number of aspects to the islander's stressful relationship to the summer visitors. Since the islander lives in a small society with the same people for all of his life, he avoids open conflict. He does not like to say no to any request. Therefore, he often makes unrealistic promises, even to other islanders, half knowing he will not be able to keep them. Often, too, the problem stems from economic anxiety. The house builder, to ensure having enough work for his men until the next summer, may overpromise himself. There is little doubt that the islander often resents the contrast between his own meager means and the conspicuous consumption he sees about him. Occasionally, such feelings break out into the open. During World War II a rich widower living in a very large house asked Herbert Garenson, builder, to add a wing to it. Herbert inspected the house, quizzically studied its owner, and made up his mind. "No," he said. "I won't build it. It's already too big for one person."

A latent cause of conflict stems from a difference in values that generally exists between the summer people and the islander. The summer visitor is more conscious of the insistencies of time than is the islander. To a much greater degree he lives by a schedule determined by the commuter train, the daily round of appointments, the lunch date, the 2:35 appointment with the psychoanalyst, or the

8:40 curtain at the theater. Even his children back in Larchmont or Newton are tied to their own schedules, the flute lessons, the dance lessons. For the islander, few tasks are rigidly time bound. His children must get to school on time, and that is about all. Because he is generally paid by the hour, he expects some leeway on the job. Examples of the islander's latent resistance to the authority of off-islanders, summer residents, or officials of the Commonwealth are observed in two seasonal activities. It is common for islanders to cut their own Christmas trees in untended fields owned by summer people or in the state forest, an activity that is illegal and punishable by a fine. To interpret this as theft based on economic need or a character defect misses the point, as is confirmed by the fact that the practice is engaged in yearly by Dr. Nathan Wesley, a respected physician. A clue to the meaning of the act once appeared on Dr. Wesley's tree, topped by a defiant notice reading "courtesy of Governor Peabody," at that time the governor of Massachusetts.

Another means by which islanders attempt to maintain their sense of identity and individual freedom, despite their loss of economic independence and of access to their lands, is suggested by the findings of a linguistic study of the island done in 1961-1962 (Labov 1963). Throughout its 320-year history of continuous settlement and perhaps influenced by its resistance to Boston ways, the island had preserved many archaic speech traits that were typical of southeastern New England before 1800. Among the patterns preserved was the pronunciation of the r in words such as *card* and *board*. This contrast with the practice in Boston and other parts of southeastern Massachusetts had led to the comment that the Vineyard was an "island of r-pronouncers in a sea of r-lessness." The pronunciation of some vowels and diphthongs were often, and still are, different from the standard speech of southeastern Massachusetts. Word survivals of seventeenth century English were found by the study, and even today the word *tempest* for storm is occasionally heard in Chilmark.

Most important, the study found that speech patterns in islanders resisted the changes which had occurred in New England speech over the past two hundred years. As islanders lost status and power to their summer visitors, rather than altering their speech to conform to the style of the increasingly powerful group, as others in similar situations have done (Labov 1972), islanders increased the frequency of old speech patterns, particularly among the "Chilmark fishermen, the most close-knit group on the island, the most independent, the group which is most stubbornly opposed to the incursions of the summer people." As early as 1838 a clergyman also noted that "the old stock of Islanders . . . some of whom have never set foot upon the main-land . . . have a language and pronunciation of their own" (Devens 1838).

In the speech of a group of high school students, it was found that those who planned to remain on the island used a greater number of traditional forms of speech than those who planned to leave the island upon graduation, who used forms closer to mainland patterns. The inference was made that those who planned to remain on the island had patterned their speech on that of the older up-islanders, heirs of the old traditions who served them as a model or reference group, while those who planned to make their careers off-island unconsciously adopted the speech styles of their summer visitors or mainland incomers. These inferences based upon sociolinguistic studies also reveal much about island character.

Conflict of Social Roles

The belief is common that the complexity of human relationships varies with the size of the place in which one lives. It is true that the number and variety of people one encounters are greater in large communities than in small ones. But the differences in role relationships between large and small communities involves more than a difference in size (Frankenberg 1966). Relationships in large communities are likely to be peripheral, simple, and well-defined. The dweller in a small community may encounter fewer people, but the relationships he has are more complex. The problems involved in this complexity are best understood within the concept of social role.

An important difference between urban and rural societies is that in urban societies the individual is involved in single role relationships with a great number of people, whereas in rural communities he performs in multiple roles with fewer people. In the city the shop-keeper is a shopkeeper and nothing else; in a rural community the shopkeeper may in addition be a classmate in one's adult education course, a member of the finance committee of one's town, the parent of a playmate of one's child, and a client or customer. In brief, the dweller in a rural community may interact with fewer people, but each interaction is close and complex.

Since behaving in multiple roles toward one person is exceedingly complex and is characterized by much ambiguity, people on the island have learned to segregate their roles. In talking to one another, they generally signal the role in which the discussion is occurring and, so far as possible, maintain that role for the duration of the discussion. An example is the interaction between a high school student and the neighbor who taught in his school. Though the child had been accustomed since childhood to calling the adult neighbor by his first name, at school he called him Mr. Bartman. On occasion, when the child remained late for some extracurricular activity and missed the school bus, the teacher drove him home. During the 15- or 20-minute trip, the child continued to address him as Mr. Bartman, but as soon as they had turned into the dirt road that the two families shared, Mr. Bartman became "Johnny" again.

Despite the skill that many people living on the island have acquired in segregating their role relationships and the expectations which flow from them, the sources of conflict are always present, and this leads to stress. Suppose, for example, a mother wishes to complain about a teacher before the school committee of which the teacher's wife is a member. The parent is confronted with the problem of dealing with a school committee member in two roles, as a teacher's wife and as a member of the school committee. On such occasions, she is likely to remain silent out of fear that the school committee member will not be able to segregate her roles. Professionals in a community are often placed in such complex positions.

Status Inconsistency

Status is the position relative to that of others which a person holds in the opinion of his neighbors. It places him at one level or another and affects his prestige and power in the community. Above all, it affects his sense of self, his self-esteem. Much of what is vital to a person contributes to the measure of his status. Among them are appearance, dress, hygiene, speech, occupation, education, possessions, religion, kin, and friends.

Three qualities are basic to a satisfactory status: it must be high enough to permit ready satisfaction of basic needs, it must be relatively stable, and the factors that determine it must be internally consistent. The basic needs for food, clothing, shelter, and intimacy are less likely to be satisfied without stress by one of low status than by one of higher status. The greater difficulty of those in low status positions in satisfying their needs for food, clothing, or shelter and their comparative lack of competence in securing sexual satisfaction and love without the risk of losing self-esteem produce anxiety and damage to that self-esteem (Sullivan 1953). Rapid changes in status, whether downward or upward, are also stressful and conducive to at least a transient increase in psychological symptoms. Inconsistencies in some of the major factors that determine status, as between occupation and education, make for a continual state of stress.

Within the last decade, of the four islanders who were graduates in engineering from the Massachusetts Institute of Technology, only one was employed as an engineer, and his job required that he travel to work by boat to the mainland. The other three, working far below their level of training, would certainly have been in a state of status inconsistency in communities where engineers are employable. Though each may have been aware of his downward occupational mobility, the professed and well-understood desire to live on the island no doubt mitigated the effect of his status inconsistency.

The position one holds in the social scheme is constantly in evidence in a small place. The residential segregation of people by economic position in urban and suburban regions determines that most of their significant relationships are with those of the same status. While this fact may inhibit the possibilities of upward mobility, it also may reduce the interpersonal stresses associated with low status positions. The rural dweller, the islander in this case, cannot so segregate his life. He associates daily with those of higher status, and he may daily experience the fact that even one of his siblings is in a higher position.

Rapid changes in status occur in islanders, as they do elsewhere, but they produce special problems for him. A city dweller who "marries up" or who inherits a large sum of money can, and usually does, move from one status to another as he moves from one address to another. He moves his home, acquires new acquaintances, and alters his style of life. While he experiences the stress of adaptation, he does not publicly and daily experience the change in his position. The islander whose position changes rapidly, however, remains in the same place and with the same people, and his attempts to cope with the new position into which fortune has placed him might be amusing if they were not often so poignant. When Samuel Whitlow, a house builder, after a few fortuitous real estate deals became, by island standards, a rich man, he found it difficult to adapt to his new position. His good fortune was widely known and he was expected to show some sign of it. But he did not feel comfortable in custom-made clothing, and he wore a suit only to weddings and funerals. He disliked travel and thought he was already eating as well as any man could. He found the solution to his problem in a motor car. Now he rides the few streets of his town in a Cadillac, still wearing the work clothes he has been accustomed to all his life. The fact that he must make what is for him an unpleasant journey off-island to have his car serviced he accepts as one of the necessary burdens of success.

By status inconsistency is meant a serious incongruity among those elements that go to make up an individual's status position, so that he lacks some of the major attributes common to the social position in which he finds himself. For example, his cultural interests and aspirations may be higher than his social status, and because of this he experiences a dissonance in his daily life. One study, for example, showed that psychophysiological symptoms were frequent in women of high education married to men at lower level occupations, a common island occurrence, and were similarly frequent in men of low education in occupations of high level (Jackson 1962). The two chief consequences of this circumstance are frustration and uncertainty. The person who is in a state of status inconsistency often finds himself frustrated by exposure to expectations he cannot or is unwilling to meet. On the reverse, he is often uncertain as to what he may legitimately expect of others. Such seemingly small transactions as who calls whom by a first or family name, or what one wears in whose home on what occasion, point up the difficulties of the state. A study in Israel reported high scores on a symptom inventory of in-migrants whose occupation and education were not consistent (Abramson 1966). This is not an uncommon finding on the island. The average education for women is significantly higher than for men. Part of this is due to the excess of women over men in the higher age groups, women who have moved to the island after the death of a husband or who have survived him there after retirement. But some of it is owing to a status inconsistency in young women. It is a common occurrence for a college girl employed on the island as a waitress for the summer to become attracted by an island lad whose competence and manliness appear to be beyond her previous experience. This makes for status inconsistency in her life, since her educational and cultural aspirations are inconsistent with the new status she occupies upon marriage.

A noteworthy example of status inconsistency, temporary in nature, is seen each summer. The perennial summer visitor to the island usually has a deep desire for feeling rooted there. In the service of this impulse, he cultivates a first name social relationship with native islanders, often those who are employed by him. It is not uncommon for a native islander working for a summr visitor to finish his job at 5:00 in the afternoon and dash home to change in order to return to the same house as a guest at his employer's cocktail party, and then perhaps a few nights later he may work as the bartender at another summer party now serving many of the same people with whom he met on a plane of presumptive equality a few nights before.

Cultural Confusion

It has been suggested that cultural confusion may be a factor in the production of psychiatric disorder (A. H. Leighton 1959). A number of studies have shown that high rates of such disorder are associated with migration to other cultures and that the longer the individual is resident in the new culture, the lower are the rates (Ødegaard 1932; Murphy 1965). Even more significant, it has been demonstrated that the rate of schizophrenia is higher in people of Italian origin, for example, if they move into a community with relatively few Italians than if they move into one with a large proportion of people of that cultural background (Mintz and Schwartz 1964).

By the word *culture* is meant a coherent set of customs, values, and beliefs. Save in times of rapid social change or when there is a large in-migration of people of another culture, cultures tend to become coherent, which is to say that the values, customs, and beliefs are shared by most members of the community.

Martha's Vineyard is populated largely by people of two cultures, those of so-called Anglo-Saxon stock and those of Portuguese origin. Those of Anglo-Saxon stock are identified not as Yankees, the common term in New England, but as "old Americans," because the island was part of the province of New York in the colonial period, and its county name, Dukes, is part of the triumvirate of county names that includes Kings and Queens in New York City. The second largest ethnic group, the Portuguese, derive not from the Portuguese mainland but from the Portuguese islands. Their forebears came during whaling days, and for a time they used the name of one of the Azores, Fayal, for Martha's Vineyard.

Although the old Americans and the Portuguese or "new Americans" have shared the island for a long time, each group maintains the primary elements of its identity. Nonetheless, there are many areas in which cultural confusion is significant. Persons of Portuguese origin of the first and second generation make up close to 14 percent of the population (U.S. Bureau of the Census 1972); with the third and fourth generation added, their proportion of the population approaches 30 percent. There has been much intermarriage, which leads to cultural uncertainty. Women of Anglo-Saxon background married to Portuguese men often make a point of noting their maiden names. There has been a significant Americanization, perhaps better called Anglo-Saxonization, of Portuguese names; names such as Rogers or Campbell may be either old American or Portuguese. Relatively little is known of the Portuguese culture even by persons of Portuguese ancestry, and few of those know of the exploits of the Portuguese navigators and seamen or have any identification with the homeland. The island schools, perhaps in response to the self-derogation of the Portuguese population, make no particular mention of Portuguese culture, and the language is not taught. Only a very few islanders any longer speak Portuguese.

An additional source of cultural confusion for those of Portuguese origin lies in the problem of color. People whose families came from the Azores or the Madeira Islands are Caucasians. The minority whose ancestors came from the Cape Verde Islands, a small group of islands off the coast of Africa, are often darker in complexion and, in parts of the United States where Portuguese sensibilities are not known, might be classified as black Americans. The so-called "black Portuguese" almost always identify themselves as white. Though the victims of prejudice by those of Azorean and Madeiraian origin perhaps as much as by their Anglo-Saxon neighbors, they struggle to maintain their belief in a white identity. When some years ago a governor of Massachusetts wanted to have a survey of race and ethnicity among state employees in order to increase job opportunities for blacks, he found it necessary to ask that each state department classify people as white, black, or Cape Verdean. It would have been politically hazardous to put the Cape Verdeans in one or the other category.

One of the frequent signs of ethnic derogation is the large number of ethnic jokes and derogatory statements directed at the Portuguese. They are basically the same comments as are applied to other ethnic groups in different parts of the country. The most common element in them is a derogation of the ability of people of Portuguese origin. Unfortunately, people of Portuguese origin are themselves participants in self-derogation, partly in a protective way, as in gallows humor, and partly because they seem to be persuaded of the validity of the derogation. The general response has been to adapt as rapidly as possible to New England ways, sacrificing the sustaining elements in their own culture except for the richness of ties within the extended family. They make no demands on the school system that it give recognition to Portuguese culture and language, and they publicly celebrate Portuguese religious festivals less often than is customary in other parts of Massachusetts where there are significant Portuguese populations.

But perhaps as a result of becoming as American as the old Americans, they have increasingly assumed a role in island affairs, serving as selectmen and members of town committees, as members of the board of county commissioners, and achieving the highest political office the island can bestow, representative to the Massachusetts legislature. Another sign of their acculturation is their more than occasional transfer from the Catholic to the Episcopal Church. This often occurs as the result of intermarriage between members of the two religious groups but frequently also when both husband and wife are of Portuguese extraction. It is likely to occur when a family finds itself in conflict with Catholic dogma, as when they feel compelled to use birth control techniques not approved by the church. It results in a widening of their social horizon and opens new areas for social relationships.

Another group of longest residence, though smallest in number on the island, is the native Americans, now limited to about one hundred and forty persons (U.S. Bureau of the Census 1971). Most of the Indian population lives in the town of Gay Head and controls its political system. Intermarriage over the centuries has made it unlikely that many persons of pure Indian stock are left on the island. The names common among them are Anglo-Saxon and one Dutch name alleged to have been brought to the island from Dutch Guiana. As with other small minorities, they are in a constant struggle to preserve their cultural identity against the centrifugal forces generated by the majority culture.

Migration In and Out

Moving one's household from one place to another has become a common occurrence for the American family. It is estimated that approximately one of every five Americans moves each year. About half of the islanders were born in other places and thus were at one time or another migrants to the island. Of those living on the Vineyard in 1970, one in every six had lived elsewhere five years before

(U.S. Bureau of the Census 1972). In addition, an unknown number of individuals had moved to and then left the island within that five-year period.

As with all changes in life requiring adaptation, moving one's household is stressful. The change of locale, the separation from friends and social groups, the need to adapt to new people and new customs, demand much of the individual. For children, the sudden immersion in a new school, where a period of initiatory scapegoating by the resident children is common, may be particularly stressful. There is an aphorism in the moving industry that for household effects, three moves are equal to one fire. The observation may be applicable to the moving of people.

People come to live on the island for many reasons, and those reasons determine to a significant degree the nature of its population, its human resources and its problems. More and more often they come to escape the pressures of the city, to enjoy the island's beauty, or to pursue the bucolic myth. The young people who have arrived in swelling numbers in recent years are often alienated from their families and from the common culture. Families sometimes come during periods of crisis, in the hope that a new environment will repair a creaking marriage. Those who because of personality disorders or alcoholism have been extruded from their families on the mainland may come with the assurance of a monthly remittance so long as they remain on the island. Thus, while the island adds to its human resources by immigration, it also receives a great number of people who bring their predicaments with them.

Out-migration also is often selective. The family with a retarded child is much less likely to leave than one with normal children since the island's tolerance for differences makes it a more benign place for the different. The out-migration is selective in respect to personality, for the young people who leave the island after graduating from high school are more likely than those who stay to be dynamic in personality (Mazer and Ahern 1969) and not traditional in values. Some of them return after a few years, but relatively few of the college-trained, since the island occupations that can use their education and specialized training are mainly limited to law, medicine, and education. There are few places in the island community for those in the sciences and engineering, or for those trained for large-scale business enterprises.

The process of migration, particularly to a community as variant as the island, may be associated with much stress. In the first place, the island is so different from the urban and suburban communities from which many of its migrants come. Its very geographic insularity is felt by some as stressfully confining. Old people often become anxious during weather that cuts them off from the resources of large city medical centers. The adjustment of a city child to an island in-group of youngsters with different values and beliefs, and even with games whose names are often localisms, may be painful. Accustomed as the city or suburban dweller is to living in a place where almost everyone is an incomer and where affiliation to place is not intense, he often finds it difficult to be considered an outsider for years and to find that the house he has bought and lives in is still known as the Mayhew house after its inhabitants of decades ago.

In time, often sooner than he expects, the incomer begins to think of himself as an islander. He does not find that the barriers to his acceptance as a part of the community are as high as he expected. If he shows an interest in the affairs of his town, his talents are quickly put to use. If he has skills the community needs, they are called upon. He soon notes that his children are adopting the local speech patterns. And in himself he finds that an eagerly awaited trip to Boston or New York ends with a quickening of the pulse as he boards the ferry at Woods Hole on his return and that his recognition by crew and fellow passengers is as comforting as any emotion he has known. He is home.

The Family

Just as the family may be a source of nurturance and emotional support, and presumably is so more often than not, it may also be a source of stress. Delinquency, suicide, accident proneness, and other psychiatric or parapsychiatric states have been associated with broken homes (Monahan 1957; Chen and Cobb 1960). Although the broken home is usually defined as one disrupted by separation, divorce, or death, it may be that long before the first two of these events occurs, family relationships have become so dysfunctional that their adverse effects are even greater than in families that have actually ruptured.

The dysfunctional family is not uncommon on the island and has a fairly specific pattern in some homes. In such families the husband is often a presence in the household but hardly functions in either a conjugal or paternal role. He provides monetary support but often does not reveal his income, similar to the families described in Bethnal Green, London (Young and Willmott 1957). His workday often ends at a local bar with his work mates, while his wife delays serving supper until the children become fretful. By the time he comes home, he has had too much to drink and stares unseeingly at the TV set until sleep overtakes him. At midnight, or sooner, he may take some food and go to bed on the couch, or with his wife who, though awake with anger, may pretend to be asleep in order to insulate herself from his unwelcome attentions.

Summer is a time of considerable stress for many families. Even before their summer visitors arrive, many islanders are engaged in arduous preparations. The poor who own no home must move from the one they occupy in the so-called "off-season" to one far more primitive, often without the certainty that they can return to the same house or even to the same town in the fall. If they move to another town at summer's end, their children, if below high school age, must enter a new school, and some island children attend three or four schools before reaching high school. It is common for home owners of modest means to build a primitive house generally called a camp for summer occupancy, since the rental of their own home may make a substantial contribution to their yearly income.

While the family is often a source of stress, it is also an important source of support and nurturance. A key distinction for families on the island is whether they are primarily nuclear or extended. Nuclear families are most often those who have moved to the island after vacationing there for some years. They rarely have any kin on the island, and the support generally available from other family members may be quite distant. Extended families are either those whose members were born on the island or those who have married into island families. In either case, there are generally a large number of relatives available for mutual help, in both good times and bad. The constant and daily support that extended families can provide was shown in a classic description of family relationships in East London (Young and Willmott 1957). The importance families place on their extended relationships was also suggested by a study in Cleveland, where it was found that economic opportunity was not the only significant factor in determining the migration to that city; the presence of kin who could be helpful to the new arrivals was similarly important (Sussman 1959).

The most isolated variety of nuclear family on the Vineyard is that in which one person has moved to the island after the death of his or her spouse. The move to the island is usually prompted by the possession of a dwelling which was used in summers, in the belief that life can be better coped with alone in a small community with a supporting network of community relationships. But this means that children and siblings may be far off and not readily available in times of difficulty. The expanding family with children that moves to the island is in a similar position, though there is more mutual support. Frequent among such families are those who come to the island for a specific task, such as school teachers, state policemen, and persons who enter old or established new businesses.

The case of Joan Hood is an example of the difficulties that nuclear families with no island ties, particularly those who have lived there only a short time, experience in time of trouble. Mr. and Mrs. Hood and their two small children came to the island because the utility company that employed him offered him a somewhat better opportunity there. It was necessary, however, for him to attend courses off-island, which absented him from home for periods of a few days at a time. Mrs. Hood, a shy woman of Polish ancestry who had grown up in New York State, found it difficult to make friends. Her large extended family remained in the area of her birth in northern New York. When four or five months after the family's arrival Mrs. Hood grew extremely anxious and began to experience paranoid feelings, it became necessary for her husband to take on more and more of the burdens of the household. He was no longer able to attend the courses and meetings required by his company. Mrs. Hood's sisters, who could have been supportive, were far away, and the island community had not yet built up the network of human services that might have served her needs. Her inability to care for her children and the restrictions her illness placed on Mr. Hood's work caused him to quit his job, and the family returned to northern New York State where there was a warm, old-world, extended family to step into the breach.

Contrast the situation of Mrs. Hood with that of Mary Hurst. When Mrs. Hurst, a widow in her fifties, became depressed and was no longer able to take care of her house, there were thirty-nine local relatives she could name in her familial network. Six of her brothers and sisters, all married, lived on the island, as did her mother. Most of them lived in the same town, and their children were accustomed to visiting their Aunt Mary frequently. Since she had no children and was the oldest of their aunts, she had performed a grandmotherly function for years. When because of her depression it was deemed wise to have someone with her at all times, there was no need for her husband to give up his job or to hire someone to stay with her. Members of her family shared the task along with the day-by-day chores of cleaning the house, grocery shopping, and preparing meals. In her case the presence of the extended family made it possible for her to be treated on the island rather than in a hospital, and her husband's job was in no way affected.

The difference in the supporting network systems among islanders was shown in a study done in 1962. Thirty-seven consecutive patients attending the island's mental health clinic were asked to name all of their relatives who lived on the island. That all had more relatives than they could name was evident, but it was assumed that if they could identify one by name, that person might be part of a supportive network. When the two groups were divided into the native born and those born off-island, the twenty-seven native-born patients had an average of twenty-six relatives on the island, the number ranging from seven to sixty. The ten patients who had been born off the island had an average of sixteen relatives on the island, the number ranging from three to thirty.

The test was particularly significant because some of those born off-island had lived on the island for many years, having married islanders and therefore having acquired by marriage an extended family. Because none of the ten patients born off the island were older than fifty, that group did not include those who had come to the island in their later years, in which case no family network is present at all.

A tentative observation may be made on the relationship of extended families to psychiatric and parapsychiatric disorder. It was noted early in the experience of the Mental Health Center that the town of Oak Bluffs had a rate of treated psychiatric disorder only one-third that of Edgartown, Vineyard Haven, or up-island. It was known, too, that Oak Bluffs is the town with the highest percentage of residents of Portuguese ancestry. It seemed a reasonable assumption that further research would find not that the people of Oak Bluffs were either relatively immune to psychiatric disorder or more reluctant to seek psychiatric help when it occurred, but that they probably expressed their disorder in acts which brought them to the attention of social and legal agencies. The research did not confirm this supposition; the people of Oak Bluffs had no higher rates of attention by social and legal agencies than people in other towns. The inference is that the people of Oak Bluffs, largely of Portuguese ancestry, with a smaller proportion of native blacks, have more supportive family networks and may indeed have even larger families than other islanders. In fact, in the case of the twenty-seven extended families of native-born patients in the study, the fourteen with Portuguese family names had, on the average, twenty-nine members, as against twenty-two members for the thirteen families with Anglo-Saxon names.

Retirement

Retirement is a transitional state, which requires adaptation and therefore may be stressful to the individual. Social maladjustment and acute emotional disturbance have followed retirement, and suicide rates for men rise sharply after their sixties (Susser and Watson 1971). The island has a proportionally larger number of inhabitants age 65 and over than have most American communities. While some natives of the island over 65 may continue to work, the largest proportion of that age group is composed of people who have come to the island to retire. Almost all of these have been summer visitors with homes that were suitable for year-round living.

In moving to the island, they face not only the usual problems associated with retirement but also the special problems that stem from the migration process itself. The stresses of moving from one place to another, from one house to another, of giving up old relationships and establishing new ones, are severe. A further important problem for the island retiree is that generally his friends during the summer have been other summer people, and even the few year-round islanders he knows, such as service employees or tradesmen, are often unaware of his occupation. He meets new people after retirement, and they too do not know who he is or what he has done. This was observed during a check of the 1965 census, during which it was noted that the local clergymen and town clerks, while they knew almost all of the retired in-migrants, often did not know their preretirement occupations.

Since Americans generally classify people and assess their social class position by placing them occupationally, retired people try to find opportunities to assert their past occupational identity. They may do this by volunteering for public service groups that can use their occupational skills. At times they do it by displaying symbolic extensions of their occupation, as in the case of the Episcopal clergyman who, though completely retired, continued to wear his ecclesiastical vestments daily. In the neighboring mainland town of Falmouth there was for some years a bronze sign on the front of a house on Main Street which noted, "Dr. James Fowles, retired Dentist."

The Limitations of Leadership

Human desires are often not clearly expressed, and the many desires of the members of a community do not arrange themselves unaided into a communal consensus or into a hierarchy of needs. Even when a consensus has been reached, action is not self-starting. The function of a leader in a democratic society is therefore not to impose his wishes on the community but to discover where its best interests lie, to find the resources within it for articulating them, and to locate people who have the necessary skills to fulfill the community's wishes. A good leader eases his own tasks by helping others with such qualities to come to the fore.

Leadership is thus a process requiring a perceptiveness of the needs of others and an ability to seek and articulate the commu-nality of their needs. A less common requirement is to be able to step aside when others appear competent to do the job almost as well, though perhaps not as well, as the leader himself. The position also requires a relative absence of self-aggrandizing impulses, save where they find fulfillment in the successful conclusion of the leadership task itself.

Good leadership, in short, is an essential instrument in the satis-faction of individual needs when they can only be satisfied by com-munal action, and its absence almost ensures their frustration. Effective leadership can be a self-regenerating process for a com-munity, and the absence of such leadership can deprive the com-munity of available resources. It has even been suggested that one important characteristic of disintegrated communities is that they have few and weak leaders (A.H. Leighton 1959).

An analysis of leadership on the island leads to the conclusion that it has generally been weak. The presumed leaders of the com-munity, the selectmen, are essentially executives of the decisions of the annual or special town meetings, where legislation is made. While the selectmen may introduce articles in the town warrant in the hope of passage by the town, the town meeting process itself makes uncertain the result of any vote except when there has been long preparation by a series of public hearings. Under the system of town government, the fact is that the selectmen in the past have rarely initiated new programs. This may be due in part to the tradition of island conservatism and in part to the fact that select-men are all underpaid part-time employees. They have become active, and then only in the last few years, in response to threats from the outside, in most cases the threatened ravages of the island by land developers.

There has been a notable lack of what Walter Lippman (1955) called the sense of the "public interest" as against self-interest. Obvious conflicts between the business interests of town officers and their public interest are frequently overlooked. Further, the fact that the island is divided into six towns with six separate town meetings and six boards of selectmen makes it more difficult to confront those problems that are island wide. The securing of a regional high school to replace three inadequate smaller high schools came about only after many years of a long and ravaging battle. Obvious forms of cooperation between the six towns in the fields of public health, water exploration and conservation, development of an island police force, and the regionalization of the entire school system have not yet been accomplished, though they are occasionally discussed.

The fragmentation of the government into six towns often makes it difficult to arrive at consensus on a common problem. The establishment of a visiting nurse service for the island was thwarted twenty years ago by the fact that the town meeting of the largest town voted against it, despite the approval of five of the six island physicians. In short, the governmental process is so fragmented that other means have been devised to establish needed services.

5

The Resources and Needs of Islanders

While Martha's Vineyard is traditional in outlook and small in population, its site within megalopolis and its dependence on a vacation economy make it extremely vulnerable to outside forces. Similarly, its small population makes it especially sensitive to catalytic human influences for good and for evil within it. Along with the Commonwealth of Massachusetts and the United States of America, of which it is often reluctantly a part, the island has recently undergone much change. Much, too, has changed as a result of internal forces, namely, the pragmatism of its native people and the catalytic influence of its incomers. In order to understand these changes, it is necessary to go back and view the human situation as it existed in the spring of 1961 just before the island undertook to establish a human service network for its people.

The Economy

Perhaps the most significant fact of island life at that time was neither readily noticed nor often admitted. Dukes County, 99 percent of whose population lived on Martha's Vineyard, was in 1959 the lowest income county in the Commonwealth of Massachusetts. Twenty-three percent of its families earned less than $3,000 a year, the poverty line according to the standards of the period. Twenty-seven percent of its married women with children under age six were in the labor force, the second highest rate in the state and another sign of its economic problems. Similarly, its median family income was $4,745, the lowest figure in all of the counties of the Commonwealth, which meant that half of the island's families earned less than that income (U.S. Bureau of the Census 1961a).

The fact is that the island's poverty was superficially invisible. The substantial, well-kept houses of its summer visitors, seen from the island's roads or lying along North Water Street in Edgartown, West Chop in Vineyard Haven, and East Chop in Oak Bluffs, though usually occupied only two or three months a year, gave the impression of prosperity, while many islanders lived in substandard houses, heated by kerosene stoves, far enough from the paved roads to be invisible. The more comfortable citizens of the island seemed reluctant to recognize the problem, while many of the island's summer visitors preferred to think of their neighbors as quaint rather than poor, since it better fit their dream of the island as another Eden.

A notable characteristic of the people of the island was their resistance to change, a characteristic that they themselves sometimes called islanditis. While the wages of artisans were significantly lower than across Nantucket Sound in Falmouth, there was virtually no attempt to develop organizations that might raise their wages. They may have felt keenly the unfairness of working next to unionized workers often brought from the mainland who earned more than they did for the same work, but they did nothing about it, in part because of their strong feelings about independence. The same characteristic made it difficult for islanders to approach other economic problems communally, because it would have required giving up strongly held values for a common purpose.

Education

One of the marks of a confident, striving community is shown in the demands it makes for its children. The people of the island demanded relatively little. Their concern for their young people in 1961 appeared to be directed more to keeping them out of trouble than to enhancing their potentialities, a position consistent with the value that man is born essentially evil and needs to be restrained for the purposes of civility. As a result, islanders demanded little of their school system. The few parent-teacher associations that existed soon fell into inactivity. The fact that a much smaller proportion of the island's high school graduates went off to college than on the neighboring mainland appeared to trouble neither the population nor the school authorities. Those young people who expressed the wish to go to college often found themselves encouraged to seek admission to small colleges with low standards, perhaps a measure of the lack of confidence of the school system in itself. Though Massachusetts would have provided school adjustment counselors at no cost to the local school system, the opportunity of securing such services was not taken; for many years the system had only one guidance counselor in the high school and none in its elementary schools. State law required that special educational services be provided for the educationally retarded, but the school system avoided the rulings of the law by not reporting the presence of children with such needs in its classrooms.

Preschool education was limited. The three up-island schools provided no kindergarten for children of that sparsely settled area, which needed them most. There were a few nursery schools in the larger towns operated either privately or by a church, but the number of children they accommodated was slight and their teachers were largely untrained. Facilities for young people of high school age were equally limited. Though the community recognized that its children were isolated, the school system, with the exception of a few teachers, made little effort to arrange for trips off-island; the traditional graduating class trip to Washington had long been discontinued.

Medical Services

The medical services of the island were based on the presence of six general practitioners and a 38-bed hospital built in 1928. Certain specialized services were shared by the general practitioners, one of them performing virtually all of the surgery done at the local hospital, except for tonsillectomies done by another. Anesthesia was administered by still another practitioner. A roentgenologist came from Boston two days a week for the X-ray work, and an arthrologist and other specialists came at more or less monthly intervals.

The ratio of practitioners to residents of the island was approximately one per thousand population, a figure lower than that of the United States as a whole. During the summer, the ratio was approximately one to five thousand, and although summer visitors are likely to have few serious medical problems, they added to the burden on the physicians because of the great number of accidents that occur among vacationers.

The hospital had no free clinic save for a monthly arthritis clinic sponsored by the arthritis foundation. Although the local physicians were often criticized for not establishing free clinics for that segment of the population which could not afford private care, they did in fact provide low cost services simply by the failure of indigent people to pay their bills. This method humiliated and penalized the conscientious and often kept them from seeking needed care. As a result, there was much shifting of patient from physician to physician, with a return to the doctor of one's choice after the patient had managed to clear his indebtedness.

The special problems of a resort community also affected the operation of the hospital. While it was rarely full during most of the year, summer saw it overburdened with patients, its sun porches and even corridors accommodating extra beds. As a small hospital, limited in both resources and specialized services, it had to refer many of its patients to mainland hospitals for special care.

Psychiatric Care

In the spring of 1961 the island had no psychiatric services, and the securing of emergency psychiatric care was often difficult. The nearest hospital that would accept psychiatric patients of low income was the state hospital at Taunton, Massachusetts, three-quarters of an hour by boat and fifty-five miles distant by road. The difficulty of even getting to that hospital was compounded by the limited boat schedule during the winter. In 1961 there were periods when the last boat left at 4:00 p.m., and the problem of coping with an agitated, paranoid patient until the next day was often formidable. The Martha's Vineyard Hospital would not officially admit psychiatric patients, basing its refusal on its charter, which forbade it to admit the "alcoholic" and the "insane." Despite this, alcoholic patients were occasionally admitted if attendants supplied by the local chapter of Alcoholics Anonymous maintained a twenty-four hour vigil at the patient's bedside whether or not such attendance was medically necessary. The island's physicians occasionally admitted patients with anxiety or depression by sending the patient to the hospital under a false diagnosis, which often required the patient to undergo the discomfort and expense of laboratory and X-ray work he did not require. Though the nurses were aware of the deception, this practice carried with it certain risks. If a patient's physician were otherwise occupied or off the island during an emergency, the physician on call might be misinformed by the chart as to the patient's real problem.

In the case of acutely disturbed psychotic patients, hospitalization in the local hospital was not an option, and once the physician had made a decision to send his patient to a state or private hospital on the mainland and if the last boat of the day had already left, he was confronted with making a suitable overnight arrangement that would protect both the patient and others. Not infrequently, agitated psychotic patients were kept overnight in a cell in the county jail. The cell in which such patients were generally kept was attached to the sheriff's office, through which visitors to the jail often passed, affording the patient little or no privacy. Medication might be prescribed by the family doctor, but there was no nursing care available during the patient's overnight stay in the jail.

Social and Intellectual Resources

Once the tourist season was over and the summer people, lectures, and films had gone, the island entered a period of general cultural aridity. During occasional winters there might be movies on Friday or Saturday evenings, but they were generally poorly attended, either for economic reasons or because the booking system provided few films worth seeing. At intervals the people of the island had an amateur theatrical group or a small orchestra for a winter or two, but these enterprises did not last. Though each town had its own public library and every islander might borrow books from any one of them, each library was operated independently; there were some evenings in which two libraries were open, and others in which none were open.

The relative absence of additional means of intellectual stimulation were evident. Opportunities for young people in the lower income groups to visit the museums and other cultural repositories of the cities were extremely limited. The great political passions that affected the rest of the nation hardly touched the island. In 1961 there were no branches of national organizations such as the Committee for a Sane Nuclear Policy or the National Association for the Advancement of Colored People. Only the League of Women Voters made valiant attempts to interest the citizenry in issues beyond the island.

There was no provision for a meeting place for young people on weekends or evenings. The corner drugstores with their soda fountains, a traditional meeting place for American youth, closed at 6:30 in the evening. The only store open later was the liquor store. Since the young people of the island often had homes too cramped for entertaining, they took to the roads, cruising from Edgartown to Gay Head to Vineyard Haven and around again, enlivening the occasion with illicitly obtained alcoholic beverages, the law in Massachusetts at that time limiting the sale of such beverages to those 21 or over.

Social Services

Although the Commonwealth of Massachusetts had a great variety of agencies that provided human services for its citizens, visits to the island by their representatives were infrequent and intermittent. The island did support a mainland organization for the prevention of cruelty to children, but its headquarters was on the mainland and its service available only at intervals. The public welfare departments were almost entirely concerned with the disbursing or, just as often, the withholding of welfare funds. The amount of social casework practiced was minimal, due primarily to the preoccupation of the welfare workers with their economic function and the absence of social work consultation for them. The fact was that, despite the low income earned by islanders and the high rate of poverty, the people of the island had a comparatively low rate of welfare recipiency as compared with the Commonwealth as a whole. In acute catastrophic emergencies, as when a family lost its possessions through fire, the local Red Cross or Salvation Army chapters responded to the call, but their efforts were generally limited to providing economic support in crises. There were no visiting nurse or home health care services to supplement the overworked medical profession's efforts, despite the high percentage of those age 65 or over in the community.

The Support System

Despite the striking lack of formal community resources for people in need, there were significant supportive elements in island life for those in difficulty. The common destiny which islanders shared made mutual support in distress perhaps more common and effective than in larger places. Since the social network of islanders was close-knit, it provided an ever-present system of social support. The special problems of living on an island often forced people into social cooperation. When children needed orthodontic services, a dental car pool was made up so that one parent and one car rather than five could convey the children to New Bedford and back, and during one period they were taken by fishing boat. The support system also found expression in the many Vineyard voluntary associations to which islanders belonged and which, whatever their stated purpose, remained systems of mutual support for their members.

This, in brief, was the human services system in the spring of 1961. With the coming of a pychiatrist in the summer and the formal opening of the Mental Health Center that fall the multiple needs of the clinic's patients and the perceptions of its pychiatrist began to reveal the gaps in the island's services. An extensive study of the human predicaments experienced by islanders was begun in 1964, upon receipt of a grant, which gave evidence within a year that there were a great many islanders in serious psychological difficulty who did not reach either the family physician or the island's psychiatric service. Indeed, they often reached facilities and agencies that not only lacked the resources with which to help them, but whose ministrations were often damaging to those whose self-esteem was already quite meager.

II

The Predicaments

6

The Faces of Disorder

Who are the Vineyarders who suffer from psychiatric disorder? How do we know? Who decides? These are some of the questions which confronted those who wished to provide help for the people with disorder on Martha's Vineyard. There is little doubt that Daniel Benedict in his paranoid self-imprisonment was a victim of disorder. But was John Castaldo, a man who alcoholized himself into insensibility as his way of coping with stress? Was Sophia Barden, who jeopardized the lives of others every time she drove her car?

At one time the presence of psychiatric disorder was determined by diagnosis by a physician or psychiatrist or by admission to a mental hospital. But such a definition excluded more than it included. It would have excluded four of the five islanders in the sketches. It would even have excluded Daniel Benedict who certainly suffered from a major disorder but who did not consult a physician.

In the study of disorder, the definition depends on the purpose of the particular study. Since the island studies were concerned with the suffering caused by disorder, they could not be limited to those who made their distress known by visiting their family physicians or the psychiatric service. Therefore, the studies attempted to count all those whose distress is revealed in one or another of the many ways human suffering comes to the attention of the community or its agents.

If those suffering from disorder, whatever the idiom in which it is expressed, can be counted, the size of the problem facing the community can be known. And if it is possible to determine why a particular sex, age group, marital status, social class position, or family constellation is associated with high rates of disorder, it may make possible the development of means for increasing the coherence and decreasing the stress in the lives of those in the vulnerable categories.

The Epidemiological Method

The method used in the island studies was that of epidemiology, which is both "a body of knowledge about the occurrence and behavior of disease in populations" and "a method of study to determine causes and courses of disease affecting the individual and the community" (Plunkett and Gordon 1960). Human ecology, to which it is closely related, concerns itself with the interactions between man and his environment and, in the case of psychiatric disorder, mainly between man and his social environment.

In order that counts of disorder in one population may be compared with those in other populations, the counts are expressed in rates, namely the number of instances of the disorder in a standard unit of the population. Since populations rarely consist of such standard units, rates are determined by dividing the number of those found with the disorder by the number of such units in the population and are expressed as cases per 100, 1,000, or any other convenient unit. The rates reported for the epidemiological studies of the island are expressed either as percentages (rate per 100 persons) or as rates per 1,000 population.

A number of kinds of rates have been used in epidemiological studies. Those used in the island study were limited in number. The commonest rate was the one-year prevalence rate, namely, the number of those experiencing the event or disorder in a one-year period per unit of the population at risk. The term *at risk* refers to the number of people in a population who may possibly develop the disorder in question. In the island study the population at risk was often the entire population; in other cases it consisted of those in specific sex, age, marital status, or social class groups.

The second kind of rate used in the island study was the one-year incidence rate, which is the number of new cases of the event or disorder occurring over one year per unit of the population at risk. Incidence rates are of great usefulness in epidemiological studies where the onset of the disorder is clear. Since many episodes of psychiatric disorder are insidious in onset, incidence rates are diffi-cult to determine. The onset of treatment has sometimes been used to date the beginning of the condition, but the practice is question-able because it may confuse actual onset of disorder with health-seeking behavior and other factors.

The Burden of Disorder

Mental illness is one of the great public health problems of our time. Few other human disorders reach its prevalence. Between a fifth and a quarter of the populations that have been studied most intensively were judged to be significantly "impaired" (Srole 1962; D.C. Leighton et al. 1963; Helgason 1964; Hagnell 1966). Ten per-cent of Americans have in the recent past spent some part of their lives in mental hospitals. In addition to the burden placed on the community by the care required for those who are so impaired, the waste of human resources in creative work not done, in joy aborted, and in relationships unfulfilled is immense.

The damage done to the individual, to family life, and to the com-munity by mental illness is nowhere so visible as in the small com-munity. Because of the Vineyard's high tolerance for deviance, many who in larger places would be sent to mental hospitals live within the community. Alcoholism and marital discord almost always come to public attention. The effects of these conditions on family life are known to the schools, the welfare agencies, the police, and the courts, while major personality disorders are often brought to the attention of the community at large in its daily life, occasionally even at its town meetings.

There is another aspect of mental illness which commands the particular attention of those concerned with the public health. Such illness behaves much as a communicable disease, particularly in a population as small as the Vineyard's. While its communicability cannot be traced with the same precision as an outbreak of typhoid fever, so long as human beings live in families and in communities, each psychologically disordered person contaminates the lives of all within his interpersonal field. There is evidence that the children of the disordered grow up at a greater risk of becoming impaired (Buck and Laughton 1959; Kellner 1963) and that psychological disorder in husband or wife in time induces both social isolation and disorder in the other partner (Kreitman et al 1970b, 1970a).

It has long been known that all of those suffering from psychiatric disorder do not identify themselves by seeking psychiatric or other medical care. In order to become a voluntary patient, one must breach a series of barriers: he must be aware of his distress, find out the location of a mental health clinic or private practitioner, know how to make and keep appointments, possess the fee, secure transportation, and finally, after surmounting all other obstacles, have the perseverance to go through the clinic intake process, which often is of such complexity and seeming irrelevance that only the extremely well-motivated survive it to reach a therapist. In brief, the more minor the disturbance, the more likely is the individual to be able to secure treatment. In consequence of these and other circumstances, only a fraction of those suffering from psychiatric symptoms ever reach a therapist (Gurin et al 1960). What happens to the others? Do they suffer quietly, contaminating the lives of those with whom they live, or do they reveal their distress by means that bring them to other than the standard resources?

One as yet meagerly explored presumption is that a significant proportion of disturbed persons reveal their disturbance unknowingly in acts which come to the attention of other than medical resources. Such an act, called a psychosocial or parapsychiatric event, is an individual experience which reveals the presence of psychiatric disorder in an idiom that does not usually bring the person to the facilities where psychiatric diagnoses are made. As a consequence, disorders expressed in the parapsychiatric mode have been included in only a few studies in psychiatric epidemiology.

As early as 1916, however, a mental health survey dealt with such conditions as school retardation, truancy, unruliness, sexual immorality, criminality, vagrancy, welfare recipiency, inebriety, drug abuse, and domestic maladjustment (Rosanoff 1917). Later, an assessment of mental health needs in a rural and semirural Ohio county included military draft rejections, school maladjustment, juvenile delinquency, adult crime, and divorce among the events recorded (Mangus and Seeley 1955). Sexual offenses and bodily assaults were counted in a census of psychiatric cases in two communities in Wales (Carstairs and Brown 1968). Similar predicament studies have been done in a Massachusetts suburban community (Devitt et al 1953). A mental health survey of a rural county in Tennessee included, in addition to instances of psychiatric disorder, events such as miscegenation, sexual delinquency, promiscuity, larceny, forgery, personal violence, and a series of petty offenses such as cheating, lying, and fighting (Roth and Luton 1943).

The inclusion of events such as unruliness, sexual promiscuity, and miscegenation point up how culture-bound our notions of disorder may be. Certainly the definition of sexual promiscuity has altered over the past thirty years, and to define miscegenation as a conduct disorder could either be a reflection of the mores of the time and place or be a psychiatric judgment that in Tennessee of the 1930s interracial marriage was so dangerous and defiant a variety of behavior as to be classifiable as a psychiatric disorder.

In a study of the psychiatric implications of accidental poisoning in childhood in rural low-income counties in New Hampshire and Vermont, data were recorded for the same parapsychiatric events that were used in the Vineyard studies (Sobel 1970). Over a five-year period, the same period as that of the Vineyard study, the rates of occurrence of parapsychiatric events in households were: single-car automobile accidents, 31 percent; fine, probation, or jail, 28 percent; school diciplinary problems, 24 percent; automobile license cancellation, 15 percent; desertion, separation, or divorce, 12 percent; premarital pregnancy, 11 percent; and other events of lesser magnitude (Sobel 1975).

The Recognition Process

The perception of distress by the subject and the definition of "caseness" by the psychiatrist are not entirely matters of personal definition. Each is also a social judgment. The perception that one requires the help of a trained person called a psychiatrist or other mental health worker is not a conclusion based on the awareness of distress alone. It depends on a myriad of other factors, such as beliefs, values, geography, economics, the availability of clinical resources and whether or not the subject has important business with the world which a recognition of disorder would impede.

Many of those who suffer from illness, according to medical criteria, do not become patients, because the definition of illness is also as much a social as a medical matter. As S.R. Kellert (1971) put it, "The negotiations that initially determine who makes his way to the physician's office occur within the community with very little in the way of medical consultation." He cited K. T. Erickson as pointing out that the first screening is often provided by a network of relatives, teachers, friends, and a variety of others, and that "whether or not a heavy drinker views himself as a candidate for medical help, for example, will depend in part on whether he is of Irish extraction or Jewish, whether he lives in a ghetto or suburb, whether he works as a night club entertainer or a school teacher— and all these considerations together make up a tissue which may be called 'the social screen' because it acts to filter the traffic moving to and from the doctor's office." This view is given support in a study which found little difference in psychiatric symptom scores between two groups of people, those who went to a medical group and those who went to a social agency (Allodi and Coates 1971).

For the psychiatrist, too, the determination that one is or is not a psychiatric case is a social judgment. The importance of the "recognition process" in relation to mental illness has been reviewed both cross-culturally and in the United States (Edgerton 1969). For example, the same act in two boys may be viewed differently, depending on the psychiatrist's understanding of the social process involved in the act in question and the class position of the subject.

The year-round Vineyard child of parents on public welfare who can expect little for Christmas will find his theft of a toy from a shop interpreted quite differently from that of a privileged child of the Vineyard summer. Changing social attitudes toward human problems may also affect the definition of disorder. The inclusion of miscegenation in the Tennessee study is one example, which illustrates Pascal's comment that "Justice on one side of the Pyrenées is injustice on the other." Or a psychiatric clinic laboring under a heavy burden may without a deliberate change in policy find itself raising the criteria for admission and so, in effect, "decreasing" the incidence of treated psychiatric disorder in its community.

The great majority of epidemiological studies, whether of treated or of total instances of mental disorder, show higher rates in females than in males (Bahn et al 1966; Bruhn et al 1966; D. C. Leighton et al 1963; Kessel and Hassall 1965; Kramer 1966; Tonge and Cammock 1961). Yet the higher female rates of treated disorder cannot be assumed to reflect higher actual rates of psychiatric disorder in women than in men. What they may reflect is the degree of awareness of distress and the degree of willingness to seek help in the two sexes. The culture has different expectations of men and women with respect to their tolerance for distress, and this may be what such studies reflect, at least to a degree. Women also have higher admission rates to general hospitals than do men, have more surgical procedures, make more visits for dental care, spend more for medical care, experience more disability days, and report more chronic illnesses than do men (Anderson and Feldman 1956; Nathanson 1975), yet have significantly lower mortality rates.

In brief, epidemiological studies are designed for human purposes. It is essential that the investigator design the study with a clear human need in mind. If he seeks data in order to estimate the need for conventional pyschiatric facilities, surveys on the prevalence of psychological suffering in the person's awareness or clearly evident to others, as in psychosis, or surveys on cases defined by psychiatrists are certainly relevant. Epidemiological studies of those who act out their difficulties, experiencing parapsychiatric or psychosocial events, are relevant if the investigator's purpose is, as it was on the Vineyard, to design new resources for those who, because of the nature of their disorder and other factors, do not and cannot enter the conventional mental health clinic. And total prevalence studies, those which examine total populations or samples of populations for the presence of disorder, are probably most useful for providing the correlations between impairment and the sociocultural environment in order to suggest programs of social intervention and community development that may prove helpful in the primary prevention of psychological disorder.

The Uses of Epidemiology

The application of the epidemiological method to psychiatric disorder is of recent origin. The discovery that pellagra and its mental symptoms are associated with a specific dietary deficiency was one of the earliest findings. The mental disorders associated with syphilis and alchoholism and the various chemical faults of metabolism that lead to mental defect are examples of direct and simple associations. But most types of mental disorder are multifactorial, that is, they result from the concurrence of a number of events acting in the person over a period of time.

As a rule, epidemiological investigations of psychological disorder do not discover specific one-to-one relationships between cause and disorder. Instead, they discover broad associations which generally hide within them many possible causative factors. Suppose, as appears to be true, that many disorders are related to social class position. Since social class is a construct devised by sociologists to help illuminate sociological inquiry, it would be naive to suggest that high or low social class position in itself causes the disorder in question. What may be important in the association between social class and disorder rates are behavioral patterns which are correlated with social class. For example, if child-rearing patterns vary significantly with social class, they may well be factors in the varying incidence of disorder with social class. If stress is greater in one social class than in another, the stress may be the hidden but crucial determinant (Uhlenhuth et al 1974). If low social class position is associated with self-derogation, this may serve to increase rates of psychosocial deviance (Kaplan and Pokorny 1969).

Or if low social class position is associated with isolation and few social supports, these may be the crucial factors (Tischler et al 1975a, 1975b). In brief, epidemiology may reveal powerful associations between disease prevalence and the demographic characteristics of a population, which then must be analyzed for the factors that act upon the individual, such as child-rearing, stress, loss, or the quality of the support system, which may directly affect psychological ill- or well-being.

The studies on the island have the virtues of clinical definition and social relevancy, for the subjects either sought help or came to public attention. The absence of this sort of relevance occurs in nonclinical total prevalence studies and even in the clinical surveys. Although the symptom inventories used in the two major total prevalence studies, the Midtown Manhattan and the Stirling County, were empirically validated, the Langner instrument's disordered sample used in the first study consisted of 139 neurotic and remitted psychotic patients (Langner 1962), while the sample of the Health Opinion Survey used in the second study was 78 clinically diagnosed neurotic patients (Macmillan 1957). The use of such groups for validation is likely to produce an instrument which secures a higher rate of positive responses from women and shows more sensitivity to disorders in awareness than to psychotic and sociopathic disorders.

While both major surveys also secured data by interview, neither made extensive attempts to secure data on psychosocial problems. This is also true for psychiatric interviews, which rarely make routine inquiries concerning antisocial behavior. The most elaborate and inclusive manual on psychiatric case study available suggests making inquiries on lying, stealing, and truancy for children, but recommends no attempt to gather data on antisocial or similar events in adults (Menninger 1952), which is also a common limitation of the sections on history-taking in most texts in psychiatry. Whether such attempts to gather evidence of psychosocial acting out in the true prevalence studies would have been successful is in some doubt, since the respondents had little motivation to air experiences of which they were likely to be ashamed.

Even though it might be expected that patients seeking psychiatric help would be more motivated to reveal as much of themselves as possible, the fact is that psychiatrists accustomed to treating largely middle class patients in private practice and community clinics are relatively innocent of the great range of psychosocial problems of those at the bottom of the socioeconomic scale. Members of the middle class themselves, with criminal and paracriminal activities alien to their own experience, it does not occur to most psychiatrists to ask their patients about criminal arrests, violence against others, theft, or incarceration for public drunkenness; indeed, the assumptions under which most interviews are conducted make such inquiries taboo.

Since with even the most extensive interviewing, subjects may withhold information on their antisocial depredations, a search of public records would seem to be an important part of such studies. Indeed, the only data on psychiatric disorder for many is to be found in the records of nonpsychiatric agencies (Allodi and Coates 1971). Both the Midtown Manhattan and the Stirling County studies secured some information at this level, the former from the city's Social Service Exchange and the civil courts, the latter from teachers and hospitals, but in neither case did the screen appear to be wide enough to catch the many other psychosocial events presumptive of psychiatric disorder.

The problem of determining the burden of psychiatric disorder in a population is thus a formidable one. Aside from the purely technical problems involved are the issues of definition and relevance. To define disorder as limited to those in mental hospitals, as was once the case, omits the great mass of those in distress. To include those in outpatient treatment widens the net but largely excludes those either who are unaware of the nature of their distress or who for complex social reasons lack the social and economic resources necessary to be enrolled in such facilities. The methods that have been used in the attempt to survey the total prevalence of disorder in certain communities suffer from a number of defects, the most notable being the issue of clinical relevance. For example, symptoms that one person can override in the course of a busy life lived with enthusiasm may be totally disabling to another. The method used in the studies of the island attempted to adhere to human relevance by counting both those who are aware of psychiatric suffering and seek help, and those whose distress is expressed in means that bring them to the attention of the social institutions of the community. Since the term *psychiatric disorder* involves a social definition, it is not to be expected that any one epidemiological method can suffice for all purposes. The method used must bear a functional relationship to the human purposes of the research, for one rarely wants to know how many suffer from disorder without some human purpose in mind.

7

The Study of Disorder

The purpose of the studies of Martha's Vineyard was both epidemiological and ecological. Since the research was conducted by a mental health clinic, it was always directed at serving human needs. Its overall purpose was to determine the amount and variety of psychological and psychosocial disorder within the community in order to devise methods for preventing the occurrence of such disorder, for ameliorating it when it does occur, and for building a human service network to fit the actual needs of the population. Under this general purpose were stated the more specific epidemiological goals of the research, all involving the study of the predicaments of presumptively psychological origin of the roughly 6,000 people who were then year-round inhabitants of the island.

The investigations were directed toward five ends. The first was to make a dependable count of those in the population who would seek psychiatric help if the usual external obstacles to securing this help were largely eliminated. The second goal was to determine the number of those who consult their general practitioners for psychiatric disorders. Third, the plan was to count those in the population who experience parapsychiatric or psychosocial events, because of the probability that these events are expressions of psychiatric disorder out of awareness, and if possible to determine whether such events are in fact presumptive evidence of psychiatric disorder. The fourth goal was to compare the characteristics of those with psychiatric disorder in awareness and those experiencing parapsychiatric or psychosocial events, in order to determine whether they come from the same or different segments of the population, and to discover the demographic characteristics of each group as compared with the demographic characteristics of the general population. And the fifth aim was to determine whether psychological predicaments, both psychiatric and parapsychiatric, cluster in certain families called high-rate families and how such families differ from those with low predicament rates.

The Register

The basic instrument of data collection and the source of most of the information for the island studies was a register of human predicaments, containing psychiatric and parapsychiatric subregisters (Mazer 1966). It was maintained in full for a period of five calendar years from 1964 to 1968. During that period it served as the repository of information about every year-round islander who experienced one or more psychiatric and parapsychiatric events and included basic social data for each of these persons. The psychiatric subregister has been continued to the present. For some of the studies, shorter periods were used for reasons of practical necessity. For example, it was considered too burdensome a demand for busy general practitioners to participate in a research study over so long a period, though their participation was in fact of a high order.

The psychiatric register is a device that was established in a number of communities in the late 1950s and early 1960s for providing a current, continuous recording of treated mental disorder for various purposes (Bahn 1962; Gardner et al 1963; Nielsen et al 1965; Baldwin et al 1965; Wing et al 1968). Such a register, however, can record the presence of psychiatric illness only in those who are aware of their disorder or in whom the illness is severe enough to require intervention by others, and where the facilities available make it possible for the impaired person to be registered in a psychiatric facility. Those who act out their difficulties without awareness generally reach community agencies other than psychiatric facilities and consequently go unrecorded as psychiatric cases. Those who suffer quietly but nonetheless affect the lives of others they live with are similarly unrecorded, save perhaps where intensive total prevalence studies have been done.

Since a psychiatric register can record cases of psychiatric disorder only after they have been identified, it requires the presence in the community of psychiatric facilities available to every inhabitant without economic or other barrier. Waiting lists for admission to clinics will effect the count of treated psychiatric disorder, since some will drop off such waiting lists and others will recover before their places are reached. The distance of psychiatric agencies from those who use them is also of importance. It has been shown that even for mental hospital admissions, which are generally more mandatory than out-patient admissions, the rate of admission from a community is inversely related to the distance of the community from the hospital (Goldhamer and Marshall 1953; Bille 1963; Sohler and Thompson 1970). Neither of these obstacles to securing a total count of treated psychiatric disorder applied to the register maintained for the island. In addition, the register recorded the occurrence of each parapsychiatric event experienced by islanders.

As an islander entered the register for the first time, he was assigned a unique code number. This individual number was linked to the subject's name in only one place, a card in a rotary file kept locked separately from the predicament and household files. For those re-entering the register after the first predicament, the individual's number was found in order that the predicament and social data might be recorded in his coded file. The data recorded on the subject's predicament card were the nature of the predicament, its date of occurrence, and the source of the data.

Since one of the purposes of the study was to determine whether psychiatric and parapsychiatric events clustered in families, it was necessary that individuals entering the register be placed within their nuclear family. In order to do so, a household file was established in which virtually every household was represented by a card listing a unique household number, the names of its members, their sexes and ages, frequently their religious affiliations, the occupation of the head of the household, and their town of residence. The family file was originally based on a religious census conducted by the island's churches in 1962. In that survey, based on door-to-door visits, cards were completed on approximately 75 percent of the island households and 85 percent of the island population. The file was later completed by data from the household cards prepared for the 1965 census of population of the Commonwealth of Massachusetts.

All of the data for each subject, including the subject number, household number, and all predicament and social data, were eventually collected on one 80-column card per year. This permitted analysis by both individual and household for each year. For some of the analyses the accumulated data for the five-year period were collected on one card for each subject.

The data on each subject were recorded on special 8½ x 11 inch optical scanning sheets, so designed that a notation made by a no. 2 pencil in an appropriate block activated a sensing device on an IBM 1230 Optical Mark Scoring Reader, which when connected with a 534 Card Punch translated the pencil notations into appropriately placed holes in a standard 80-column card. Analysis of the data was accomplished by two means. For some analyses IBM sorters and computer printouts from which data could be counted were sufficient; for others the data were processed by a Univac computer.

Psychiatric Events

For the purpose of the register, a psychiatric event was defined as the experience of consulting a psychiatrist, being hospitalized in a mental hospital, being hospitalized in a general hospital for a psychiatric condition, or consulting a nonpsychiatric physician for a psychiatric condition. Thus, psychiatric disorders were recorded under two categories, psychiatrist and general practitioner.

The first category includes those who were seen by the island's only psychiatrist, by a psychiatrist off-island, or by a psychiatrist in a general or mental hospital. Since those seen in a general hospital are usually on brief admissions for transient crises, they were classified as out-patient psychiatric contacts. If transferred to a mental hospital, they were recorded as experiencing in-patient psychiatric events. The second category of psychiatric disorder includes those who were seen by one of the island's general practitioners for a psychiatric disorder confirmed by the psychiatrist.

The studies were based on the recording of every episode of psychiatric disorder in the community treated by a mental health worker. Until near the end of 1968 the psychiatrist-director of the clinic was the only mental health worker in the community. Since that date, the term *mental health worker* has included the psychiatrist, two psychologists, and the part-time help of a social worker, all members of the clinic staff. From July 1, 1961, until the present a procedure has been in use which assures that every episode of treatment of an inhabitant by a mental health worker is recorded in the register. An inhabitant is defined as one who lives more than one-half of each year on the island, thereby eliminating summer visitors.

Most often patients began a period of psychiatric treatment or service in the island's mental health center, occasionally in the private practice of the psychiatrist, less often in a psychiatric hospital, sometimes in a general hospital for a psychiatric condition, and much less frequently in the office of a psychiatrist on the mainland. A period of psychiatric service was defined as beginning with one or more consultations with a mental health worker and ending, in the case of outpatient treatment, on the day of the last visit, but only if the patient was not seen subsequently for ninety or more days. This procedure was used in order to make the term *period of service* have functional meaning and to avoid the inflation of such events by abortive attempts to stop treatment. The period of service in a mental hospital was considered terminated on the day the patient left the hospital, if he did not return within ninety days. Consultations with psychiatrists or psychologists in general hospitals were classified as outpatient experiences.

The low income of the population served to make the securing of psychiatric service off the island quite rare. Since the island is served by a community mental health clinic with modest or no fees, there is no economic barrier to the securing of psychiatric treatment locally. Between 1964 and 1968 five of the six local practitioners regularly reported the number of islanders in a period of psychiatric service off-island. The absence of reporting during that period by the sixth doctor, the local surgeon, had only minor effect on the completeness of the survey (Mazer 1969b).

The first entries for psychiatric treatment in the register are called primary rather than first admissions to indicate that they represent first admissions only to this service rather than to any psychiatric service in the past. Since there had never been a psychiatrist on the island, previous psychiatric service had been secured infrequently, usually in mental hospitals. In the case of patients in a period of service in a mental hospital, only patients who entered the hospital five or fewer years before July 1, 1961, were included, a procedure adopted in other such studies (Gardner et al 1963; Srole et al 1962). The rates of psychiatric disorder were computed on the basis of the census data for the entire population secured as of January 1, 1965; this census was more advantageous than either the 1960 or 1970 censuses because it included basic data on the entire population not available in the other censuses. Further, the changes in the population between 1960, 1965, and 1970 were not notable.

The diagnostic categories used for the symptom patterns were those of the first edition of the *Diagnostic and Statistical Manual: Mental Disorders (DSM)* of the American Psychiatric Association. The term *hypochondriacal reaction* was also used, even though it is not a main category in the manual, because it is in common use by local general practitioners to describe the symptom pattern seen in patients who complain of a great variety of bodily symptoms which frequently appear to be expressive of an underlying depression (D.C. Leighton et al 1963).

Parapsychiatric Events

The island study was concerned with suffering caused by psychological disorder however it revealed itself. Because many in distress first came to the attention of educational, social, or legal rather than medical services as the result of a failure in performance or disruptive behavior, called a parapsychiatric experience, they were included in the study. For the purpose of the register, a parapsychiatric event was defined as any episode or continuing condition which brought an individual to public or semipublic notice and for which there was presumptive evidence that psychological factors were in operation. In brief, the presence of significant psychological disorder was noted in whatever idiom it revealed itself, whether by entrance into a psychiatric service or by experiencing one or more of fourteen parapsychiatric or psychosocial events often believed to reflect the presence of psychiatric disorder.

The parapsychiatric events regularly recorded were:

Fine (adult)
Probation (adult)
Jail (adult)
Juvenile delinquency conviction (to age 17)
Desertion, separate support, divorce
Premarital pregnancy
Single-car accidents
Driver's license withdrawal
Chronic alcoholism
Acute public drunkenness with temporary jailing
Suicide (attempt)
Suicide
Major disciplinary problem, high school
Educational underachievement, high school

These fourteen predicaments certainly did not include all psychological predicaments occurring among islanders. They were chosen because they were reasonably definable and because the data on them could be secured regularly within the resources available for the study.

Most of the parapsychiatric events recorded are defined by their titles. Premarital pregnancy was defined to include children born within seven months of the marriage date, as well as those born between seven and eight months ten days after the marriage when the infant showed no evidence of prematurity by birth weight. Automobile accidents, which are presumptive of psychological stress and disorder (Seltzer et al 1974; Shaffer et al 1974), were limited to the driver in a single-car accident, to eliminate the problem of determining culpability in multiple-car accidents. Automobile license withdrawal in the Commonwealth of Massachusetts is a prerogative of the Registry of Motor Vehicles and is done on the basis of presumptive evidence that the individual is not a safe driver. It often follows automobile accidents, particularly where alcohol is a factor, and involves a good deal of judgment on the part of the local registrar. Major school disciplinary problems were those defined as major in the school code and regularly recorded in the disciplinary file of the principal of the high school. Educational underachievement was considered to be present when performance on the Iowa Test of Educational Development was 20 percent or more below that predicted by the score achieved on the Otis Intelligence Test. Grades were not used in assessing underachievement because they were significantly influenced by the "track" or "streaming" plan then in use in the school system and by the practice of so-called "social promotions" based on other than educational qualifications. These items were limited to the high school for practical reasons.

The occurrence of each and every parapsychiatric event is not necessarily indicative of psychiatric disorder. An episode of juvenile delinquency, for example, may in a slum area be normative behavior for an adolescent youth. A divorce may in some instances represent a healthy correction of a previous neurotic error. However, when treated statistically, which is to say in the mass, the events listed as parapsychiatric are presumptive evidence of psychological disorder. However, this presumption is a hypothesis which was also tested in the research.

Social Class Position

Since social class position has been associated with the occurrence of psychological disorder, such data were recorded in these studies. Because the social data available to mental health researchers may be limited, particularly that concerning the populations at risk, simple scales are generally preferred to complex ones. British mental health workers have most often used the occupational classification of the Registrar General, which establishes five social class levels. The most commonly used scales in American investigations have been those based either on occupation, the Alba

Edwards scale, or on a modification of a weighted tri-factor scale employing education, occupation, and quality of residence.

Since the use of occupation alone or of an index based on occupation and education is almost as useful as the tri-factor scale (Hollingshead and Redlich 1958), the island studies were based on occupation alone, each subject being placed in one of seven occupational categories (Hollingshead 1957). The occupation of each inhabitant of the island at one point during the research was secured. When occupations, such as typewriter repairman or caretaker, were encountered that were not included by Hollingshead, they were placed in one of the categories by their similarity to another occupation in the economic system and written into the Hollingshead list to ensure consistency in classification. Since to divide a small number of cases into seven cells would in some of the studies have provided insufficient data for valid analyses, occupational positions were often combined to form two or three groupings. Because the level of occupational position may increase with age, which was not controlled, the social class data may suffer from this limitation.

The use of an occupational scale alone has an advantage other than simplicity. It preserves the distinction between class and status, while the use of two or more factors blurs the distinction. Pending the development of a more precise and pertinent occupational scale, the Hollingshead seven-step scale used alone is the best available instrument for measuring social class position (Haug and Sussman 1971).

The criteria of social class position are used as measures of systems of values, styles of life, and relative prestige and power in a community. They take no account of judgments that are based on one's family history and the personal qualities known to one's neighbors, factors which may be of importance in establishing one's actual status in a small community. Finally, what is really at issue is not how one's position in the social class hierarchy is crudely correlated with rates of impairment, but how it affects the individual in respect to stressful events, child-rearing practices, the quality of relationships, or other experiences that may more directly influence psychological ill- or well-being.

Sources of Data

Since there was only one psychiatric facility on the island, there was little difficulty in counting every islander who received psychiatric treatment locally. A monthly survey of family physicians ensured that the number of persons who secured psychiatric care on an ambulatory basis off-island and those who were hospitalized without the intervention of the one local psychiatrist were recorded. Those experiencing parapsychiatric events entered the register by means of a periodic search of public records. Data were secured at stated intervals from the courts, the educational system, the registrar of motor vehicles, and other sources.

The research studies were designed to determine and serve the needs of the people of the island. This, it was felt, justified the collection of so much information about islanders although its collection raises ethical problems (Cooper and Morgan 1973). Since the investigator was also the island's clinical psychiatrist with a long experience in the requirements of confidentiality, every possible measure was taken to protect the identity of those who were included in the register. Machine processing and similar methods made this possible. Moreover, much of the information was already available in public records. The dates of marriages and births appearing in town reports led to inferences concerning premarital conceptions. The dockets of the courts are public records and may be seen by any islander, if he has not already been sufficiently informed by his reading of the island's weekly newspapers. Finally, an ever-present safeguard lay in the fact that the researcher was not a temporary resident who would leave when the studies were completed, as is usually the case in both community and epidemiological inquiries, but was a committed member of the community who would continue to live among those who were the focus of his clinical and research concerns.

The clinic was opened at the end of 1961 and the research was begun at the beginning of 1964. This allowed time for the role of the researcher as the island's psychiatrist and director of its mental health center to become established. Having provided a needed and never before available service to more than one hundred and fifty islanders for over two years, he had dissipated much of the initial suspicion that attached to the introduction of a psychiatrist into the community. By 1964 he was seen not simply as a psychiatrist but as a citizen, husband, father, and no doubt in other roles beyond his awareness. In addition, he had served on a number of local committees and had appeared as guest speaker before local groups on perhaps fifty occasions, a task generally assigned to professionals entering the island community for their first year or so of residence.

During the two-year interval before the start of the research the psychiatrist had also developed many functional relationships with those who were the custodians of the data that would later be required. The general practitioners were given a consultation service they had long needed and were relieved of the time-consuming and often frustrating burden of caring for many of their psychiatric patients. Advice, both formal and informal, was given freely to the probation officer and the clerk of the district court about problems for which the techniques of the court were not appropriate. Consultations for clients seeking disability assistance established relationships with the welfare workers, and consultations with high school officials concerning the school's disciplinary code and similar matters smoothed the way for later research collaboration.

The initial problem was to win the consent of the custodians of the data so that the information required would be made regularly available. The winning of such consent is important, even when the information needed lies in records in the public domain. For example, while the town clerk may be required by law to permit anyone to see the records of births (except for illegitimate births), or the clerk of the court may be obliged to let anyone study the criminal docket (except for cases of juvenile delinquency), each official can place many obstacles in the way of the investigator. He may find himself too busy to search out the records, or he may discover that his own clerks require the ledgers at the moment the investigator wishes to consult them. Further, much of the information was not in the realm of public information, some of it requiring the approval of the judge of the district or probate courts, and all of it requiring a high degree of trust in the investigator by the source of information.

If the data collection procedures are to work without repeated delays, it is necessary for the investigator to understand the problems of the official who is to be the source of information. The common practice, therefore, was to give the potential informant a general idea of the nature of the research without spelling it out in detail. Emphasizing the importance of the enterprise and of the role of the custodian of the records had two purposes. First, it increased the accuracy of the data supplied. Second, it armored the custodian, should criticism be directed at him for his collaboration. It was found necessary to reassure the source of information that its confidentiality would be respected and preserved. This was done by outlining the precautions to be taken, including the use of code numbers rather than names once the data had been collected and the use of machine data-processing methods.

Reassurance was offered still more effectively by nonverbal than by verbal means. The collection of information at the town hall, the court house, or a physician's office was never done casually. Printed or mimeographed forms were always used, some divisible, with name and code number on one part and data and code number on another. The reason was not that the informants required such precautions—they had not asked for such measures—but simply to reassure them as to the researcher's care of the data. The information collected was never casually inserted into the investigator's coat pocket. A brief case was always carried for this purpose and the procedure treated with some solemnity. In short, every effort was made to anticipate the anxieties an informant might have, to relieve his anxieties by acts rather than by words, and to arm him in advance against criticism.

The initial contact for what was to be a request for information was always done by a formal visit to the custodian of the information. Care was taken not to make a request immediately and certainly never to require a yes or no answer. A negative response, once uttered, is difficult for a public official to retract. Once said, it marshals a dozen reasons to justify itself. Instead, the investigator discussed the importance of the work, the significance of the contribution the official might make, and talked around the subject leisurely, making an occasion of the visit, in the hope of eliciting and dealing with whatever anxieties the informant might have before his help was requested. This usually resulted in the allaying of anxiety, the assurance of the official's interest in the project, and frequently the offer of help before it was even requested. On the one occasion when the potential informant suggested that the decision be made by a superior, this was agreed to immediately and the superior seen, using substantially the same procedure.

In fact, there was much less reluctance to cooperate than had been anticipated. Town clerks, for example, are the custodians of great masses of information about the residents of their towns. In the towns of the island they regularly transcribe all information on birth, death, and marriage certificates into large ledgers which are almost never consulted. The possibility that their careful and persistent work might be finally put to a useful purpose was welcomed with enthusiasm. When the 1965 state census was reviewed with respect to occupations, it was found that the clerks had a wide knowledge of who the people were in their towns and what they did for a living.

In brief, the winning of consent and the active cooperation of those whose help was vital for the social research done in this small community was only secondarily a technical matter. Of primary importance was an appreciation of the concerns of those whose help was needed, so that they felt no danger as a result of their help. Developed relationships were more important in securing cooperation than were the statutes requiring cooperation. Finally, each agreement to help was recognized as a contract, which could be breached only at peril to the research.

8

Psychiatric Disorder in General Practice

The relationship between the physician and his patients in a small community has been movingly described by an English practitioner in a rural area in Yorkshire: "Such is the lie of the land in the pleasant dale in which I live that a climb to the summit of one of our noble hills enables me to make out almost the whole of my practice and I clearly remember a glorious evening in early summer when I clambered up one of these. The sun was setting and it lit up the pile of an ancient castle, once the prison of history's unhappiest queen, our little lake seemed to lie at my feet, and one by one I was able to identify most of our gray villages with their thin pall of smoke, and as I watched the evening train creeping up the valley with its pauses at our three stations, a quaint thought came into my head and that was that in all these villages, there was hardly a man, woman or child of whom I did not know even the Christian name and with whom I was not on terms of intimate friendship" (Pickles 1958).

The intimacy of the Yorkshire physician's relationship to his patients is not unknown on the Vineyard. Almost every islander identifies one of the island's general practitioners as his physician, and at this time four of the island's six practitioners have been in practice for from twenty to forty years. Since doctor-patient relationships are long-standing, four of the island's present practitioners have seen children at whose delivery they presided grow into adulthood. They and their patients have grown older together, and the vicissitudes in the lives of neither are secret from the other. Since each practitioner numbers many of his friends among his patients, the finding of serious or fatal illness in them often shatters the professional detachment that protects the physician's equanimity.

The general practice studies undertaken on the Vineyard owe much to the fact that they were conducted on an island. Because of this, it was possible not only to determine the experience of the general practitioners with respect to psychiatric illness but also to compute rates of disorder per thousand population, since the population at risk, the entire population of the island, was known. The determination of such rates is possible in an island community because all or virtually all of those consulting a general practitioner do so locally.

European and North American Studies

The role of the general practitioner in caring for those with psychiatric disorders has been studied most thoroughly in Great Britain. There are probably two reasons for this. First, relative to the United States there are proportionately fewer psychiatrists practicing outside of mental hospitals in Great Britain (Cooper and Brown 1967); hence the general practitioner assumes a larger role in the treatment of the emotionally disturbed. Second, the patient assignment and record-keeping methods of the British National Health Service make it easier to count those with psychiatric disorders in general practice. Since the number at risk in any one practice or combination of practices can be known, the count may be converted into rates or cases per unit of population, a circumstance that rarely exists in the United States. Seven general practice surveys from Great Britain found one-year prevalence rates ranging from 4 to 13 percent of populations at risk (Shepherd et al 1966). A four-year study of a physician's own general practice in a rural area in the general vicinity of Oslo revealed a mean yearly rate of mental disorder of 5.4 percent of the population at risk (Bentsen 1970). These figures give the range of the proportion of the populations identified as psychiatrically disordered by general practitioners.

The surveys of psychiatric disorder in general or nonpsychiatric practices in the United States have generally provided data on the proportions of all patients seen who had psychiatric disorder during the period studied. Since the size of American practices, the populations at risk, are generally not known as they are in the European studies, the rates for the populations studied are not available. The findings of nine American surveys (Table 1) show that, for all ages, from 3 to 19 percent of all patients seen were considered to have psychiatric disorder. For patients 15 years and older, the range was 5 to 17 percent. These findings are not rates per unit of population but rather proportions of patients seen who were thought to have psychiatric disorder. The findings of the studies are not entirely comparable, because of variations both in the economic and social class characteristics of the practices in the periods studied, and in the criteria for determining the presence of psychiatric disorder. In addition, it is not clear in all cases whether steps were taken to avoid counting the same patient twice if he had consulted more than one physician engaged in the survey. The highest rate was found in a study based upon physicians' recollections rather than upon actual counts. Further, only three of the studies covered a period longer than three and a half months, which introduces the possibility of seasonal and other temporal variations (Mazer 1967, 1969b; Vobecky et al 1972). These and other problems characterize general practice surveys (Kessel 1962; Shepherd et al 1966).

So far as is known, only three North American studies have given data on rates in relation to population at risk (Fink et al 1969; Mazer 1967, 1969b). From a fourth study in rural French-speaking Canada such a rate has been calculated (Vobecky et al 1972). In contrast to diagnosed disorder, two studies of the prevalence of psychiatric *symptoms* in Nova Scotia gave a prevalence rate of 64 percent for an island village of about 400 (Llewellyn-Thomas 1960) and of 37 percent for a town of 3,000 (D. C. Leighton 1956).

The American studies, which gave rates of 3 to 19 percent of all patients seen, may be compared with the British studies, in which the proportion of general practice patients consulting for psychiatric morbidity ranged from 6 to 23 percent, with a very high rate of 65 percent in one study (Shepherd et al 1966). The Norwegian study reported that 15.8 percent of those consulting in one year had mental disorder (Bentsen 1970). The somewhat higher rates in the

Table 1. Surveys of Psychiatric Disorder in Nonpsychiatric Medical Practice in North America

Author	Source of data	Period	% of those in practices		% of total population	
			All ages	15 & over	All ages	15 & over
Peterson et al 1950	91 general practices	1 wk.	3.0-5.3	—	—	—
Finn & Huston 1966	291 nonpsychiatric physicians	few mos.	18.5	—	—	—
Locke et al 1966	Nonpsychiatric group practice	3 1/2 mos.	—	14.6		
Locke et al 1967	79 nonpsychiatric physicians	1 wk.	7.0	9.0	—	—
Mazer 1967	5 general practitioners	3 mos.	—	—	4.6	6.7[a]
Fink et al 1969	Family group practice	3 mo.	—	5.0[b]	—	1.7[b]
Locke et al 1969	58 internists and general practitioners	1 mo.	4.2	16.9	—	—
Mazer 1969b	5 general practitioners	1 yr.	8.0[a]	—	5.2	6.9[a]
Vobecky et al 1972	Probability sample	1 yr.	6.7	—	4.1[a]	—

a. Rates calculated from additional data made available by authors.
b. Age 20 and over.

European than in the American studies are probably owing to differences in the duration of the studies. The North American studies were of one week to one year's duration; only two of the nine cited were for periods longer than three and a half months. Those reported for Britain lasted from six months to five years, and that from Norway for four years.

In contrast to the relatively low proportion of general practice patients who are reported to have actual psychiatric disorder on the basis of careful studies, the off-hand estimates made by general practitioners are notably higher. Thus, one group of general practitioners surveyed expressed the belief that a significant percentage of their patients had "some significant emotional disturbance"; the median estimate fell between 30 and 39 percent (Taylor 1960). Part of the difference between such estimates and the lower rates reported in surveys may arise from a difference of definitions; surveys generally use defined psychiatric diagnoses or "conspicuous psychiatric morbidity" (Kessel 1960), while practitioners are likely to include in their estimates those whose symptoms of emotional distress are secondary to physical illness. Further, since psychiatric patients are more frequent attenders at the offices of general practitioners than are those with somatic illness and require more time for each visit (Waterson 1965; Bentsen 1970), the general practitioner may easily acquire the impression that psychiatric patients make up a larger proportion of his practice than they do in fact. Thus, a physician practicing in a country town in West Scotland who found that only 3 percent of his patients came for primary psychiatric disorder commented that, "it must be confessed that while the disease incidence of mental illness is low, the number of consultations with patients suffering from psychoneurotic disorders is proportionately high. One tends to see that patient frequently and they take up quite a lot of time and before I found the disease incidence, I thought it was much higher than it proved to be" (Waterson 1965).

Vineyard Studies

From 1961 to the present the island has had four to six general practitioners. During the period of the general practice studies, when it had six practitioners, one of them spent part of his time as the island's general surgeon. At present, the island has six practitioners, two of whom are internists, with support services supplied by a surgeon and a radiologist. A psychiatrist has practiced on the island only since 1961. In addition, more specialized support for the primary physicians is supplied by specialists, orthopedists, urologists, and others who come at regular intervals to conduct clinics at the hospital. For care beyond the resources of the local system, islanders are sent to hospitals in Boston, in emergency by ambulance or Coast Guard helicopter.

After the Mental Health Center had been in operation for more than two years, three surveys were conducted in order to determine the extent to which the general practitioners of the community were engaged in the care of islanders with psychiatric disorder. The first survey covered a three-month period beginning on March 1, 1964, the second covered thirteen random weeks in 1965, and the third spanned the calendar year 1966 (Mazer 1967a, 1969b). The second survey, though not analyzed here, is mentioned to indicate that by the time of the third study the practitioners and psychiatrist had had considerable common experience. In addition to determining the frequency of general practitioner consultation for psychiatric disorder, information was gathered on the characteristics of the psychiatric patients in the care of the practitioners by diagnosis, age, sex, marital status, and social class position. Since the methods of the studies were similar, only that of the one-year study is described (Appendix 11).

A patient was considered to be a psychiatric patient when the primary condition for which he consulted his practitioner was psychiatric in nature. The method used to determine what was or was not psychiatric morbidity assured that there would be significant congruence between the psychiatrist and the general practitioners. That such congruence can be achieved has been demonstrated (Rawnsley 1966).

Diagnostic Categories

Of the 8 percent of the practitioners' island patients who had psychiatric disorder, the study showed that 37 percent had psycho-neurotic disorders; 29 percent had personality disorders, including the transient situational personality disorders; and 24 percent had psychophysiologic disorders. Thus, 90 percent of the patients seen by the practitioners had one of these three conditions. The psychotic disorders made up another 4 percent of patients with psychiatric disorder seen by general practitioners, and chronic brain disease of all types represented 5 percent (Appendix 12).

Twenty-eight percent of the males and nine percent of the females who consulted a general practitioner for psychiatric disorder had as the main diagnosis alcohol addiction. Among the psychoneurotic disorders, anxiety and depression were almost equal in frequency in both surveys and made up almost 80 percent of the psychoneu-rotic reactions observed. The other large group was the hypochon-driacal reactions, which made up 12 percent of the psychoneurotic reactions.

Prevalence by Age and Sex

The one-year prevalence of psychiatric disorder in general prac-tice for the entire island was 5 percent, or 52 per thousand popula-tion (Appendix 13). For those persons age 15 or older, the rate was 7 percent. The usual experience that females come to psychiatric treatment more frequently than males was confirmed, but not to the extent reported in other studies. The psychiatric disorder rate in the general practices for males of all ages was 4.8 percent and for females was 5.5 percent.

The prevalence rate by age for both sexes rose rapidly from a rate of 7 per thousand in the 0-14 year age group to reach its peak at 84 per thousand in the 35-44 year age group. When the rates by age for males and females were compared, it was found that the rates for males were highest in the 25-44 year age groups, the rates for females in the 35-54 year age groups. In the three-month study, the female rate peaked earlier than the male rate, a finding that has been noted elsewhere in general practice (Watts et al 1964). The largest difference between the two rates was seen, as has been fre-quently reported, during childhood, when the rate for males was more than twice that for females (Appendix 13).

Marital Status

As has been shown in a number of studies, the never-married and the separated-divorced-widowed marital statuses were associated with higher rates of disorder than was the married status. Those who were never married, separated, divorced, or widowed had a 50 percent greater chance of consulting a general practitioner for a psychiatric disorder than did married persons (Appendix 14).

Social Class Position

The relationship between psychiatric disorder treated by the general practitioner and social class position was measured by occupation (Appendix 15). Because of the relatively small numbers involved, the seven categories of occupation were collapsed into three groups. The rate of psychiatric disorder treated by the general practitioner was related to social class for males only, both the highest and lowest level occupations giving higher rates than the middle ranking. These data may represent a composite influence of two factors. First, there may be some real relationship between social class and the frequency of occurrence of psychiatric disorder. Second, it is quite likely that there is a relationship between social class position and the incidence of help-seeking behavior.

Psychiatric Referral

Of the 307 patients who consulted for psychiatric illness during the year 1966, 64 or 21 percent of the total were referred to a psychiatrist either in or out of the hospital. Twenty-eight males who were referred made up 21 percent of the practitioners' male psychiatric admissions for that year, and the 36 females who were referred made up the same percentage of his female psychiatric admissions for that year. Nine of the males and five of the females were hospitalized, a male/female ratio for mental hospitalization usual for this community. The greater number of males who were hospitalized as compared with females was accounted for entirely by the greater hospitalization of males for problems associated with alcoholism.

The 1966 survey showed that more than one in every twenty people of the island consulted a general practitioner for a psychiatric condition during the year. This was more than twice as many as first consulted a psychiatrist during that year, even though psychiatric service was readily available, geographically accessible, and at low cost within the community. It is evident that in this community, and no doubt in others, the burden of treating psychiatric patients is being and must be shared by the general practitioner. Since there was only one mental health worker, the psychiatrist, present during the study, it is possible that with no choice available, some potential psychiatric patients may have chosen not to enter treatment by personal self-selection. That this hypothesis may have validity is suggested by the fact that later additions to the staff of the clinic appeared to attract a new clientele, particularly the young and those with marital problems.

Both the three-month and the twelve-month surveys gave similar prevalence rates for psychiatric disorder in the general practices of the island. The fact that the prevalence rates for the two periods were almost identical is not surprising, because persons suffering from psychiatric disorders are known to be more frequent attenders at medical offices than are those with somatic disorders (Shepherd et al 1966; Bentsen 1970).

If a psychiatric patient on the island should make six or eight visits to his family physician over a year, it is likely that he will be recorded at least once in each three-month period and will appear in both a three-month and a twelve-month survey, given the pattern of general practice visits in this community, which tends to distribute a series of visits over a long interval. While a psychiatric clinic is likely to consider admissions in terms of episodes of care with a continuous series of weekly or biweekly visits from inception to termination, the general practitioners of this community often discuss the presenting problem with the patient, prescribe medication, and leave the making of another appointment to his discretion. This spreads a series of visits over a longer period, which would tend to make quarterly and yearly rates similar.

The higher rates for female than for male subjects is a common finding in general practice studies. It may be owing to actual differences in frequency of disorder between the sexes, to a greater awareness of distress in women than in men, or to cultural differences that make it easier for women than for men to seek help. The female role in the rearing of children may also cause women to become more aware of their emotional difficulties as they critically observe their own transactions with their children.

The island studies were not designed to determine the percentage of the practitioners' patients who suffered from psychiatric disorder. In order to secure such data it would have been necessary to record all patients entering each practice during the studies, a procedure which under the circumstances was not politic to attempt. Such a percentage can be calculated, however, if one knows what proportion of the population consults a practitioner during the survey year. From the data of an American survey which found that 64.8 percent of the rural nonfarm population living outside of standard metropolitan statistical areas consulted their physician in a year (NHS 1969), it is calculated that 8 percent of all patients consulting their practitioners during the year did so for psychiatric disorder, a figure which is within the range of other reports (Shepherd et al 1966). Of great significance is the fact that during the one-year survey the general practitioners retained approximately 80 percent of those who consulted them for a psychiatric disorder; had they not retained so many, the demand on the psychiatric service would have been beyond its capacity at that time.

9

Psychiatric Disorder in Mental Health Practice

In the year 1855 a report by the Massachusetts Commission on Lunacy noted that there were only nineteen Vineyarders who were mentally ill (Jarvis 1971). Since the population at the time was 4,798, this established a prevalence rate of but 0.4 percent. The information in the report came from the island's physicians and the overseers of the poor. It is safe to suppose that those counted as mentally ill suffered from the psychoses or were grossly retarded, for the neuroses and character disorders had not yet been generally recognized.

By the turn of the century, the existence of the neuroses began to be described in American textbooks of psychiatry. The physicians of the island may also have had their interest in mental disorder stimulated by reports of the lectures given by Sigmund Freud at Clark University in Worcester, Massachusetts, in 1909. But until 1961, when the island acquired its first mental health service, only those with the more disabling disorders received specialized treatment, requiring an expensive and time-consuming journey to a mainland city and sometimes hospitalization in a mental hospital.

Islanders who now identify themselves as suffering from psychiatric disorder can attend the island's mental health service. Since the population is confined, with mainland facilities relatively inaccessible, islanders almost always seek care locally. The usual barriers to the securing of mental health care are minimal. Neither great distances, economic obstacles, nor waiting periods for service now exist. Since 95 percent of the population are within fifteen miles of the clinic and 85 percent are within ten miles, and since almost every household possesses a motor vehicle, the admission rates are not believed to be significantly affected by distance. Fees are based on family size and income and are never permitted to impede treatment. Those asking for an appointment are always seen within a week, often within hours, and immediately if necessary.

There have been numerous studies of the prevalence of psychological disorder in defined places both rural and urban. Because rural populations can be defined and demarcated more clearly than can urban populations, the former have been the subject of more community surveys than have the latter. The rates of disorder found in rural surveys show wide variations, far greater than do those in general practice surveys, where the highest prevalence rates are only four times the lowest rates. The spread of disorder among the rural communities surveyed in North America and northern Europe, omitting two studied that recorded only symptoms, ranged from 1.1 to 28.6 percent of the populations (Dohrenwend and Dohrenwend 1969). It strains credulity to attribute the 26-fold difference between the lowest and highest rates reported to actual variations in the populations studied. It is far more likely that the explanation for the difference lies in variations of method.

Rates and Varieties of Disorder

The psychiatric disorders for which islanders come to the clinic were studied over three time periods, 1962-1966, 1967-1971, and 1972-1973 (Appendix 16). Between 1962 and 1973 the personality disorders, including the transient situational personality disorders, made up 39 to 50 percent of the conditions; the psychoneurotic disorders, 23 to 33 percent; the alcoholic disorders, 9 to 12 percent; and the psychotic disorders, 6 to 10 percent. The organic brain disorders, mental deficiency, and drug dependency contributed smaller proportions of patients.

The segregation of the clinic's experience into three time periods revealed that problems for which islanders come for treatment have changed notably with time. The transient situational personality disorders, mostly disorders of children, showed a marked increase between the first and second time periods. The number coming for marital problems rose significantly for each interval (Appendix 17). Drug dependency, which was not seen before 1967, made up almost 10 percent of all admissions in the 1967-1971 period and then dropped sharply as changes in patterns of drug use and police practice occurred.

The one-year primary admission rates for the three time periods were roughly one, two, and three percent of the population, respectively. These may be counted as one-year incidence figures. Since some clinic patients had been continued in treatment from the previous year and others were readmissions, the one-year prevalence rates were significantly higher, namely two, four, and six percent of the population for each period. All three periods, particularly the two later ones, showed unusually high rates for community clinic practice in Massachusetts. The high rates may be attributed to three circumstances, the high visibility of the clinic in a small community, the absence of other mental health or family service agencies, and the clinic's practice of providing prompt, responsive service to all who come rather than selecting only those who match its existing programs.

First Admissions

A number of analyses were made of the information continuously collected on primary admissions and readmissions to the clinic from 1961 to 1974. For the period 1961-1966 the mean first admission rates per year per 1,000 population in round numbers were:

Primary admission rate   12
All person admission rate   15
All episodes rate   17
One-year prevalance rate   22

The one-year prevalence rate, the most stable of all from year to year, gives a significant measure of the demand for service by the people of this community; on the average, 2 percent of the population were in psychiatric treatment each year in 1961-1966.

Of the patients seen for psychiatric conditions during this period, one in three had a psychoneurotic disorder, one in five had a transient situational personality disorder, one in six had one of the personality disorders, one in eight had an alcoholic disorder, and one in ten had a psychotic disorder. Males had alcoholic disorders and transient situational personality disorders more often than females, while females much more often had psychoneurotic disorders. Persons with psychophysiological disorders rarely reached the psychiatric service and, on the evidence of the general practice studies, remained within the practices of general practitioners.

The usual experience that female rates of admission are notably higher than male rates was not confirmed except for one age group, 25 to 34. Indeed, the data show that with time, the proportion of males to females seeking treatment gradually increased. In 1962, for example, the male-female ratio was 0.81, and in 1966 it was 1.38. The fact that the proportion of males to female patients admitted as first admissions gradually increased from 1962 to 1966 is believed to be a sign of the increasing acceptance of the Mental Health Center by the community. If it is assumed that men are more reluctant to seek help than are women, the change in the sex ratio of primary admissions over time may indicate the growing willingness of men to seek such help as the center became an accepted community institution.

A High Rate Group

Perhaps the most striking finding of the period 1961-1966 was the high rate of admission to psychiatric service of women between age 25 and 34, for more than 18 percent of all women in that age group consulted a psychiatrist during the first five and a half years of study (Mazer 1970a). A number of other studies have also shown that females in this age group seek psychiatric treatment more frequently than do any other age groups in either sex (Bahn et al 1966; Bruhn et al 1966; Kessel and Hassall 1965; Kramer 1966; Tonge et al 1961; Shepherd and Gruenberg 1957). Since these women were almost all married and mostly engaged in the rearing of young children, the possibility that psychiatric intervention might improve disturbed mother-child relationships marked them as a strategic group for public health concern.

Of the 54 young women who sought help, six came for marital problems. Of the remaining 48, two-thirds were diagnosed as having psychoneurotic disorders; depressive reactions were present in 61 percent of them. Two of the women suffered from alcohol addiction and two from schizophrenic reactions. Thus, they suffered from psychoneurotic reactions generally and from depressive reactions specifically in a much larger proportion of instances than in the island's population as a whole.

Information was available on the marital status at the time of admission of each of the 48 women with psychiatric disorder and of virtually all females in the same age group on the island as of January 1, 1965. As a result, their rate of disorder by marital status could be calculated. The lowest rate was found in the currently married; the rate was a third higher in the never-married; and the rate in the divorced-separated was more than three times that of the married.

The social class position of 47 of the 48 patients with psychiatric disorder was compared with the 258 of the 263 women in the general population in the 25-34 year age group for whom social class data were available. The criterion used for social class position was the occupation of the head of the household. The risk of becoming a psychiatric patient was not significantly different for the two social class groups into which the seven occupational classes were collapsed.

Recent in-migration was significantly more common among the women patients in this age group than among all women in the same age group who lived on the island at the time of the 1965 census. Seventeen percent of the patients, as compared to five percent of all women in their age group, had migrated to the island within the year of admission. Similar findings were reported in a study on the Danish island of Samsø (Nielsen et al 1964). A very high rate of subsequent out-migration was also characteristic of the patients in the Vineyard study.

Almost half of the 38 Vineyard women with psychiatric disorder who had ever been delivered of a child had conceived their first child while unmarried. This rate is higher than the premarital pregnancy rate for the same age group on the island (Mazer 1967b). Of 101 children alive at the time of admission of their mothers, more than one-quarter were the result of premarital or nonmarital conceptions. When such unconventional pregnancies were related to place of birth, it was found that a higher proportion of island-born women as compared with mainland-born women had had such pregnancies, a difference that was statistically significant. Since the mainland-born women came mostly from large towns or cities, the difference in the two groups may simply reflect the higher rate of premarital pregnancy among rural people.

Six of the patients were pregnant at the time of admission. Three had been delivered of an infant within four months of admission. Five of the women had experienced the death of a parent, brother, child, or ex-husband in recent weeks or months. Three of them, though they desired children, were involved in a sterile union; two of them later adopted children. Although comparative control data are not available, it may be ventured that the women in this study were experiencing a high rate of stress.

In summary, the 48 women of age 25-34 who came for psychiatric treatment over a five and one-half year period had a higher rate of divorce and separation than did women in the same age group in the general population, a higher rate of premarital and nonmarital conceptions, a higher rate of in- and out-migration, and a frequent history of recent stress. Nineteen percent of these women were either pregnant or had been delivered of a baby within six months prior to admission, and an additional ten percent had experienced the death of someone close to them within days or months before coming to treatment.

Since the 38 women who were mothers had in their care a total of 101 children, 95 percent of them below the age of 12, the possibility of effective treatment of the women posed an unusual public health opportunity. Since many of them came for treatment soon after a stressful experience and most for the more benign psychiatric conditions, it is probable that the treatment of this group of young

women caring for a significant number of children could be among
the most productive efforts of the mental health service.

Lowering Clinic Barriers

It had been assumed that if external barriers to the securing of
psychiatric treatment were eliminated, primary or first admission
rates would soon become stabilized. The experience of the period
from 1962 to 1967 seemed to bear this out (Fig. 1). That the highest

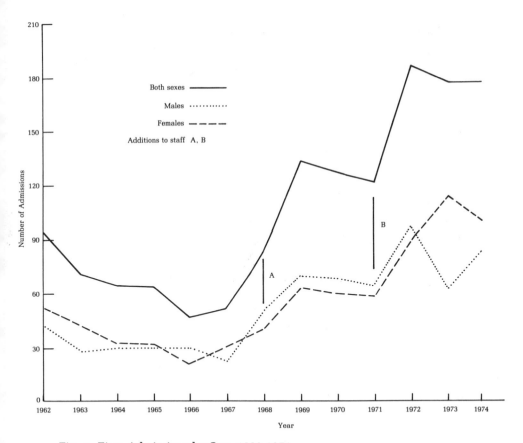

Fig. 1. First Admissions by Sex, 1962-1974

rate came in the first year is believed to be due to a backlog of patients with difficult problems who were until then in the care of general practitioners, an experience of many new psychiatric services. The hypothesis that first admissions by year would become stabilized was based also on the belief that help-seeking behavior was not likely to change over the short run. However, this assumption proved not to be justified. The rate of first admissions began to rise in 1968, appeared to level off between 1969 and 1971, and then showed an abrupt rise in 1972. Both of these increases in primary admission rates were associated with the addition of new professionals to the staff.

The first rise, which doubled primary admission rates by 1969, coincided with the addition to the staff in 1968 of a psychologist in his mid-twenties who had a sensitive understanding of the problems of young people. To make the mental health service easier for the young to accept, the clinic established within it what was called the Youth Counseling Service, housed in quarters separate from the clinic building. The offices were on a prominent corner of the main street of Edgartown above a drugstore, with a separate entrance from the street. At the outset, the psychologist spent many evenings there holding open house. The lighted windows of his office attracted attention, for the office and the liquor store were the only enterprises in town open during the winter evenings. He also spent much time at the Youth Center on weekends, making himself known to the young people of the island. From the beginning it was common for young people to drop into his office in the evening, chat with him, talk with each other, and sometimes do their homework on the large table in the waiting room. They were not enrolled as patients unless they said that they had a problem for which they wanted help.

The second increase in rates, which trebled the basic rate of the 1962-1966 period, was associated with the addition to the staff in 1971 of another psychologist, a man in his forties who had served as a priest of the Episcopal Church on Martha's Vineyard twelve years before. He had since become interested in mental health work, taken further training in clinical psychology, and left parish work. Because he had been a member of the community in the past, he was known to a significant proportion of the population, and it was also known that he was a clergyman.

The causes of the precipitous increases in primary admission rates, each after the addition of a new mental health worker to the staff, were suggested by the data on diagnosis and age (Appendices 17 and 18). The addition of a younger psychologist to the staff was followed by a sharp increase in the proportion of outpatients assigned diagnoses of transient situational personality disorder and marital problems and in the actual number of persons admitted each year with these diagnoses. Even more striking was the change in the pattern of admissions by age group. During the first period, 1962-1966, the highest admission rates were in the 25-34 year age group. During the second period, 1967-1971, the highest rate of admissions was in the 15-24 year age group, the admission rate in that age group increasing almost four times for both males and females. The only other notable increase in rates was a 45 percent increase among males of age 25-34 years.

The addition of a psychologist who had previously served as an island clergyman was also followed by changes in admission patterns. The proportion of psychiatric patients in the various diagnostic categories did not change significantly, save for a decrease in the rate of drug dependency in the 1972-1973 period. The number of admissions for marital problems per year increased by 122 percent over the 1967-1971 period, and for the transient situational personality disorders by 50 percent. The rates of disorder by age group increased markedly in each group up to age 34. The greatest increases were in the 25-34 age group, with increases over the 1967-1971 period of 135 percent for males and 209 percent for females. A significant proportion of this increase was due to those coming for marital problems.

It is inferred, therefore, that the addition of a young and understanding professional to the staff made it easier for young people to bring their difficulties to the agency. Identifying the operation as a "youth counseling" instead of a "psychiatric" service may also have made it easier for young people to come, since by doing so they no longer had to classify themselves as patients. The location of the office in a separate building from the Mental Health Center for the first year may have been of some influence in the increased rate of admissions among young people, for later, when the two services moved into the same quarters, the rate of youthful admissions decreased, if only slightly.

The addition of a second psychologist to the staff had two main results. Because he had served as a clergyman of an island church, he was perceived as an appropriate person to help with marital dysfunction, a problem often seen by islanders as within the competence and duty of the clergyman. Since he was no one's pastor, islanders could seek his help without the embarrassment that they often felt when consulting their own pastor, with whom they might be on some degree of intimacy. Because he joined the staff of the clinic after skillful service as director of the island's Youth Center, where he had done counseling, it was natural that young people continued to consult him.

When the clinic started, it had been assumed that once all of the known external barriers to seeking professional help for psychiatric disorder were removed, the clinic could then depend on a relatively unchanging first admission rate, unless measures were taken through public education or other means to increase the rate of help-seeking behavior. The serial addition of two professionals to the staff and the association of their coming with increases in rates of admission and changes in age distribution and diagnostic categories of the patients showed that the hypothesis was incorrect. This does not suggest that every addition to the staff of every clinic will be followed by increases in admission rates. In a large community with a large staff, additions to the staff of the mental health clinic may mean only that prospective patients can secure appointments more readily or more frequently. In a community as small as the island, however, professionals are very visible. Early in their coming to the community, they are usually interviewed by the island's weekly newspapers, and during the first year or two of their stay they are invited to address many community groups. They are seen, they are heard, their presumed capacities for giving help are assessed. Personal reactions to them, positive or negative, are experienced. They are observed functioning in many roles beyond that of mental health work. Their relationships with their friends, their wives, and their children are noted and may become role models for others in the community.

As a result of the two staff additions, a choice of therapists became available. Those who had not been prepared to seek help from a psychiatrist of definable age and character now had the option of seeing others from different professional backgrounds, of other ages, and with different personalities. The clinic's practice of permitting patients to choose a therapist whenever possible also helped in making entry easier. It is believed that these findings apply only to small communities. Since the occurrences and policies resulted in an increase in the number of those who sought help for their problems, one may conclude that a clinic manned by a single professional has inherent handicaps, that a range in age and professional affiliation is desirable among a clinic staff, and that the public visibility of members of the clinic staff may facilitate entry to it. The advantages resulting from the public visibility of the clinic's staff can only occur when the clinic serves a population small enough to be a community, a circumstance absent when clinics serve catchment areas of 75,000 to 150,000 persons.

In 1973 there was a change in the proportion of males to females. This was owing to two circumstances. First, a greater number of women came for marital problems. Second, there was an increase in the number of girls reaching the clinic. For the first time in the clinic's history, the number of girls exceeded the number of boys. Although it has long been the experience of clinics that boys enter psychiatric services more often than do girls, the difference may be due simply to the way in which the disorder is expressed; boys have behavior problems and come to public attention, whereas girls suffer equally but less obtrusively.

The causes of the change in the relative number of boys and girls coming to the clinic in 1973 is not known with certainty. During that year, however, the clinic for the first time had the part-time clinical services of two women, a social worker and a mental health aide. This was perhaps responsible, in part at least, for the reversal of the sex ratio for this age group.

Psychiatric Readmissions

Because the Mental Health Center was in an unusual position as an immediate and available source of help, it was possible to make one important modification in usual clinic practice. If a clinic carries a waiting list or has a complex intake procedure, the therapist may hesitate to discharge a patient until he is reasonably certain that the patient can manage on his own. This may add unnecessary hours of therapeutic work to the clinic's case load and defer the patient's chance to function on his own. Because the island clinic was committed to readmit a patient immediately without the need to repeat the intake process, it was decided at the outset to attempt to discharge patients early, though provisionally, with a knowledge on their part that they could readily return should they need further help. Thus, the decision to terminate treatment, usually made by consensus, was often phrased by the therapist as, "Well, then, suppose you try it on your own and call me if you need further help."

Since the mental health profession has not agreed on a standard definition of readmission, it was necessary for the clinic to design one. If readmission is simply a return to treatment after the mental health worker and the patient together, or the former alone, have decided that treatment is over, the return to treatment a week or two later must be counted as a readmission, with the result that readmission rates are meaninglessly inflated. In order to avoid such inflation and yet permit freedom in discharging patients early, readmission was defined as a return to treatment 91 days or more after the last visit. By this definition, no one was discharged in the records until 90 days after his last visit. This procedure made readmission a meaningful event; it meant that the individual had managed without psychiatric care for a significantly long time. It made it more likely that a return to treatment was due to another episode of stress or to a failure of the equilibrium achieved rather than simply to the continuation of old symptoms. In either event, the operative question was, "What occurred to make you decide to return at this time?"

While there are other definitions of readmission, for the purposes of the clinic the readmission rate for each year was calculated as the number of persons readmitted that year divided by the total of all first admissions and readmissions that year times 100. Such a datum is important in determining whether the service is reaching new cases as they occur or is largely treating the same clientele with chronic or recurring disorders. During the first full year, 1962, there were no readmissions from 1961. Since that time, the readmission rate has varied between 22 and 46 percent per year. During the four years 1970 to 1973 it stabilized between 34 and 38 percent. The average readmission rate for the twelve-year period 1962-1973 was 32 percent. In short, one-third of all persons admitted each year had prior treatment in the clinic.

Such clinic readmissions can be interpreted in a number of ways. If the therapeutic encounter has as its goal not only the relief of the presenting symptoms but also the reorganization of personality so as to make recurrences unlikely, then all such readmissions would be considered relapses or therapeutic failures. This point of view about readmissions was taken in one study, where more than 50 percent of all readmissions were therefore counted as relapses (McPartland and Richart 1966). Since the clinic whose readmission experience was described was in a moderately large city with other similar facilities, it is quite likely that some of its patients were readmitted to other clinics on the second or third time round and did not enter its readmission statistics; had they, the rates might have been even higher.

The main therapeutic technique used in the island clinic is crisis intervention with reestablishment of a functioning equilibrium. The goal is not the immunization of the individual from the consequences of stress forever more, if indeed such a goal were a reasonable one. In addition, since the clinic deals with a fairly stable population and as time goes on will have treated a larger and larger proportion of that population, it is to be expected that a significant proportion of all admissions each year will be readmissions. In view of these circumstances, the fact that one-third of the patients are readmissions is considered a reasonable and manageable proportion.

Social Class Position

There have been more than two score studies of the relationship between psychological disorder and socioeconomic status (Dohrenwend and Dohrenwend 1969). In the majority of such studies the highest rates of disorder occurred in those in the lowest socioeconomic position. When psychiatric conditions are divided by diagnosis, however, further differences are evident. Schizophrenia, for example, is highly associated with lower social class positions, whereas treated psychoneuroses are more frequent in higher status positions. In the island studies the relationship between admission to the clinic for psychiatric disorder and socioeconomic status was measured by the occupation of the head of the household (Appendix 19). Neither in males nor in females were there any significant differences in rates in the three occupational groupings used. Since the study was one not of total prevalence but rather of treated disorder, one cannot conclude from this finding that there was no relationship between psychiatric disorder and socioeconomic status. Since most total prevalence studies show higher rates among those in lower status positions, it appears to be a fair inference that those in the lower social class positions on the island were simply less likely to seek service.

Social Mobility

The frequency of psychiatric disorder has been related to social mobility, particularly to downward mobility (Ødegaard 1975; Langner and Michael 1963), and such findings are often interpreted as due to downward drift in occupational level as a result of illness. Other studies have reported higher rates of disorder in both downwardly and upwardly mobile persons than in the socially stabile or nonmobile (Kleiner and Dalgard 1975). The higher rates associated with upward mobility may be the result of stress during the period of upward striving.

There have been a number of studies in which social mobility has been measured by comparing the patient's occupation with that of his or her father, though this method has limitations (Susser 1968). Since under normal circumstances many people improve their occupational positions with time (Rogoff 1953), the ideal study would compare occupational position of son or daughter and father at the same period of life. In addition, occupations in general are moving upward, and a control group of nonpatients' occupations in relation to that of their fathers would be a desirable addition to the studies.

The data for the five-year period 1967-1971 was analyzed as to social mobility. Using the full seven-category occupation scale, the number of zero changes, upward changes, and downward changes between occupation of patient and the patient's father were recorded for the five disorders for which there was a sufficient number of cases to give the results validity. The data showed a notable downward mobility in four of the conditions: the psychotic disorders, personality disorders, alcoholic disorders, and marital maladjustments (Appendix 20). In the psychoneurotic disorders there appeared to be no notable change in average mobility. Two hypotheses have been put forward to explain such observations. The first suggests that downward mobility owing to ill fortune or other external factors may equally with the strivings of the upwardly mobile produce sufficient stress as to cause disorder. The second hypothesis, the so-called drift hypothesis, suggests that people with psychiatric disorders drift downward in their occupational position as a result of disorder. Certainly one with a major illness, such as a psychotic disorder, is handicapped in occupational competence, and the alcoholic disorders cannot but have the same effect (Langner and Michael 1963).

Marital Status

The relationship between marital status and psychiatric disorder has been the subject of quite a few studies (Srole et al 1962; D. C. Leighton 1963; Shepherd et al 1966; Baldwin 1971; Ødegaard 1946). Virtually all show lower rates in the currently-married than in the never-married or in those whose marriages are disrupted by separation, divorce, or widowhood. The rates per thousand population in each status of those age 15-54 were calculated for the island population (Appendix 21). The currently-married, as has been found in other studies, showed the lowest rate, with the divorced next, the never-married three times the married rate, and the separated seven times the married rate. The number of widows coming to treatment was insufficient for a meaningful computation of rate. The separated, whose rate of disorder was seven times that of the married, are usually under great continuing stress. Those who are divorced have been through the divorce process and have had time to make the adaptation from one status to another, to have passed through the crisis, and in many instances to have resolved it. The separated, on the contrary, remain in psychological limbo. They are in a state of decision and indecision. They are usually in legal conflict and even more frequently, in a community with a low median income, are in economic distress, for until the court has made an adjudication or until the parties to the divorce have reached an agreement, the husband often uses his economic leverage as a legal instrument. In short, the separated are subject to many current stresses and therefore show the highest rates.

Migration

There have been many studies on the relationship between psychiatric disorder and migration from place to place (Mezey 1960; Murphy 1965; Ødegaard 1932; Malzberg and Lee 1956). Migration from country to country is often associated with higher rates of psychiatric hospitalization than are reported for the same group in the home country or in the adopted country. Further, with time, the admission rates of those in the adopted country gradually fall. This finding supports the stress hypothesis. In addition, those who move to a community in which there are a large number of people from the same ethnic background have lower rates than those who move to a community in which they remain ethnically isolated.

The rate of admissions per 1,000 population for those who came to the island clinic during the five-year period 1967-1971 in relation to where they had lived five years before gave some information on migration and treated psychiatric disorder (Appendix 22). The lowest rate of disorder was found in those who were living in the same house where they had lived five years before. Progressively higher rates were found in those who were now living in another house on the island and in those who had moved to the island from mainland Massachusetts, and the highest rates were found in those who had moved to the island from another state.

The fact that people who had moved from one house to another had higher rates than those who had remained in the same house is consistent with a Baltimore study (Tietze et al 1942). Moving from one island town to another may simply be a sign of economic stringency, the inability to own one's home. However, since the social network of the islander is mainly in his own town, moving to another town may be experienced as a significant loss. Moving from another part of Massachusetts to the island, however, involves a still more major transition. One's family and friends are left behind. It may be necessary to make severe occupational readjustments and to suffer economic loss. Often, it is believed, such migrations occur not simply in search of a better life but also in an attempt to repair a family already in crisis. The same considerations apply, though in even greater degree, to those who have moved from another state to the island, the group with the highest prevalence rate of all.

10

Comparison of Psychiatric and General Practice

The psychiatric practice and general practice studies on the Vineyard during the first years of the clinic's operation showed that by far the larger burden of psychiatric disorder, in numbers of patients at least, was borne by the general practitioners of the community (Mazer 1965, 1967a, 1969b). It thus becomes pertinent to inquire in what respects the general practitioner's case load is the same or different from that of his psychiatric colleagues.

Islanders suffering from psychiatric disorder do not reach either a general practitioner or a mental health worker at random. The relatively small percentage of the psychologically impaired who do reach such assistance indicates that there is a self-selection process from the start. Further, a variety of factors are involved in both the selection and referral processes. One large-scale American study indicated that clergymen were first consulted more often than other caretakers (Gurin et al 1960). A study in Boston gave evidence that general practitioners treated the majority of the psychiatrically disordered in that city (Ryan 1969). It is probable that on Martha's Vineyard a general practitioner is, more often than not, the first professional consulted by those in psychological distress, though there are exceptions. If the patient's practitioner is unsympathetic to the emotionally disordered or uncomfortable in their presence, his patients may come to the Mental Health Center at the outset. A few patients have been encountered who have two practitioners, one for somatic ailments and another for alcoholic or psychiatric disorder.

The general practitioner may give clear signs, consciously or unconsciously, of his discomfort with emotional disorder, or he may show his interest by setting aside double appointments during office hours or arranging for longer evening appointments for his patients. On the contrary, he can find ways of inhibiting the stream of emotional material by quickly suggesting psychiatric referral or diverting the patient in other ways. One practitioner feared that once he permitted a patient to reveal much personal material, he was likely to lose him, since later visits or social encounters might prove embarrassing to the patient.

A number of other factors are influential in determining the referral of patients to psychiatric resources by the general practitioner. Discouragement with the results of his treatment of the patient, anxiety about the possibility of suicide, fear of the disordered thinking of the psychotic person, or a problem in the patient that resonates with the practitioner's own difficulties in life might each influence referral, in addition to a perceptive appraisal of the patient's need for psychiatric consultation.

In order to determine whether those with psychiatric disorder who consulted their general practitioner were in some way different from those who consulted the clinic staff, two groups of data were compared. The first was the information collected during the one-year study of psychiatric disorder in general practice (Mazer 1969b). The second was a tabulation of all patients with psychiatric disorder who had seen a psychiatrist, generally on the island but occasionally off it, whether in the hospital or out, during the period July 1, 1961, to December 31, 1968. These two groups were compared with respect to sex, age, diagnosis, marital status, and social position, using occupational level as a measure of social position.

Sex

The data show that a somewhat higher proportion of patients treated by psychiatrists were male than were patients treated by general practitioners. For every 100 females treated by a psychiatrist there were 94 males; for every 100 females treated by a general practitioner for psychiatric disorder there were only 77 males. The difference, however, between the male-female figures could have occured by chance from 10 to 20 times per every 100 and therefore cannot be considered statistically significant.

Age by Sex

The data also give the distribution of general practice and psychiatric patients by age group for both sexes (Appendix 23). For each sex, those who consulted a psychiatrist were significantly younger. For males, the peak age group of general practice patients was two decades later than for psychiatric practice patients, and for females one decade later.

Two major factors are thought to account for this difference between psychiatric practice and general practice patients. On the island, as in most communities, a higher level of education has been achieved by the general population in recent than in past decades. If educational level is associated with the willingness to seek psychiatric help, the better educated, younger segment of the population would be more likely than their elders to see a psychiatrist. A second, perhaps even more important factor has to do with diagnostic selection. In this community, general practitioners rarely retain children in difficulty; it is their common practice to refer them to the Mental Health Center. This has been a tradition in Massachusetts, where state outpatient services are often limited to services for children.

Psychiatric Diagnoses

Self-selection by diagnosis is made by both patient and general practitioner. Patients with psychophysiological disorders did not, during the initial period, ever consult a psychiatrist. This was not unexpected, since patients developing psychophysiological disorders are assumed to be engaged in repressing awareness of anxiety. In addition, general practitioners feel a special competence with psychophysiological disorders and on the island rarely refer them to the Mental Health Clinic. They may also feel a reluctance to make such referrals since they then risk the antagonism of a patient who has announced by the expression of his illness that he prefers to present his anxiety in a disguised fashion.

The data on diagnoses show that the psychiatrist saw a predominance of the patients with psychotic and personality disorders, the latter largely the transient situational personality disorders of childhood and adolescence (Appendix 24). The general practitioners, in contrast, treated all of those with psychophysiological disorder and saw somewhat more patients with alcoholic disorders than did the psychiatrist. Approximately one-third of the psychiatric practice of each group consisted of those with psychoneuroses.

The data also show that 78 percent of those who were treated by general practitioners for psychiatric conditions were limited to three diagnostic categories, the psychoneuroses, the psychophysiological disorders, and alcohol disorders. This suggests that if general practitioners who handle the greatest burden of psychiatric disorder are to be effectively trained for their tasks, the training should emphasize the threatment of these categories of patients, with less emphasis on the treatment of the young and the psychotic.

Social Class Position

The distribution of patients by social class position was not significantly different for those who consulted a mental health worker and those who consulted a general practitioner.

In summary, comparison of the practices of the general practitioner and the psychiatrist produced two significant findings. First, almost four out of every five patients in the care of the primary physicians were suffering from psychoneuroses, psychophysiological disorders, and alcohol disorders. Second, patients with psychoneurotic disorders were shared almost equally between the two resources, whereas patients with personality and psychotic disorders were treated mostly by mental health workers. These findings have implications for the further training of general practitioners in the treatment of those with psychiatric disorder.

11

The Prevalence of Human Predicaments

Mental health workers have long been aware that many of those with psychological disorders express their difficulties not in awareness but in acts. One category of such difficulties is the group of disorders classified as sociopathic. The concept of accident proneness is an example of another category. It is probable that those experiencing disorder out of awareness are often uncounted in clinical surveys. The total prevalence surveys, which depend heavily upon distress in awareness, may therefore inadequately explore the psychosocial difficulties of their subjects, since the two main symptom inventories used (Langner 1963; Macmillan 1957) neither include items that disclose anger and irritability nor elicit data suggestive of the psychoses or sociopathic states (Phillips and Segal 1969).

If the clinician or epidemiologist is to identify disorder out of the subject's awareness, he must ask the relevant questions. The clinician knows, for example, that in assessing the state of a man with an alcoholic disorder, information on automobile accidents, arrests, work history, and marital problems may tell more about the disorder than a precise record of the frequency and volume of alcohol used.

In the few studies of psychiatric epidemiology that have included psychosocial events presumptive of psychiatric disorder, no evidence is given that the psychosocial events were in fact indicative of the presence of such disorder. Although the statistical evidence for the association between parapsychiatric events and psychiatric disorder is persuasive, individual parapsychiatric experiences are not necessarily indicative of psychosocial disorder. Divorce, for example, may involve the correction of a neurotic or impulsive decision made in the past. Further, the parapsychiatric events included in the island study by no means exhaust the ways in which human beings express psychological distress.

The evidence of the island study is that parapsychiatric events occured much more often in psychiatric subjects than in the population at large (Mazer 1972a). When such events occur without psychiatric consultation, they are considered to be expressions of disorder out of awareness. This makes them a public health problem for which there are as yet no appropriate resources. A study was made of all those living in the island community for a five-year period 1964-1968 in an attempt to differentiate more critically between those experiencing predicaments who consult a mental health worker and those who do not. Such a differentiation can help either to eliminate the barriers that keep those experiencing such events from the existing sources of psychiatric aid or to design new means of reaching them.

The study compared two groups of people in the same community, those who take the avenue that brings them to mental health facilities, and those who use the parapsychiatric idiom for the expression of their difficulties and who reach agencies not equipped to help them (Mazer 1972a, 1972b, 1974). Those who chose the psychiatric and parapsychiatric routes were compared with respect to sex, age, and social class position for the entire population.

Over the five-year period 1,317 of the 5,959 persons in the year-round population of the island came into the register for one or more of the sixteen predicaments under study. Thus, 22 percent or roughly one in five experienced one or more predicaments. The data on chronic alcoholism were based only on patients who came to the psychiatric facility and so do not represent the total rate for the condition in the community; other of the events recorded no doubt suffer from similar but less evident limitations in completeness.

Sex

The rates by sex and the sex ratios were calculated for each of the sixteen predicaments (Appendix 25). Rates of over 25 per 1,000 population were more common for males than for females. Rates of this magnitude were found for males in the following predicaments, in descending order of frequency: fines, psychiatric episodes, school disciplinary problems, probation, acute public alcoholism, single-car accidents, chronic alcoholism, and school underachievement. Female rates of this magnitude occurred only for psychiatric episodes and school underachievement.

A concise way of noting the comparative experiences of males and females is through the use of the sex ratio, a number obtained by dividing the male rate by the female rate. A sex ratio above 1 indicates a higher male rate, a value below this figure indicates a higher female rate. Sex ratios of 5 or higher (male rates more than five times female rates) were found for predicaments that bring the individual into conflict with the legal system; men came to the attention of the legal system 7 to 16 times more often than women. In order of decreasing ratio, sex ratios were: jail, 16; probation, 11; acute public alcoholism, 9; fines, 8; juvenile delinquency, 7; single-car accidents, 5.

Predicaments in which the sex ratio was close to 1 were psychiatric episodes, mental hospitalization, school underachievement, suicide attempts, marital dissolution, and premarital pregnancy. The latter two had such sex ratios since they always involve couples. The remaining predicaments had intermediate sex ratios.

Age by Sex

The prevalence of predicaments was closely related to age, with the highest rates for most predicaments in the 15-24 year age group (Appendices 26 and 27). Thus, during the five-year period, 37 percent of all males on the island between 15 and 24 years of age were fined by the district court. Thirty-two percent of all boys in the high school during that period were recorded, according to the definition used, as having had school disciplinary problems, with 22 percent showing underachievement. Predicaments that had their highest rates in the male 15-24 year age group, in descending order of magnitude, were fines, school disciplinary problems, school underachievement, probation, single-car accidents, premarital pregnancy, auto license suspension, juvenile delinquency, and jail. For females, the highest rates in the 15-24 year age group were, in descending order; school underachievement, premarital pregnancy, school disciplinary problems, fines, and single-car accidents.

For males, acute public alcoholism was a phenomenon which ranged fairly evenly in rate from 15 to 54 years of age. Chronic alcoholism reached its highest rates between 45 and 64 years, dropping sharply thereafter. Psychiatric episodes in males occurred most frequently in the 35-44 year age group, as did mental hospitalization. In females, psychiatric episodes occurred most often in the 25-34 year age group, a decade earlier than in males. Marital dissolution for females was most common in the 25-34 year age group. Mental hospitalization for females, however, occurred most commonly between 45-54 years of age, as did chronic and acute public alcoholism. The high rates for those conditions in that age group may be related to the occurrence of menopause and the increasing rate of widowhood at that time.

Social Class Position

The prevalence rates by social class position for persons of both sexes experiencing the sixteen human predicaments were calculated for the five-year period (Appendix 28). The predicaments were ranked according to the influence of social class position, as determined by the value of P in the chi square test, which was used as a statistical measure of the degree of association between the prevalence of the predicament and the social class position of the subjects. The P value expresses the probability that an apparent relationship of two variables can occur by chance. A P value of 0.01. for example, means that the association could occur by chance only once in one hundred times. If an association between two variables can occur by chance five or fewer times in one hundred, the association is by convention considered statistically significant.

The data show that the prevalence of eleven predicaments was related to social class position, ten of them inversely; that is, the lower the social class position, the higher the predicament rate.

For no predicament was the highest rate found in the highest social class position. The findings are:

$P < 0.001$ Court probation, acute public alcoholism, fines, marital dissolution, premarital pregnancy

$P\ 0.01\text{-}0.05$ Single-car accidents, auto license suspension, jail, mental hospitalization, juvenile delinquency, psychiatric treatment.

$P\ 0.1\text{-}0.6$ School underachievement, suicide attempts, school disciplinary problems, chronic alcoholism, suicide (no statistically significant association between the predicament and social class position)

In summary, the first ten predicaments showed a significant inverse relationship to social class position, the lower the position, the higher the rate. No statistically significant association was found for school underachievement, school disciplinary problems, suicide attempts, chronic alcoholism, and suicide. Only for psychiatric treatment was the highest prevalence rate found in the highest social class position; the lowest rate was found in the middle position.

When the social class data were analyzed by sex, the inverse relationship between the two variables was maintained for males in cases of probation, acute public alcoholism, fines, jail, auto accidents, premarital pregnancy, juvenile delinquency, driver's license suspension, marital dissolution and psychiatric treatment. For females, the inverse association held up only for marital dissolution, premarital pregnancy, and fines.

The inverse relationship between the prevalence of a predicament and social class position may occur for one of two reasons. First, the event itself may occur more frequently in the lowest than in the highest social class position. Second, the event may occur with the same or lesser frequency in the lowest class position but be made more socially visible and recorded more often because of the manner in which society handles such events in different social classes. The finding that psychiatric admission rates were little different for the highest and lowest social class groupings, while mental hospitalization in the lowest group was almost twice that of the highest group, may be due both to the higher rates of major disorders in the lower class positions and to differences in the way in which disorder is handled. Upper class people probably get treatment earlier, often have the resources to hire others for home care, and may be shielded from acting out their disorders publicly in ways that provoke hospitalization.

In a small community, the handling of acute public alcoholism is often affected by both age and class. A young fisherman who staggers down the main street may be taken to the county jail to sober up, while the lawyer or merchant is likely to be driven home in the police car. In the case of marital dissolution, the actual class bias may be even larger than that found in the study. Legal fees and the difficulty of maintaining two households on a small income make divorce economically unfeasible for many in the lower class positions. And, it is likely that for some predicaments the higher rates in the lower social class positions may be due both to biased handling on the part of social institutions and to greater prevalence.

Although total prevalence studies of psychiatric disorder have shown that those in the lowest social class positions have the highest rates of impairment, it is likely that on the island such persons seek psychiatric treatment at lower rates than do those in the higher class positions. The reasons may be many, including variations in the awareness of distress, absence of the belief that expertise can solve such human problems, the pressures of daily life which put psychological distress in a low priority position, or the difficulty in surmounting even the relatively low hurdles that exist between the desire to see a mental health worker and the steps that must be taken to reach one. The question is, how do people in such position express their difficulties? It is a common observation on the island that anger is more likely to be expressed in action than in words among working class people, and fist-sized indentations in composition board walls or cardboard coverings for window panes shattered in anger are not infrequently observed in their homes. The data suggest that there are sex, age, and social class differences between those who express their psychological distress by seeking psychiatric help and those whose distress is expressed in acts which bring them to the attention of the social, educational, legal, or other institutions of the community.

The data also show that those whose distress is expressed in parapsychiatric events are most often young, very often male, and almost always in the lower social class positions. These findings suggest that the extensive development of community mental health clinics to provide treatment for those who know they need help may not at all approach the problem of the significant proportion of the population who signal their distress in another idiom.

12

Parapsychiatric Events and Psychiatric Disorder

A major question of the research was whether psychiatric and parapsychiatric subjects come from two different subgroups of the total island population (Mazer 1972b). If the two groups could be distinguished by demographic characteristics, it might result in a description of those with disorder out of awareness which would help in bringing them within the orbit of therapeutic services. The studies indicated that those whose distress was expressed in parapsychiatric experiences were most often young, male, and in the lower social class positions as compared to psychiatric subjects. The question then arose whether persons with distress in awareness, the psychiatric patients, have fewer parapsychiatric experiences than do subjects experiencing parapsychiatric events alone.

An ideal design for testing this question would begin with the identification of functionally impaired persons by elaborate home surveys as was done in the Stirling County and Midtown Manhattan studies (D.C. Leighton, et al 1963; Srole et al 1962). A comparison of the frequency of parapsychiatric events in two groups of impaired persons, those who consulted a psychiatrist and those who did not, both of the groups being matched in degree of impairment, would more or less decisively answer the question. But since such studies have shown that only a small percentage of those rated as impaired were currently consulting a psychiatrist (5.4 percent in the Midtown Manhattan study), the pool from which the two groups would have to be selected would have been quite large, far exceed-

ing the resources of this or any other study yet attempted. Therefore, the research on the island tested the question by less critical
techniques.

The data for the total population used in the other island studies
were not considered suitable for this one. In-migration, out-
migration, birth, and death during the five-year period 1964-
1968 made the population at risk variable in composition. Even
had the total population remained constant in numbers, the population under study would naturally have varied from year to year. A
significant in-migration of high risk persons during one year might
easily bias the results. Because of these considerations, the population whose predicaments were the basis of analysis consisted of
those who had been at risk within the community for the entire
five-year period. This group was secured by removing from consideration all those who were born, died, in-migrated, and out-
migrated during the period. The total population studied was thus
reduced to 4,519 and the number of subjects to the 867 persons who
experienced either a psychiatric or a parapsychiatric event, or
both.

In order to make a comparison of the two groups, a parapsychiatric score was computed for each subject. The score is simply the
total number of parapsychiatric events experienced by a subject.
While such a score gives equal weight to items that may be of
unequal implication so far as psychological disorder is concerned,
this face value procedure seemed the only one possible in the
absence of data which would justify weighting the items. It is also
recognized that for some individuals a parapsychiatric experience
may not always reflect psychological disorder, as in the case of
certain divorces. However, the numbers involved in the study
should compensate for such occasional exceptions.

Frequency of Parapsychiatric Events

The first question at issue was whether or not the list of events
described as parapsychiatric are reflective of psychiatric disorder.
If they are not, they should occur no more frequently in psychiatric
patients than in the general population. However, more than twice

as many psychiatric patients as members of the total population at risk had one or more parapsychiatric experiences, or 33 percent as compared to 15 percent (Appendix 29).

In brief, the parapsychiatric events recorded occurred much more often in persons who had consulted a psychiatrist than in those who had not. While occasionally a parapsychiatric experience led to psychiatric consultation, this was an uncommon route. The data imply that the experience of parapsychiatric events is presumptive evidence of psychiatric disorder.

Psychiatric Admissions

In another test of the question whether disorder in awareness is associated with fewer parapsychiatric events, consulting a psychiatrist one or more times was used as an index of disorder in awareness, and the experience of parapsychiatric events without psychiatric consultation was used as an index of disorder out of awareness. Since entry into the "parapsychiatric only" group required the experience of at least one parapsychiatric event, only the 94 psychiatric subjects with one or more parapsychiatric events were used for comparison. This procedure assured that both groups had the same entry requirement, one parapsychiatric event. To have included the 191 psychiatric subjects with no parapsychiatric experience would have biased the analysis in favor of the hypothesis. For this reason, all of the analyses were based on data for the 666 subjects, both psychiatric and nonpsychiatric, who had experienced one or more parapsychiatric events. It was found that the 94 psychiatric subjects had significantly higher parapsychiatric scores than did the nonpsychiatric subjects (Appendix 30). This finding indicates that disorder in awareness was not associated with a lesser degree of acting out; on the contrary, of persons in predicament, those who consulted a psychiatrist also had higher rates of acting out.

In order to determine whether these inferences are valid or due to grossly unequal distributions of men and women in the psychiatric and nonpsychiatric categories, the data were also broken down by sex. It was found that women in predicament were almost twice as likely as men to have consulted a psychiatrist (21 percent as opposed to 11 percent). Male subjects had much higher parapsychiatric scores than did female subjects. For men, the parapsychiatric scores were significantly higher in psychiatric than in nonpsychiatric subjects; for women, the difference was in the same direction but not to a statistically significant degree.

Psychiatric Diagnoses

The generally higher parapsychiatric scores in the psychiatric than in the nonpsychiatric group were largely owing to the very high parapsychiatric scores among those diagnosed as having sociopathic disorders (Appendix 31). The high scores among persons with this diagnosis are not surprising, since acting out is a characteristic of the disorder and one of the criteria for its diagnosis.

Of the 36 persons diagnosed by psychiatric interview as having a sociopathic disorder, 35 had also entered the register for parapsychiatric events; 35 of the 36 fell among the 15 percent of the population at risk who had entered the parapsychiatric part of the register. When the data were computed with the sociopathic disorders omitted, the scores for the psychiatric and nonpsychiatric groups showed less variation.

Sex

Males were more often in predicament than females and had significantly higher mean parapsychiatric scores (Appendix 32). Nevertheless, approximately the same number of men and women came for psychiatric treatment. Thus, a significantly smaller proportion of males in predicament consulted a psychiatrist than did females, a finding revealed in a previous analysis. In brief, males experienced predicaments more frequently than did females but sought psychiatric help less often.

If, as this finding suggests, men experience distress out of awareness but in action more often then do women, the higher rates of treated disorder in women reported in the literature may in part reflect the difference in awareness of distress. Since the total prevalence studies depend heavily on conscious response to symptoms reported in questionnaires, the greater degree of awareness of distress in women suggests that they may produce more positive responses to symptom questionnaires even with the same or a lesser degree of disorder.

Age

Age was an important factor in the frequency of occurrence of both psychiatric and parapsychiatric events (Appendix 33). The high parapsychiatric scores and the low rate of psychiatric admissions in the 15-24 year age group show that adolescence and young adulthood are periods when psychological disorder comes to the attention of other than psychiatric agencies. Whether this is a reflection of the nature of adolescence and young adulthood alone, or whether it also suggests that psychiatric agencies, having been designed for older adults or for the parents of young children, somehow erect barriers to the entry of adolescents and young adults, is a question raised by these data. Those in the 15-24 year age group with almost the highest parapsychiatric scores in fact reached psychiatric resources least often. That this situation may be altered is shown by the clinic's experience when acquiring a new young mental health worker.

Parapsychiatric scores, on the contrary, were lowest at both ends of the age scale. This finding is no doubt due to the fact that the very young and the very old are not at all or less frequently at risk of some of the parapsychiatric experiences, such as auto accidents, divorce, and public drunkenness, and that when experiencing such events they are more likely to have them shielded from public attention. It is inferred that adolescence and young adulthood are periods of the greatest acting out with the least expression of distress in awareness.

Social Class Position

There was an inverse relationship between social class position and parapsychiatric scores; that is, the lower the class position, the higher the score (Appendix 34). For subjects who consulted a psychiatrist, the reverse was found; the higher the social position, the more likely was the subject with a predicament to have had psychiatric consultation. It is inferred that disorder in awareness was more common in the higher than in the lower social class positions, with the reverse being true for disorder out of awareness. The relative competence of the classes in taking the steps required to secure psychiatric care may have played an important role in the psychiatric consultation rate by social class. Even though those in the lower social class positions had higher rates of predicament, various social factors made them less likely to seek psychiatric help.

The hypothesis that those who are aware of psychological distress are less likely to display it in psychosocial acts was not confirmed. In fact, it appears that the human experiences called parapsychiatric or psychosocial are associated with and represent another mode of expression of psychiatric disorder. Of the psychiatric diagnostic categories, the sociopathic group had the highest parapsychiatric scores.

There may be two reasons for the fact that women were more often aware of the presence of psychological distress than were males. First, when in distress, women may find it more consistent with their values and beliefs to seek expert help. Second, they may be actually more aware of distress than are men. This presumption may have important implications for the methods used in some of the total prevalence studies, which depend in part on subjective responses to symptom questionnaire items, for it has been pointed out that both the Langner 22-item instrument and the Health Opinion Survey emphasize introspective and passive varieties of discomfort and contain no items expressing irritability, losing one's temper, or other assertive symptoms that are more congenial to the male role in society (Phillips and Segal 1969; D.C. Leighton et al 1963). These considerations may in part at least explain the higher rates for females reported both in total prevalence studies and in psychiatric service admission rates.

Adolescents and young adults age 15-24 years, though in distress almost as often as any other age group, sought psychiatric help least often. While acting out may be a characteristic of this period of life, psychiatric clinics may also have been designed for the capacities and value systems of middle class adults, and child guidance clinics for the same parent group. It may well be, therefore, that they are so organized as to be unintentionally inhospitable to those adolescents and young adults who, like the poor, find it difficult to hurdle the barriers which the intake process often places in their path.

Disorders in awareness tended to be a higher social class phenomenon, and acting out was more common in those in the lower social positions. Four factors may explain the difference. First, those in the lower class positions may be exposed to stress so great and so frequent as to immobilize them. Second, they may be so preoccupied with the daily concerns associated with survival that awarenes of internal distress is obscured. Third, because of their life experiences they may take a pessimistic view of the aid to be secured from social institutions and therefore seek psychiatric consultation less frequently. Finally, they may lack the competence needed to take the often formidable steps required to gain entry to a clinic and reach a therapist. It is often not realized that making an appointment, arranging to be away from home or work, preparing for the care of children, securing transportation, and making the transition through the intake and psychological testing processes, all without any evidence of help before one finally reaches a therapist, require a degree of internal organization, administrative competence, and ability to defer the satisfaction of needs that generally marks one as a fairly healthy, competent member of the middle and upper classes. Because of these obstacles, it is not surprising that the predominantly young, largely lower class members of the community reach conventional therapeutic services infrequently.

Finally, the finding that many persons express their distress in ways which may cause them to go unrecorded as suffering from psychiatric disorder suggests that items indicative of such events be included in the instruments used in total prevalence epidemiological surveys.

13

The Multi-Predicament Family

In almost every rural community there are families set off by general agreement as "no-good," "shiftless," "lazy," or "always on welfare." They come to attention by getting into public or semi-public difficulty with greater than ordinary frequency. Marital conflict translates itself into violence, and the police are called. Anger that cannot be expressed in words results in a fist slammed through a window and emergency medical attention is required. Alcohol becomes a common means of escape from the intolerable stresses of life, and assult, automobile accidents, and acute public drunkenness become public signs of what their neighbors come to believe is their inherent incapacity to cope with life.

Such families have generally been called multiproblem families by social agencies and are defined as those that become known to such agencies because of the multiple and long-term services they require (Curtis et al 1964; Brown 1962; Willie and Weinandy 1963; Schlesinger 1963). Because the definition has been based on the services rather than on the nature of the problems experienced, it has remained imprecise. As a result, few of the many studies have been comparable. A common failing is the absence of control groups, so that statements as to the characteristics of the family studied are often difficult to interpret, since it is not known whether they are equally common to families who do not come to the attention of social and welfare agencies.

The study of multiproblem families on the island avoided these two methodological problems (Mazer 1972c). First, the multiproblem family was defined in terms of the frequency, not of its applications for service, but of its experience with one or more of fifteen human predicaments occurring among its members (Table 2). Although this definition does not include all of the problems which families have, it is at least precise and replicable. Second, the group of families under study were compared with two groups of control families (Appendix 35).

Table 2. Predicaments Experienced by the 244 Members of 63 Multiproblem Households and the Total Population

Predicament	Multiproblem households		Total population
	No.	Rate per 100	Rate per 100
Psychiatric disorder			
Psychiatric treatment	85	35.8	6.0
Mental hospital	15	6.1	1.6
Suicide attempt	4	1.0	0.3
Suicide	4	1.6	0.1
Chronic alcoholism	20	8.2	2.0
Educational problems			
School disciplinary problem	22	9.0	2.7
School underachievement	18	7.4	2.8
Marital problems			
Marital dissolution	10	4.1	2.0
Premarital pregnancy	28	11.5	1.3
Sociolegal problems			
Fine	44	18.0	4.8
Probation	19	7.8	2.0
Jail	2	0.8	0.2
Juvenile delinquency	2	0.8	0.5
Single-car auto accident	14	5.7	1.7
Acute public alcoholism	10	4.1	1.7
Total	297[a]		

[a]Total is greater than 244 persons since some experienced more than one predicament.

The data on 63 multiproblem families were collected over the five-year period 1964-1968 in the register of human predicaments. The assignment of a household number for each subject, based on a virtually complete household file for the entire population, permitted the information secured for individuals to be collated for households. While the terms *family* and *household* are used interchangeably, the household was the actual unit of study. Only 9 of the 244 persons involved were not actual members of the nuclear family. For the random and matched control groups, the numbers of persons not actual members of the nuclear family were, respectively, three and none. Thus, the distinction between household and family was not a crucial one in this study.

For the purpose of the study, a multiproblem household was defined as one with two or more persons in which more than 50 percent of its members had experienced one or more of the human predicaments recorded in the register over the period. Thus, in order to meet the definition, two of a two-member family had to appear in the register, two or more of a three-member family, three or more of a four or five-member family, four or more of a six or seven-member family, and five or more of an eight or nine-member family. It was found that 63 of the island's 1,627 two-or-more-person households qualified as multiproblem households.

Predicament Rates

The predicaments recorded for the 244 persons in the 63 multiproblem households over the five-year period are given as rates per hundred persons both in the multiproblem households and in the general population (Table 2). Eighty-five persons, or more than one-third of the members of the households, had had an episode of psychiatric treatment, and 6 percent had entered a mental hospital. Eight percent were recorded as suffering from chronic alcoholism. Since this diagnosis was arrived at only as the result of a psychiatric consultation, it underestimates the rate of alcoholism in this multiproblem population. For those 85 subjects who were examined by a psychiatrist, 24 percent had chronic alcoholism, as compared with 12 percent of psychiatric patients in the same community (Mazer 1969a).

Though the rates of school disciplinary problems and educational underachievement given in the table are higher for multiproblem families than for the total population, they nonetheless understate the effective rates. If the rates are based not on the 244 members of the multiproblem families but on those actually at risk, namely, the 39 between 14 and 18 years of age, the rate for school disciplinary problems becomes 56 percent and for educational underachievement 46 percent, rates considerably higher than those for the high school population.

For similar reasons, the rates for marital dissolution and premarital pregnancy deserve special scrutiny. During the five-year period of the study, 45 members of the multiproblem households married. Ten persons had their marriages dissolved by divorce, desertion, or separation. Thus, for every four marriages entered into, one was dissolved in these families over a five-year period, though not necessarily those marriages entered into during the period. The number of persons, male and female, marrying while pregnant was similarly large. Of 45 members of these households entering marriage, in 28 cases, or 62 percent, an infant was already on the way. This premarital pregnancy rate is notably higher than the rate of 35 percent on the island for all marriages in women in the child-bearing age (Mazer 1967b). In short, the members of the multiproblem households experienced predicaments at rates which generally ranged from three to nine times the rates in the general population. Half of those on the way to making the next generation already showed behavioral difficulties and educational achievement below their potential, and were likely to produce in their own image the next generation of multipredicament families in the same community, unless means were found for interrupting the process.

In summary, as compared to appropriate control families, the multipredicament households had more male than female members, had fewer members below 15 or over 65 years of age, had larger families, had more one-parent families, experienced a higher rate of broken marriages, and provided homes for more persons unrelated to members of the families. One finding of the study did not conform to expectations, for multiproblem families did not significantly differ in social class distribution from non-problem families.

Although the 63 multiproblem households in the study carried a great burden and great variety of human problems, in relatively few was there the dependency on public welfare resources noted in other studies (Curtis et al 1964; CMF 1960). Only 7 of the 63 households, or 11 percent, received public welfare assistance at some time during the five years of the study. In four of the families the assistance was "aid to families with dependent children," reflecting the absence or incapacity of the father; in two households the aid was "disability assistance," reflecting physical illness; and in one household it was "old age assistance." There were no instances of families on general relief. These findings are consistent with the failure to find any significant relationship with social class position. The ten persons receiving some form of public welfare in the multipredicament families make up 4 percent of their membership. For the entire population of the island the figure is 6 percent, a difference not statistically significant. The greater figure for the general population probably resulted from the old age assistance given to many elderly people living alone, a group excluded from this study. This low rate of welfare assistance contrasts with the high rates that have been reported for families designated as multiproblem because they had multiple contacts with social agencies or, as in one study, because they were "troublesome families" in a low-rent public housing project.

The data of the study suggest, therefore, that defining multiproblem families by their high rate of use of community resources selects those not simply with many problems but also with an incapacity to deal with them. The method biases the data, since it necessarily selects families of low socioeconomic status. The families of the island study were in difficulty, to be sure, but they were not inordinately dependent on welfare resources, and in view of the one-third who actually sought or were persuaded to seek psychiatric help, they showed a notable ability to seek pertinent assistance for their problems. Finally, the study showed that when bias was not introduced into the selection process, there was no notable tendency for families with many problems to collect at one end of the socioeconomic spectrum.

Although the study gives some information on how multiproblem families differ from control families in family structure and other characteristics, it does not provide data which explain why certain families have high predicament rates while others do not. The role of fate, as for example in illness or in the early death of a parent, of values, and of belief systems are among the variables that must be investigated in such families in the search for the factors in operation. Such studies will require much more detailed and intensive scrutiny of such families than the epidemiologic method used in this research could provide.

The Services

14

Beyond Psychiatry

The studies of island life and the counts of the predicaments experienced by islanders were done in order to design a rational community mental health program for the people of Martha's Vineyard. The epidemiological studies showed that only a small fraction of those with psychiatric disorder reached a source of effective help. Many suffered silently as though fate had ordained it. Others expressed their distress in ways which brought them to public attention. But the attention they elicited was often unresponsive or punitive, and a sense of isolation from the community was added to their burdens.

The epidemiological studies also showed that the amount of disorder among islanders was beyond the capacity of any feasible system of mental health services alone. While a notable and growing proportion of the population identified their problems and came to professional sources of help, a great number of islanders were either not aware of their problems or could not define them sufficiently to know where to seek help. This led to two efforts. The first was to make the mental health agency more congenial to those who needed its help. The second effort was to develop a series of agencies which would respond to the needs of the islanders and which by both a formal and informal relationship to one another would try to avoid the fragmentation of purpose and effort so common among human service agencies. The research also identified those who, because of their age, sex, marital status, social

class position, or family constellation, were at particularly high risk
of developing psychosocial disorders, in order that the services
would cover the wide spectrum of their needs. And finally, the study
of the community, its strengths and its weaknesses, its coherent and
disintegrating qualities, was undertaken in the hope that means
might be found which over the long run would so improve the quality
of community life as to diminish the incidence of psychosocial disorder among its members.

Premises for a Community Psychiatry

Community psychiatry has been variously defined. To some it represents a great scientific advance, comparable to the discoveries of
Freud, and has, perhaps in hyperbole, been called "the third psychiatric revolution" (Bellak 1964). To others, it is no more than a
pretentious term for a too brief, too superficial variety of an inferior
therapy. This is often the position taken by psychoanalysts who crit-
icize the therapy provided by community mental health programs as
not going "deep" enough.

Community psychiatry, as practiced on the island, is based on four
premises. The first premise recognizes that the development of the
human personality does not end in the first six or eight years of life.
It holds that man is a social organism in constant interaction with
his fellows and the physical environment. It operates on the
assumption that whatever his genetic heritage, his character structure, and his coping mechanisms, an episode of psychological disorder often begins at a particular moment or period when some new
or greater stress is added to either the social or the physical environment for which the individual's coping mechanisms and the
community's support system are not adequate. It assumes further
that, since the individual's social network of kin, friends, and neighbors are almost always most concentrated within a small distance
from his home, the community is the strategically desirable site for
his care.

The second premise of community psychiatry holds that in
matters of human welfare, the fee-for-service economy as practiced
in medicine in general and in psychiatry in particular is inappro-

priate and indeed immoral when applied to human suffering. This view confronts squarely the rationalizations that have for long permitted so much skill to be used for so few. In brief, one of the major premises of community mental health programs is that there is a moral responsibility to distribute psychotherapeutic services on the basis of need, not wealth.

The third premise of community psychiatry recognizes more clearly than ever before that mental disorder is a public health problem as surely as are the contagious diseases of childhood. Like other contagions, psychiatric disorder may produce social disturbance or psychological disorder in others. Far worse than the infectious diseases of childhood, its effect on others and on the social order may be long-term and widespread. Thus, while the efforts of community psychiatry may be charged with not going "deep enough" for the individual, one of its major concerns is that it go "wide enough" to affect the community of individuals.

Finally, community mental health programing is a practical attempt to bring means into some rational relationship to needs. It tries to put the service where the need is, not where the funds are. As such, it explores the community to discover those groups in which the prevalence of psychiatric disorder is highest, those periods in the life cycle in which men and women are most psychologically fragile, and those characteristics of the community which are disintegrating to human capacities, in order that it may bring its resources for both prevention and treatment into most effective use.

Defining the Needs

For some time it has been commonplace for communities to conduct a survey of their needs for psychiatric and other human services in order to determine whether such services are required. This would be valid activity if communities were ever free of psychiatric casualties; the fact is that no known community does not require such services. The preliminary or ceremonial survey as usually conducted is not in fact designed to discover whether or not a community requires psychiatric service, since the answer is known in advance. It is used as a public relations device to permit those agencies and government organs which control funds to justify what they already know is required and to give mental health administrators leverage in competing for such funds with other communities (Eisdorfer et al 1968). A survey of a community's burden of psychiatric disorder need not be a useless enterprise unless its sole purpose is to determine whether or not the need for service exists. Such a survey can be a useful activity if its goal is to develop community participation, to define the community's specific needs, to determine the kind of service required, or to evaluate whether or not the service is reaching the clientele it was designed to serve.

The ceremonial survey on Martha's Vineyard, initiated in 1961, was fortunately modest in scope, for a larger effort might have delayed the opening of the clinic and lost the momentum of interest already aroused. The number of cases of juvenile delinquency for the past year was secured from the district court, and each of the island's physicians was asked to estimate how many patients he would be likely to refer for psychiatric treatment or marital counseling within a year. Both sets of physicians' data proved to be gross overestimates in the light of subsequent experience.

Another means of estimating the needs of a community for mental health and other social services is to draw inferences from epidemiological surveys carried out in similar communities. Since the results of even the so-called low-rate psychiatric surveys show a significant prevalence of disorder in all communities, even in those whose social life had led to the theoretical presumption of very little disorder (Eaton and Weil 1955), it is probable that no community, sophisticated or primitive, has achieved a sufficiency of mental health services.

Many studies, for example, have shown high rates of psychoneurosis among young adult females, so that populations with a disproportionate number of that group can expect to have higher clinic admission rates, particularly in the psychoneurotic category, than do populations with standard sex and age distributions. In short, specific age, sex, social class, or ethnic rates secured from one population may be used to estimate the services required and to predict the rates for similar communities. Such data for the island have led to projections that may prove useful in determining the eventual

demand for psychiatric services on nearby Cape Cod and may even
suggest the "mix" of child and adult therapists that will eventually
be required (Mazer 1970c). In addition to surveys, such unobtrusive
kinds of research as recording demands for service, rates of criminal complaints, single-car accidents, school disciplinary problems,
and the like may be used as indicators of the probable demands for
social services in other related communities.

Still another method for determining the demand of a community
for psychiatric and other social services fits well into the American
pragmatic tradition and was the major method used initially on the
island before the research data had been secured. The need for
service may be determined by first providing that service by means
of a small agency having the capacity for expansion in response to
demand. In short, the presence of a mental health clinic or other
social agency enables those with psychological disorder, through its
use, to identify themselves to professionals. Just as important, the
clinic enables those with covert disorder to identify it in themselves
now that a means of help is at hand. For most people, to recognize
the presence of mental illness is too frightening unless resources for
curing or ameliorating it are available. This was one of the reasons
that the investigators of the Stirling County study began by establishing a clinical service. It was also a possible factor in the extru-
sion of a mental health education program in midwestern Canada,
where the attendant discussions of psychiatric disorder had
increased its indentification in the community and hence the level of
community anxiety about it. But since no clinical facility was provided, the population had either to suffer increasing levels of anxiety
or extrude the program, which latter choice it decisively made
(Cummings and Cummings 1957).

Another factor in the rejection of the program in Canada may
have been its period. In the early fifties public understanding of
mental illness was limited, perhaps because the techniques and
facilities for its treatment were meager. Effective psychotropic
drugs were not yet in general use nor had their effects been adequately established. Psychiatric services were yet restricted to
cities. The perception of mental illness by people living in rural
areas was also quite limited. The ability of rural residents to identi-

fy psychiatric disorder has showed a progressive increase since 1950 (Bentz et al 1969). This may be due to a developing hopefulness about successful treatment as the effectiveness of the psychotropic drugs have become evident and as more clinical facilities have been opened in rural areas.

The design of programs to satisfy human needs would thus appear to be susceptible to rational processes. The needs can be defined as the result of both experience and research. The advice of experts as to the best means for satisfying them can be secured. The help of the community can be enlisted and the processes, frequently political, needed to secure the resources put into effect. The difficulty with this format is that it departs from reality. The very phrase "human needs," suggests that somewhere a list of such needs exists which can be ticked off in terms of the community of concern. But the fact is that the needs of a community to a large extent depend on the beliefs, assumptions, and values of its members. The pattern of life drawn up by experts might be utopia for some and sheer hell for others.

An incident that occurred in 1961 at a meeting of social welfare workers in a mainland rural community near the Vineyard is illustrative. The problem for group discussion was posed by an eager young clergyman who described what he considered the sad plight of a young couple with two children living on a meager income in a house with limited facilities. The problem, as he presented it, was that they were not married and that all efforts on his part to get them to legalize the arrangement had been unavailing. They did not understand why they should marry since they were content with the present arrangement. The clergyman had visited them often and made many efforts to persuade them to regularize their relationship, and he was obviously distressed at their failure to do so. One of the social workers asked if there was some problem in respect to the two children, and he admitted that there was not, at least as yet, because they were still young. Then someone asked whether the couple were in conflict, in distress, or unhappy. The young clergyman's face reddened as he replied, "That's just the trouble, they are as happy as clams." At this point, someone was moved to quote Thoreau's comment that if he knew for a certainty that a man was coming to his house to do him good, he would run for his life.

The point is that while there is much information about factors that may cause human distress and psychiatric disorder, very little is known concerning human happiness, and yet the degree of contentment and happiness may be among the great forces which make one man less vulnerable than another to the stresses that inevitably beset him. In designing programs for a community, therefore, the planners should remember that human beings have preferences and that a society is not a rational organism responsive to rational programs, but rather a collection of individuals, with common attributes to be sure, but with many variations among them. Thus, program development is not engineering. It must take into account and be subjected to the scrutiny of those whom the programs would affect. It is vital to recognize that the opinions of experts may merely be preferences based on their own beliefs and values and must not be treated as ordained truth to be imposed upon all.

Community Resources

When mental illness was identified only in those who exhibited the major disorders—psychoses, grand hysterias, and major depressions—the common approach was to exclude the individual from the community either by banishment from the town, as often occurred in colonial New England, or by confinement in total institutions which, while designed to care for the patient, often did little more than to protect the community from him. As the recognition dawned that in any community there were many suffering from psychiatric distress of a lesser degree, it became apparent that facilities other than the total institutions known as mental hospitals were needed. This awareness resulted in a great expansion of outpatient services, with the provision for small mental health centers within the community and for psychiatric beds in general hospitals. Bringing services into the community helped to diminish the sense of shame and fear that had long been attached to the idea of mental disorder. That attitude had kept many from even such help as was available, and only in the last two or three decades are mental health outpatient services becoming "respectable" agencies. The shift from private shame to public acknowledgment made possible the growth of group therapy, a semipublic experience that would have been impossible for most people to engage in a half-century ago.

In each of the historical stages of psychiatric treatment, the public's view of mental health and mental disorder dictated the nature of the service offered. When mental illness was identified only with major disorders, some even dangerous to the community and little affected by the treatment available, the total institution of the mental hospital isolated from the community seemed an appropriate measure. Now, when there is increasing concern over the threat of psychological disorder to the social and political health of the community, mental health workers have become interested in the damaging effects of poverty, in the self-derogation that occurs in the lower social class positions (Kaplan and Pokorny 1969, in the powerlessness among marginal members of the community, and in the many other aspects of social disintegration that have been shown to be related even to gross measures of psychological disorder. Today's mental health workers, struggling against a tremendous burden of new patients, also seek ways to stem the tide of those in distress. Preventive activities which attempt to teach parents something about the development of personality, which inform young couples about the mental hygiene of psychological accommodation, and which support people of low income in their striving for a more secure position in the community are all gradually becoming legitimate functions of mental health services. The teaching of parliamentary procedure, for example, may seem an irrelevant activity for a mental health agency until it is realized that unless one knows something of such techniques, he may be simply a helpless spectator in the very organization which is designed to help him.

It is becoming clearer and clearer that mental health agencies cannot directly and alone solve the mental health problems that confront a community, and that the mental health system is simply a part of the network of community agencies which overtly or covertly provide mental health services. The common belief that psychological disorders can be helped only by mental health services has two serious drawbacks. First, it defines the problem in a way that is impossible of solution, for there are not and probably cannot be a sufficient number of trained mental health workers to care for all those with psychological disorder. Second, it defines the problem in such a way that only those who seek out its services are identified as having psychological disorder. The fallacy of this assumption has been shaken by numerous studies, which show that the prevalence of psychiatric disorder in all communities examined was many times greater than that of treated disorder and that many of the disordered sought help from nonmedical services.

The shattering of the belief that only mental health agencies can treat psychiatric disorder makes it necessary for mental health workers to develop collaborative relationships with other resources which already exist within communities. For an average Massachusetts community of 10,000 persons there are available approximately 30 state-employed human service personnel to provide help when needed though not all of them may be stationed within the community (Curtis 1973). In the same community of 10,000 there may be between 300 and 400 persons engaged in delivering human services. On Martha's Vineyard, for example, with a year-round population now of over 7,800 there are available for occasional help 30 mainland state-employed workers and 150 others who with training and support may become helpful to the mental health system. These include teachers, school counselors, special education personnel, school administrators, clergy, social agency personnel, mental health workers, police, recreational personnel, court personnel, hospital workers, physicians, public health nurses, general nurses, and others.

A universal resource in providing human services is one that rarely comes into consideration. It is easy to forget that, for better or worse, human beings affect each other, and that psychotherapy was conducted by siblings, parents, friends, and neighbors long before the mental health professions existed. Such relationships can also be destructive, and whether they are healing or destructive may in significant part depend on the nature of the community in which they exist. In short, the social network can be a powerful instrument in coping with human problems, psychological or other.

Help from networks of "intimates," however, is probably most effective for those in whom the social component of the disorder is greater than the psychological. It has been shown that in periods of crisis the psychologically impaired are more likely to seek help from formal sources than from family and friends, whereas the unimpaired are less likely to do so (Lindenthal et al 1971). The inclination of the impaired to seek help from formal sources may be due to their marginal adjustment to their own interpersonal network.

As currently constituted, mental health clinics do not offer easy entry for the very segments of the population which are most in need of their services—the poor, racial and ethnic groups, the otherwise disenfranchised, and those whose illnesses involve passivity or a deficiency in the social skills required to enter institutionalized systems. Indeed, many mental health services impose formidable barriers to those applying for the title of patient. In addition, the poor and the disenfranchised may not at all perceive their difficulties as falling within the category of psychiatric disorder. The simple struggle for survival, the constant anxiety about keeping one's job or giving one's children a better chance, the fear of aging in manual workers—problems such as these may relegate to a low priority position those distressing feelings that others might recognize as psychological in origin. Yet these very psychological symptoms further impair the primary processes involved in earning a living, conducting a marriage, being an adequate parent, and living with a modicum of joy.

15

The Caretakers Move

The development of a network of human services for the people of the island began in 1960 when a group of physicians and clergymen only one of whom was native to the island began to meet informally in order to devise a plan for securing the services of a psychiatrist. During the summer of 1961 the group decided to form an organization which would sponsor a psychiatric clinic and persuaded the psychiatrist, who had been a long-time summer resident, to become an island resident. At that time the group, which had expanded to include a larger number of year-round and seasonal islanders, elected temporary officers and began proceedings for incorporation as a charitable institution in the Commonwealth of Massachusetts.

Although the organizing committee's single purpose was to establish a mental health association in order to sponsor a psychiatric clinic, it was clear at the outset that the people of the community had many other needs and few services. It was not clear to the psychiatrist that a mental health clinic should have the first priority, but he realized that the initiative already taken was as yet fragile and might not survive any attempt at delay or diversion into another channel. Since the proposed venture already had support from the medical profession and from some of the clergy, it seemed a strategic place to begin the development of the network of services that the community appeared to need.

As a result, the organizing committee made its charter broad, stating that it would assist in the maintenance of mental health

175

services and otherwise provide medical, educational, social nursing, and such other human services as were needed by the community. The name it chose was similarly inclusive, Martha's Vineyard Community Services, Incorporated.

Upon incorporation the organizing committee enlarged its membership to thirty-one, becoming the Board of Directors of the new organization. The directors were largely islanders, but a number were perennial summer visitors who had had experience in similar enterprises. The directors who were islanders represented the non-political leadership of the island. They were physicians, clergymen, educators, lawyers, bankers, and others long active in the island's community life.

Obstacles to the Undertaking

Although overtures to the Massachusetts Department of Mental Health had been met with an expression of interest, the high viscosity of governmental operations made it clear that financial support from that source would not be available for some time. Therefore, in a move consistent with island character and responsive to the immediacy of the need, the organizing group decided to raise its own funds rather than wait for federal, state, county, town, or foundation support. A summer fund-raising drive gathered in approximately $11,000, and with that sum in hand the Martha's Vineyard Guidance Center, now called the Mental Health Center, opened for service on November 15, 1961.

The establishing of a community organization which within a few months opened a psychiatric clinic was an unusual occurrence in 1961. At that time, in both Massachusetts and the country at large, it was commonly believed that a significantly long period of community organization was necessary before a clinic could be established. Two officials of the Massachusetts Department of Mental Health had held that "it usually takes two to five years for each area to develop its sound community organization" (Hallock and Vaughan 1956). By this they did not mean that a clinic could be established within that time, but only that the community organizers would by then be ready to start upon the political process necessary.

Massachusetts law requires that each professional mental health position for a clinic be included in the Department of Mental Health's budget and win passage by both legislative branches of the government and the approval of the governor. This task, even with a "sound community organization," further delays the process of securing mental health workers for a community. Perhaps frustrated by the long period of community development they believed to be necessary and by the cumbersome legislative process for establishing professional positions, the officials of the Department of Mental Health appeared to make a virtue of necessity. In their 1956 paper they noted with approval that the department had asked for and secured appropriations for "three new psychiatric teams each year designated for specific areas which have progressed to the final stage of development." Since each team consisted of three professionals, the department apparently felt that adding nine new mental health workers per year to the state's mental health clinics was about right for the time.

Had the organizing committee planned to spend two to five years in community development before asking for state funds, it is doubtful whether a psychiatric service would have been established within a decade. The people of the island live in six different towns, and island-wide efforts are infrequent. Town loyalties are strong, and cooperation between towns is rare. The fate of earlier attempts at intertown organization had made the state prescription for the development of a "sound community organization" through the political process an illusory goal in 1961. And the Department of Mental Health, itself coping with the problem of providing services to the five million residents of Massachusetts, had understandably little interest in approaching the problems of the then roughly six thousand people of the island.

The Consent of the Community

Although the project was started on the initiative of a few of the physicians and clergymen of the island and carried forward by a small organizing committee of both islanders and summer people, there was no general community support. Indeed, the history of the island's response to innovation in the recent past was not reassuring. Efforts to establish a visiting nurse service during the fifties, though supported by all but one of the island's physicians, had failed when the town meeting of the island's largest town withheld its support. The attempt to combine three small, inadequate high schools into one had barely succeeded and then only after years of an internecine battle within the community. Within a few months after the mental health service began, the people of Edgartown had voted against fluoridation of their water supply, despite the unanimous approval of their selectmen, their physicians, and their dentist, and in the face of major dental problems in their young people coupled with a scarcity of dental services. Thus, it appeared unlikely that the mental health service would at the outset have widespread community support. Consent would have to be won, and the nature of the clinic's program and its approach to the community would be crucial in determining whether the service would come to be accepted within a reasonable period as one of the island's standard resources.

The scarcity of services on the Vineyard at that time arose from a number of circumstances. Perhaps as important as any was the excessive self-reliance characteristic of islanders. They had long had to do things for themselves and had little belief that the imported expert could do things much better. In addition, they had the sense of fatedness common to people living close to the soil and the sea, always vulnerable to the vicissitudes of the weather. They were therefore prone to see the human disorders and tragedies about them as ordained by fate and resistant to human intervention. The small size of the population and its separation from neighboring communities by major stretches of water added to the difficulties, for just as the island apparently could not support the full-time services of a typewriter repairman, there was reason to believe that many human services were beyond its resources.

Whereas all islanders belonged to the Vineyard community, they took as a given that change, when required, should start with independent initiative and that cooperation, if required, should not go beyond the town level. When at a large public meeting in 1962 the proposal was made that a youth center be started as a means of decreasing the frequency of vandalism and other delinquent acts, the commonest reaction was that such problems begin at home and should be taken care of there. Even today each of the island's six towns, ranging in size from about 150 to 2,700, has its own police force, fire department, and board of health, as though crime, fire, and contagion respect town lines. Though a single high school was finally established, elementary education is still conducted in five schools operated by five school committees. Aware of the history of previous attempts at community and intertown collaboration and of the values held by islanders, the mental health organizers decided not to seek either the support of local governments or a general consensus. Instead of soliciting community approval by verbal persuasion, they decided to go ahead and open the clinic in the hope that consent would be won in time by the experience of islanders with the services offered.

The group responsible for establishing the clinic did not expect that its opening would be met with universal acceptance. There was a lively appreciation that the very idea that the people of the island might need a psychiatric service would threaten many by reminding them of the ubiquity of mental disorder in general and of their own vulnerability in particular. It was anticipated, too, that some who already served in counseling roles would feel threatened, for often those who by their calling might be expected to favor the starting of a clinic may also perceive it as a competitive function to their own (A. H. Leighton and Longaker 1957).

Opposition to the enterprise was never organized. In part this may have been owing to the composition of the board of directors, many of whom were community leaders, active and articulate. Individual attacks on the program were never responded to publicly, on the assumption that a public response might marshal the sentiments of those who opposed it. The message in a single letter to the Gazette dies within a week or two; any letter in response is almost certain to invite others and prolong the futile dialogue for many weeks. The opposition to many local programs springs from resentment at the use of tax funds for their support, particularly on the part of those with small fixed incomes. Since the organization asked nothing from the towns and depended from the outset on voluntary contributions, it did not arouse opposition on this ground.

Consideration was also given to whether the clinic should seek sponsorship or affiliation with an existing community institution. The islanders in the organizing group, knowing the history of such organizations and the general feelings about them, suggested that affiliation with an established organization, however useful its experience might prove to the new venture, would also mean inheriting old antagonisms. They therefore recommended that the mental health service and its parent organization start afresh.

An issue of importance to the organizing group was what the mental health clinic would do. The possibility that a new service would be overwhelmed by demands for direct service and would be unable to offer support to other community caretakers was considerd. One expert consulted recommended that the psychiatrist see no patients at the outset and limit his activities to consultations with community caretakers. But it was felt that, while such a position may be tenable in communities where patients can be referred to private or other clinical facilities, under the island circumstances it would be necessary to start out by offering direct services to the community. Several considerations underlay this decision.

First, because the impetus for starting the service had begun with the perceived need for a clinical service by physicians, clergymen, and a small proportion of the general public, to fail to meet this need might lose the local support already developed. Second, since the community was conservative in temper, pragmatic in outlook, and largely oriented to the present, it was believed that the best way to win consent for the Mental Health Center and other programs being planned lay in providing a service which was practical, immediate, and visible. In brief, the premise was that consent would be more readily won by providing service than by long-range promises, and that help given would gradually win for the clinic the support of its patients, their families, and members of their social network. As it turned out, the effort of the new organization to establish a community innovation, a mental health clinic, was soon met by a complementary response from the community, the participation of islanders as patients. As the number of islanders served by the clinic increased, reaching more than 1,300 by 1975, it gradually became an indispensible community service.

In attempting to respond to the problems of those who came to the clinic, the psychiatrist found that the psychiatric problems of islanders were almost always multifaceted and psychosocial. It had been assumed that the psychosocial aspects of psychiatric disorder would be more clearly seen in the small community than in cities, where patients emerge from a mass of persons only to retreat from the therapists' view at the end of an hour. The multiplicity of problems presented by the clinic's patients, their high visibility, and the surprising lack of the usual social agencies made it clear that the people of the island needed to develop a great variety of services if the human needs of even the comparatively few who reached the clinic were to be approached. Thus, the clinic soon became the instrument through which many of the community's psychosocial problems first came to definition and the catalytic agent for developing the new services that were needed.

16

The Human Service Network

The island's small population and its separation from other communities presented special problems to the board of directors. Whereas mainland communities, each too small to operate its own mental health service, have often joined in starting and maintaining one, the water barrier between the Vineyard and the nearby mainland made such a solution difficult. In fact, there was little relationship between Vineyard institutions and those of either the nearby mainland towns on Cape Cod or the island of Nantucket. When Vineyard physicians sent their patients off-island for special diagnostic or surgical services, they rarely referred them to the many specialists and larger hospitals on nearby Cape Cod, preferring the major medical centers in Boston. This choice was based in part on the personal relationships established between the island's physicians and the specialists from Boston who summered on the Vineyard. Thus, the smallness of the population, its natural demarcation, and custom suggested the desirability of finding some means whereby the services to be developed would be truly community services, located on the island and belonging to it.

The Development of Services

Martha's Vineyard Community Services was designed essentially to provide mental health services for the island, but with its charter broad enough to include other services within the needs of the community. Within a few months after establishment of the Mental

Health Center, a public meeting was called in order to try to learn what islanders felt their needs were. The meeting, held in the high school gymnasium, was attended by almost 10 percent of the islanders age 20 and over. The range of comments was wide, and issues not anticipated were raised. The meeting had a number of desirable effects. In the first place, it indicated that the new organization wished to discover what islanders themselves thought about their needs, and did not intend merely to tell them what they needed. The meeting also taught Community Services and other local institutions that they had not foreseen all the significant problems and needs of the community, and it resulted in an almost immediate response, the initiation of an adult education program by the school system.

Once in operation, the Mental Health Center had a notable effect in initiating a number of other services. Its very establishment under the most unfavorable circumstances shook the commonly held assumption that human problems were largely fated and not susceptible to human effort. Its existence showed that there were people in the community who had the competence, will, and energy to start such services, and it set islanders to thinking about their other needs.

Even more directly, the experience of the Mental Health Center through its clinical work and research programs revealed the needs for other services. And the experience of the board in raising funds for the center, through public appeal, establishing a thrift shop, and securing grants from foundations, the county, and the state, gave promise that funds could also be raised for other ventures. The roster of agencies developed under the aegis of Martha's Vineyard Community Services from 1961 through 1972, with the dates of their establishment, are:

1961	Martha's Vineyard Mental Health Center
1962	Council on Alcohol
1964	Youth Center
1965	Visiting Nurse Service and Homemaker Service
1969	Pre-Start School (Clinical Nursery School)
1970	Summer Project
	Helping Hand
1972	Early Childhood Programs

The problem of alcoholism, which had long been felt by many to be a major problem for the island community, quite soon attracted the attention of the board of directors. An Alcoholics Anonymous group had been active in the community for years, but its efforts were limited to the charter of that organization. In order to broaden the scope of efforts to cope with problem drinking on the island, a Committee on Alcoholism was established in 1962, consisting of members of Alcoholics Anonymous, a number of clergymen, other citizens, and the director of the Mental Health Center. During one period when drug abuse was of great concern, the committee also functioned in that area. In 1974 it was renamed the Council on Alcohol.

The Youth Center was started because of a concern for island young people of high school age. They have available none of the conventional meeting places, such as the corner drugstore, hot dog stand, or ice-cream shop. The drugstores close at 6:30 in the evening, and island homes are often inadequate for entertaining, providing no room where young people can get off by themselves. As a result, it was common for young people to roam the roads, just driving, often sparking the occasion by drinking illicitly obtained beer. In addition to the emptiness of the activity, islanders were concerned with two possible results, premarital pregnancy and automobile accidents. The establishment of a youth center, therefore, had been on the agenda of the Martha's Vineyard Community Services for some time, and its need was supported by preliminary findings of the research in progress. The occurrence in 1964 of an automobile accident in which two high school youngsters driving home from a party were killed when their car ran into a tree persuaded the board to act immediately, even without the assurance of adequate financial resources. Within a few months it had hired a director and secured the loan of space for the Youth Center.

That such an agency was desirable was apparent not only from the absence of places where young people could meet but also from the relatively low rate at which they used the services of the Mental Health Center in its first few years. Later research showed that young adults had probably the highest rates of disorder in the community and the lowest rates of health-seeking behavior. Thus, the organization of a counseling service at the Youth Center was one result of the clinical experience, the other being steps taken by the Mental Health Center to make itself more inviting to young people.

Proposals for new agencies were also made by members of the board of Martha's Vineyard Community Services. Since a significant proportion of them were retired people, they were particularly sensitive to the needs of the elderly, needs that were substantiated by both census data and the household analysis done by the Mental Health Center. The fact that one of every six islanders was 65 or over, a proportion 50 percent higher than that for Massachusetts, and that close to 300 of them lived alone made it clear that an agency which would provide health services in the home was preeminently desirable. Although the initiative was not taken by the local physicians, they readily confirmed the need for both a visiting nurse service and a homemaker service, which were established in 1965. While functioning as distinct services, both programs are administered by the same agency.

The needs of the island's educationally retarded children had been long neglected. In 1961 there were no special education classes in the school system, despite a state law that required them. The admission of retarded and otherwise handicapped children to the Mental Health Center brought their range of needs into bold relief. As a result of pressure from parents, encouraged by the Mental Health Center and supported by a physician and a clergyman, the school committee of one town was persuaded to start a special education class. This led to demands from parents in other towns, so that today four of the island's six schools have such classes.

Since the school system's classes for children with special needs cared only for children enrolled in school, preschool children with special needs continued to be neglected at the very age during which services might be most helpful. In 1969, when the Massachusetts Department of Mental Health offered to underwrite the salary for a teacher and teaching aide, Martha's Vineyard Community Services provided the funds for equipment, supplies, and a building for a new clinical nursery school designed for preschool children with special needs.

On the initiative of the Youth Center, aided by the staff of the

Mental Health Center, a summer program was started in 1969 for the thousands of young people who come to the island each summer. The need for such a service was shown by the clinical experience and research findings of the Mental Health Center. The problems of migratory young people, such as loneliness, housing, drug abuse, physical illness, nonmarital pregnancy, alienation from parents, the stress of migration, the threat of service in a war in which they did not believe, and the usual psychological difficulties of adolescence, all reach the island each summer. An "epidemic" of five instances of attempted suicide over one Fourth of July weekend was a dramatic sign of these stresses, and the day-to-day calls on the clinic for a great variety of services for summer young people gave further evidence of the need for a summer program. A year later, in 1970, Summer Project was established as a separate agency with its own staff but using the facilities of the Youth Center.

The discovery that there were a great number of islanders suffering from a variety of human predicaments that did not bring them to a clinical service suggested that other ways would have to be found for reaching them. On the recommendation of the Mental Health Center and in concert with the Community Action Committee, the island's arm of the federal antipoverty program, Martha's Vineyard Community Services began in 1970 an all-purpose walk-in service known as the Helping Hand. The agency was to be experimental and possibly of limited duration. Its functions were to define and to cope with the multiple problems of those members of the community who did not find themselves able to reach another resource and perhaps to discover through its experience what new resources were needed or what modifications of the functions of existing agencies would suffice. The Helping Hand functioned until 1974. A survey of its activities in that year showed that most of them were directed toward the needs of the elderly. Since a Council on Aging supported by tax funds had recently been started, the functions of the Helping Hand were transferred to that independent agency.

The growing recognition during the early sixties that the preschool years were of crucial importance in the educational and social development of all children evoked an interest on the island in preschool education in general. In 1961 the schools of only the three

larger towns had kindergartens; one or two nursery schools operated in private homes. In the late sixties a number of young women,
incomers to the island, started the Island Children's School for children from age one to six. During the same period, the island acquired a preschool under the federal Title I program.

By 1972 there were six nursery schools with an enrollment of
close to 140 children between three and five years of age. Each had
a separate sponsorship: private, parents' cooperative, federal Title
I, and Martha's Vineyard Community Services. There was much
variation in the training of teachers and little or no collaboration
among the schools. In 1972 after a staff study the board of Martha's
Vineyard Community Services started a training and coordinating
service known as Early Childhood Programs. The implementation of
the board's decision was made possible by the presence in the community of an expert in early education associated with a teacher
training college in Boston.

Transitional Activities

Although the eight services provided by Martha's Vineyard
Community Services make up a substantial network covering a
significant proportion of the human needs of islanders, Martha's
Vineyard Community Services has been able to take on additional
tasks. In 1965, when the national Head Start programs began, the
community had not yet organized a Community Action Committee
under the federal antipoverty program, so Community Services, as
an existing charitable organization with an administrative apparatus and personnel undertook to operate through its Mental Health
Center the summer Head Start program that year and, in collaboration with the Community Action Committee, the summer Head Start/
Day Care program the next year. When food for distribution to low
income people became available through two courses in cooking
given under the Federal Manpower Development Act, Community
Services was there to serve as the food distributing agency. Thus,
whenever federal or state programs were able to provide funds for
temporary programs, the existence of Community Services with a
functioning administrative apparatus and a group of experienced

board members and professional human service workers permitted the community to acquire such programs.

The roster of agencies now operated by Martha's Vineyard Community Services will not necessarily remain static, for the lives of islanders are changing rapidly, and their need for various supportive services can be expected to alter in ways that can only be dimly foretold. The history of the development of services thus far promises that the organization which sponsors them will continue to be alert to and responsive to the needs of islanders. Some agencies may change their character, others may find their functions converging, and in time the needs of the people of the island may dictate new and innovative measures for coping with the stresses that are inescapable to the human condition.

The Reach of Services

The agencies of Martha's Vineyard Community Services affect in one way or another a significant proportion of the now 7,800 people of the island. The number of persons coming into direct contact with one or another of the staff members of the agencies in 1974 was approximately 1,600 islanders, in addition to over 2,000 summer visitors of all ages. Even allowing for contacts by one person with more than one agency, a proportion estimated at 25 percent of the total, the number of islanders receiving direct service in that year was approximately 1,200, or one in every six. In addition, there were hundreds of meetings with groups of islanders and with community caretakers, physicians, clergymen, police officers, the staff of the courts, and others. Since there are only approximately 2,800 year-round households in the community, the proportion of those affected indirectly is even greater. Over the past decade it can be inferred that almost every household on the island has been affected in one way or another by the activities of the agencies of Community Services.

It was never contemplated that Community Services would provide all of the human services needed by the people of the island. What was hoped for was to establish an effective collaborative relationship with the members of other human service agencies. The police of the island, for example, have long responded in marital crises and are often aware of disordered and deviant behavior before it comes to public attention. The clerk of the district court has had long experience in dealing informally with those with alcoholic problems for which the formal judicial mechanism is ill suited. The probation officer is often consulted by parents troubled by disruptive behavior in their children which has not yet come to the attention of the court. As often as any group, the clergy of the island are reached by those in difficulty, and their commitment to service and their clinical training while in seminary make some of them sensitive to disruption in the lives of their parishioners.

Those who by the nature of their work are called upon to intervene in instances of psychological stress are often handicapped by a lack of training for the problems thrust upon them as well as by the fact that the resources of their own calling are not germane to the task before them. The police officer who is called in to intervene in domestic turmoil and finds that arrest, his main resource, is irrelevant usually has available to him only his own human sensitivities developed as an observer of the human tragedy, and these sensitivities are often not enough. The availability of the Mental Health Center, the Alcohol Counseling Service, the Youth Center, Summer Project, and other such agencies gives him welcome alternatives to initiating the judicial process.

17

The Functions of the Agencies

The agencies established and sponsored by Martha's Vineyard Community Services now meet a good proportion of the needs of islanders. Each agency functions as an independent unit, providing defined services to particular segments ot the population. At the same time they belong to a network of collaborating services under one administration, so that their resources can be used with the elasticity required of the shifting needs of a small community.

Mental Health Center

The Mental Health Center provides a wide variety of psychiatric and psychological services to the people of the island. At the beginning its staff consisted of a psychiatrist and a secretary, each employed part-time. At present, it has a full-time staff of four, a part-time staff of three, five part-time volunteers, and a number of clinical associates who work with it though their main human service functions are with other institutions of the community. The full-time staff of the center consists of a psychiatrist, two psychologists, and a secretary. Its part-time employees include a social worker and two clerical workers. Its staff of clinical associates varies in size, depending on their availability and the demands on the clinic; during the past years the clinical associates have included school guidance counselors, teachers, youth workers, the probation officer, housewives, and others with special talents. The center's main source of support comes from the Department of Mental Health of the Commonwealth of Massachusetts, which finances professional salaries, travel expenses, and a portion of the rental of the center. The second largest source of support is the parent organization, Martha's Vineyard Community Services, which in addition to its own public fund-raising activities has secured funds earmarked for the center from Dukes County, from various foundations, and from the National Institute of Mental Health for the research programs of the center. Small amounts are generated internally through modest patient fees.

The clinic is a community agency engaged in the general practice of mental health work. That is, it treats everyone who can use its service, with fees never posing a barrier to care. All fees are weekly family fees, based on family size and income, and are quite modest; a family of five with an income of $8,500 per year pays a fee of only $3 weekly. The established fee may be altered at any time at the discretion of the therapist, and in the case of those below the lower limits of the fee schedule or on some variety of public welfare, no fee at all is charged.

In addition to removing the economic barrier to care, the weekly family fee has had a desirable effect on individual treatment programs. Since the fee that the patient is charged is unrelated to the frequency of visits, the therapist is free to see the patient as often as he desires without the usual concern that a mounting clinic bill may cause a decrease in the amount spent for food by that family. In the case of a depressed patient for whom suicide is a concern, the patient and therapist may meet each other daily, if briefly, during the period of crisis without worrying about cost. It is a common experience for therapists, both in private practice and in clinics, to hesitate to suggest such additional visits, either because they are concerned about the patient's economic situation or because they fear that their own motives will be misinterpreted.

One unusual feature of the center is its attitude toward applications for help. The staff does not screen applicants to determine whether they fit the clinic's programs or are admissible on other grounds. It is assumed that any islander who has mustered the courage and resources to come to the clinic has some problem for which he needs help. The issue is not whether the applicant is or is not suffering from psychiatric disorder, but what kind of help he needs and how best his needs can be met.

The individual therapeutic services offered by the Mental Health Center are not unique. What is perhaps unique is the large number and variety of programs available to so small a population, as well as the fact that the resources of the entire network are readily at hand no matter by what route the client enters the system. This does not mean that the clinic offers all of its services constantly. It attemps to respond to what its staff perceives as the current needs for specific kinds of programs by community, sex, age, and interest groups. Among its programs are psychotherapy, generally crisis-oriented therapy, group therapy, family therapy, drug therapy, drug rehabilitation programs, and an extensive consultation service to the school system, in addition to consultative services to community caretakers in general. Preventive group experiences initiated by the center have been a part of its program since 1969.

The Mental Health Center has always monitored the data that come into it, in order to assess whether it is or is not meeting its own goals. For example, an analysis of its patients by social class position showed no difference in rate of admissions among the three social class groupings. Yet since the total prevalence studies had shown that the highest rates of disorder occur in the lowest socio-economic groups, it was concluded that the clinic needed to make special efforts to reach those groups. The clinic's long-term program of research into psychiatric and parapsychiatric problems, supported by the National Institute of Mental Health, resulted in a series of publications on psychiatric epidemiology, on the delivery of psychiatric services in rural areas, and on the particular problems of the therapist operating in a small community. The research findings have also influenced the clinic's own practices, resulting in an increase in the admission of certain needy groups. Thus, the self-monitoring system built into the clinic's operational practices has produced self-directive changes in those practices.

At the beginning it was felt important to establish effective working relationships with the island's general practitioners, and for this purpose monthly evening meetings were held with them during the first year of the clinic's operation. These relationships have since been strengthened through joint consultations concerning the physicians' patients, through collaborative work at the Martha's Vineyard Hospital, and through an emergency psychiatric service available to the hospital staff. Although consultation has always been offered to the general practitioners about psychiatric patients in treatment in their own practices, they have availed themselves of it infrequently, perhaps because of their high rate of referral of such patients to the clinic. It is also suspected that they are reluctant to ask for the psychiatrist's time without paying him, accustomed as they are to fee-for-service medicine. This suspicion seems confirmed by the fact that the general practitioners made use of the opportunity for such psychiatric consultation when they and the psychiatrist were engaged in the collaborative study of psychiatric disorder in general practice. When the psychiatrist was in their offices for the purpose of this research, they would often ask for advice on the handling of one or another patient they were seeing.

The surprisingly high rates of psychiatric disorder revealed by the total prevalence studies made clear that there was little hope of making progress against the toll taken by psychiatric disorder without effective means of primary prevention, an effort that began to be feasible as the staff increased in size. By primary prevention is meant the sum of those measures which, when applied to the people of a community, give some prospect of decreasing the rates of disorder within it. Although there are measures that promise to be effective in primary prevention, they have rarely been applied in any systematic way. Since most mental health clinics are responsible for large communities with staffs quite small in proportion, their staffs are usually overwhelmed by the immediate clinical demands upon them or are discouraged by the obvious magnitude of the task of trying to alter the fabric of a large community. Despite such considerations, preventive programs may be designed which are frugal of scarce resources, by focusing on high-risk groups with the mental health center acting as a catalyst for community action programs. A deliberate attempt to decrease the incidence of depression among the elderly in an urbanized area adjacent to Boston is a current example [Cardoza et al 1975].

The measures that the Mental Health Center has taken in the area of primary prevention include consultation with teachers and other community caretakers, educational programs on mental health for community organizations, and group experiences for those in the community who are not identified as having psychiatric difficulty but who belong to high risk or strategic groups. In order to ensure that those eligible for one or another variety of public welfare assistance receive what the statutes and regulations provide without further damage to their self-esteem by the welfare system, the clinic often directly or indirectly takes on an advocacy role on behalf of its patients.

Since 1969 the clinic has offered at low or no cost group experiences for members of the community who fall into groups that are at greater than average risk of developing psychiatric disorder, or for groups who are strategically positioned in relation to others. High rate groups so far conducted by the clinic include young couples married or not, adolescents, young people on legal probation, parents in one-parent households, foster parents, and newcomers to the island. Strategic groups so far conducted include schoolteachers in the first year of teaching, new parents, parents of adolescent children, parents of hyperkinetic children, parents in one-parent households, and foster parents.

Many people in the community may be identified as being in both a strategic position with respect to others and at a high risk of experiencing disorder. For example, a single parent coping with small children alone is often subjected to great stress while also being in an unusually strategic position with regard to the psychological development of the children. All those who deal with the needs of human beings—human services agents, gatekeepers to public welfare or unemployment funds, and virtually all those who facilitate or frustrate the satisfaction of human needs—are unusually strategic in the lives of others, particularly the poor and the otherwise disadvantaged. And finally, each human being, whatever his calling, exercises a strategic role in the lives of at least a few others.

In each preventive group the staff is alert to the presence within the group of potential leaders, with the intent of inviting them to become coleaders of the group in the second year, and leaders on their own thereafter. In a community having as many problems as does the island and with so many opportunities for self-isolation, few efforts are as worthwhile as the development of a continuous series of self-generating group experiences. In this way, the clinic multiplies its resources for preventive work by offering to such groups consultation services, meeting space, and the means of communicating with others interested in joining.

The use of agencies other than the Mental Health Center in sponsoring preventive group work is desirable, and a program of such sponsorship has been started. Preventive group work initiated by the center will ultimately be transferred to other more appropriate community institutions, whether part of Martha's Vineyard Community Services or not, for it is likely that the tasks of preventive psychiatry are best done within the natural arenas of daily life rather than in the specialized enclave of a clinic. Thus, a group on self and sexual development for adolescents has been transferred to the high school's programs. Another group for single parents with young children might be effectively conducted by another agency of the network, Early Childhood Programs.

In addition to its formal and informal relationships with the agencies of Martha's Vineyard Community Services, the Mental Health Center and its staff have functioning relationships with other strategic community institutions. As citizens, members of its staff take part in the operation of their towns by serving as officers or members of town committees. Effective functioning relationships exist with the police departments of the four largest of the island's six towns. This connection is of some importance because of the multiple roles that police officers play on the island. It is now common for police officers to seek the advice of members of the staff of the clinic. If a police officer has only two options, either to charge and prosecute an alleged offender or to take no action, he may have to do the former, though his judgment and sensibilities inform him that the problem is other than criminal. As soon as the Mental Health Center began to offer other options to the police officer, many so-called "crimes" received different handling. The fact is that the police officer has a great deal of discretion in applying the law, and in the small community in which he also lives, his concerns are more likely to be rehabilitative than punitive.

Since many of the clinic's patients are of low income, the staff is in frequent contact with both welfare and legal services. If one of the clinic's patients is unable effectively to argue his or her case at the welfare office, a member of the clinic staff may accompany the patient. When patients require legal services through the federally supported legal service whose headquarters is on the mainland, the clinic supplies space for the legal counsel on her periodic visits to the island. When the island had an active Community Action Committee operating under the federal antipoverty program, members of the clinic participated actively in its work. One of the more useful undertakings of the staff of the clinic was to assist low income women in learning the rudiments of parliamentary procedure in order that they might make themselves heard more effectively in an organization which was dominated by sophisticated middle class people. When a task force was organized on Cape Cod to explore the possisilities of starting a family planning program and of securing funds for it, the clinic designated one of its staff to represent the island in the development of the program.

Although geography dictates that the Mental Health Center be as self-sufficient as possible, it is part of the larger network of services supported by the Massachusetts Department of Mental Health. It is one of the psychiatric facilities in the mental health area covering Cape Cod, Martha's Vineyard, and Nantucket. For acute psychiatric problems where hospitalization is needed for periods up to a week or two, the facilities of the Martha's Vineyard Hospital are now available. For longer term hospitalization, islanders are served by the Taunton State Hospital and occasionally by private hospitals. It is expected that within a year a small mental health center containing 24 in-patient beds will have been opened on the nearby Cape just over an hour's distance by boat and car from the island.

Council on Alcohol

The Council on Alcohol was the second offspring of the parent organization, Martha's Vineyard Community Services. In the late sixties when drug dependency was common, the Dukes County Community Action Committee approached the problem through its own drug committee. Since the problems of drugs and of alcohol both have to do with addiction and are related in other respects, the two committees joined under the sponsorship of Martha's Vineyard Community Services. As the school system took a greater role in drug education programs, that part of the work became its responsibility, with the Council on Alcohol now concentrating its attention on the problem of alcoholism. Until recently, its activities, while helpful, did not receive sufficient support to have a substantial effect on the problem. The council now conducts educational programs, provides attendants to remain with alcoholics while they are in the local hospital, and acts as a referral and transfer agent for alcoholics who require detoxification at the state's center on the nearby mainland. At present it is an alcohol counseling service with a transitional residential care unit operated under contract and with funds largely provided by the county government. The council collaborates effectively with the Mental Health Center, the Youth Center, Summer Project, and others.

Youth Center

The Youth Center is housed in a substantial building in Vineyard Haven, the largest town on the island. Its primary service is to young people of high school age, though at present it has a small introductory program for eighth grade students. It is open six days a week, with a membership of approximately 250. While it is used mainly as a meeting place for young people, with a cafeteria open on weekends, it provides a number of recreational and educational activities. Television, table tennis, and pool are ever current activities, but at times courses have been given in weight lifting, self-defense, black studies, and sex education, and groups of young people have been taken on trips to museums on the mainland. A yearly trip to the Taunton State Hospital and visits to the local courts and the county jail have been popular, particularly for those young people who have shown an interest in making a career of human service. The young people's board of the Youth Center sponsors the support of a foster child. A collaborative course with the police in human development is part of the center's program to foster constructive relationships between the police and young people.

Counseling services for young people with problems are available in a private office at the Youth Center by the director and his associate, one male and one female. Consultation to the counselors is provided by the staff of the Mental Health Center.

The Youth Center has made one important innovation among the agencies sponsored by Martha's Vineyard Community Services. Its policies are largely set by its clients. The youth board elected by the members is involved in every phase of decision making with respect to programs, administrative operations, and disciplinary decisions whenever these are necessary.

Visiting Nurse and Homemaker Services

One of the community resources of which islanders were once deprived was a public health nursing service that could supplement the physician's care in the patient's home. Such public health nursing services have long been common in American communities, but an effort to establish one on the island two decades ago had been unsuccessful. The need for such a service was evident. In the first place, the island had insufficient practitioners, particularly during the summer. All their offices were in the villages on the northern edge of the island, which put them at some distance from their up-island patients, more than twenty miles in the case of those living in Gay Head. In addition, the high proportion of the population in the older age groups, approximately 18 percent over 65 as compared with 12 percent for the state, argued for the need of visiting nurse and homemaker services. After a long period of preparation and with the advice and initial financial help of the Massachusetts Department of Public Health, Martha's Vineyard Community Services established a Visiting Nurse Service and a Homemaker Service. The nursing service operates as an adjunct to the island's medical services and accepts patients on referral by the family physician. Patients are visited in their homes and given general nursing care in addition to whatever special services the family physician prescribes. The service is also involved in maternity and well-baby care, health promotion, disease control, health counseling for the elderly, preventive chest X-ray examinations, and physiotherapy for those who cannot leave their homes.

Because the island has more than 300 older people living alone, it was felt important that the nursing service be complemented by a homemaker service. The home health aides employed by that service provide housekeeping services, including the preparation of meals, for families where the homemaker is either in the hospital or unable to perform such tasks and for persons living alone and incapacitated. The home health aides are employed only after a training period in which other agencies collaborate.

Pre-Start School

In 1969, through a partnership agreement with the Department of Mental Health, Martha's Vineyard Community Services established a clinical nursery school, called the Pre-Start School, for children with special needs, with a particular focus on island children who appear to be mentally retarded. The partnership arrangement is similar to that under which the Mental Health Center operates; the state provides professional salaries and some money for equipment, supplies, and food, while the local organization provides the physical facilities and supplements the food, equipment, and supply budget.

The program consists of a daily morning nursery school program on five mornings a week in the home of the service, a building that is owned and used during the summer by a cerebral palsy camp. Transportation is provided at no cost to the parents by the public school system in accordance with Massachusetts law. The afternoon teaching program is a home-based program for children whose school program can best be supplemented at home and who are under three years of age.

In addition to providing a wide variety of services for the children themselves, the staff of the school provides counseling services for the parents and an in-service training program for the teachers in the public schools who will later be involved in teaching the children. In order that the children, most of whom will live out their lives on the island, not be isolated from their age mates, part-time students are brought from a standard nursery school and some Pre-Start School students attend classes at other nursery schools two mornings a week.

Summer Project

Summer Project is operated as a self-help program for young people, with three paid staff members and sixty or seventy volunteers during the summer season. It provides service throughout the day, offering a walk-in service from 10:00 A.M. to 10:00 P.M. and a night line from 10:00 P.M. to 10:00 A.M. A low-cost or free medical clinic operates three evenings a week, and psychological counseling is provided two or three evenings a week by the staff of the Mental Health Center and at other times by Summer Project's staff. Legal and welfare counseling has been offered by a law student. A dental clinic is open one evening a week. Employment information, temporary housing, and emergency babysitting are other services provided for and by young people, and a boat ticket is always available for a young person wishing to go home.

But the youth who work for and use the services of Summer Project also serve the island community. A group of them give services to the island's elderly population, shopping, doing household repairs, and providing transportation. When alcoholic or psychiatric patients in the local hospital need attendants at any time in the day or night, a corps of volunteers registered with Summer Project performs that service at no cost to the hospital or to its patients.

The operation of the program year-round during the current year, 1975-1976, has been made possible by a state grant. Project, as it is now called, provides for the needs of the 18-30 year age group who are mainly recent migrants to the island. Living on meager incomes, often in marginal housing, and isolated from family and peers by their migration, they find in its programs, staff, and other participants the community they so desperately need until they can become part of the island community or until they are prepared to re-enter the larger world from which they sought a period of escape. Whether the year-round program will continue beyond the current year will depend upon whether funds are available for its support.

Helping Hand

The Helping Hand, founded as an agency to provide social

resources for a wide variety of human problems, operated with an open door ready to hear anyone with any kind of problem. Its staff did not pretend to be able to solve all human problems but made an effort to secure help for the individual involved either directly or by referral to a more pertinent service. Because the studies of the Mental Health Center showed that the people of Oak Bluffs used mental health services at approximately one-third the rate of the other towns, it was assumed that perhaps their needs were expressed in an idiom which did not bring them to the existing agencies of Martha's Vineyard Community Services. For this reason, and because the town had no visible agency of Community Services, it was decided that the quarters of Helping Hand be located in Oak Bluffs and be of sufficient unpretentiousness as to make them easy to enter. The use of the service by islanders grew rapidly. Members of the community sought information on employment, community events, transportation, housing, and town government, all activities that are outside the charter of Martha's Vineyard Community Services. The other categories of information sought concerned medical services, social security, public welfare, domestic problems, and legal assistance. During the year 1973 the largest amount of service provided was for the island's councils on aging. Therefore, since only ten percent of the activities of Helping Hand clearly came within the Community Services charter, and since other agencies were covering most of the social welfare field, it was decided in 1974 to turn the functions of Helping Hand over to the developing councils on aging. Of some weight, too, in the decision to change the nature of the service was the growing economic stringency under which the parent organization was operating.

Early Childhood Programs

In 1972 Martha's Vineyard Community Services established Early Childhood Programs to provide expert consultation to the teachers and parents of the children of the six nursery schools. The program at present includes meetings with the teaching staffs of the schools on both clinical problems and curriculum enrichment. Parents of nursery school children are seen individually for problems concerning their children. The director of the program meets regularly with the boards of the nursery schools and conducts workshops and individual conferences for the teachers. Through a collaborative arrangement with Wheelock College, Wheelock students are placed in nursery schools as part of their training, making their own contribution to the schools in which they work. A library specializing in the problems of young children and in nursery education and practice is available for the use of teachers and mothers. Once each year an all-day conference is held on the problems of children of nursery school age, the last one having been attended by over 200 islanders, who represented a significant proportion of the families with preschool children.

18

The Common Purpose

Those in the helping professions set out to treat human beings in distress, yet often find themselves seeing a series of problems or predicaments and missing the person. Part of this difficulty arises from the need to analyze complex issues into smaller, more manageable components. The difficulty, too, is that human needs cover a wide spectrum, while professional skills are compartmentalized.

The problem in securing the help required from different agencies in most communities may lie in the fact that interagency relationships are either nonexistent or formal. Issues such as agency domain, institutional inertia, and professional specialization can produce impermeable boundaries between independent services (Halpert and Silverman 1967). Further, because of independent financing, contracts between agencies may have to be negotiated. But contracts define and hence exclude, because as soon as the duties of each party are defined by contract, that which is not included tends to be excluded, and the possibilities of open, original, and innovative relationships are diminished.

One major virtue of a multiservice agency such as Martha's Vineyard Community Services is that it takes upon itself the responsibility of filling in the gaps in human services which exist in the community. The interaction of its agencies as needs arise for the clients of each soon reveals the gaps in the network of services. In addition, the organization may mobilize its agencies into a research effort to determine where deficiencies exist. Community Services has done this in two ways. First, its Mental Health Center conducted a five-year study of a wide variety of human predicaments experienced by islanders. This study demonstrated that a significant proportion of the population displayed their problems in ways which did not bring them to the appropriate social welfare agencies. Second, Community Services established an experimental agency that could both provide services and discover needs for which there were no services. This agency, the Helping Hand, was designed as a telephone and walk-in service for any sort of human need, particularly those not clearly identified by the subject as being within the scope of an existing agency of which he knew.

Another advantage of a multiservice organization is that it readily permits collaborative relationships to develop between the professionals who serve in its agencies. The rationale for bringing a variety of human services into one building is generally that it permits a client to receive help for all of his needs at a one-stop service. This is considered important, particularly with low income people whose loss of time, pay, and self-esteem while being shuttled from one agency to another may be quite damaging. But there is another reason which is rarely noted, the opportunity for those working at the same task but with a variety of allegiances and different sources of funding to circumvent the need for formal contractual relations by direct and frequent association.

Multiple Use of Personnel

Besides consultation provided by one agency to another in multiservice organizations, there are additional ways in which agencies administered and funded by one organization can help each other. The development of organizational and administrative techniques appropriate to a small community must to some extent be learned. While the general principles are known, usually based on experience in business and industrial organizations, their application to human service organizations requires modification, and their adaptation to communities of small size with idiosyncratic characteristics often demands significant modifications of organizational and administrative tactics. In a multiservice organization, it is not necessary that each new agency learn anew by trial and error what has already been found to work with others. As each new agency of Martha's Vineyard Community Services was established, it had available to it the experience that had already been gained. This sharing of experience was often effected by placing upon the new agency's operating and advisory committees staff members and committee members of other agencies within the Community Services network.

The agencies of Martha's Vineyard Community Services are staffed by professionals with a wide variety of skills which may be used within the network. The research facilities of the Mental Health Center have been used to analyze the functioning of other agencies in order to determine whether agencies are in fact doing the job they set out to do. An analysis of the records of the Visiting Nurse Service, for example, gave that service information comparing its clientele by social class position with the community as a whole, in order to determine whether it was in fact reaching those it was designed to reach, among them, people of low income. The experience of the Mental Health Center in grant application writing has been used by the Council on Alcohol, the Youth Center, and Summer Project. When the clinic requires attendants for its patients hospitalized locally, the long experience of the Council on Alcohol in that area is regularly used. In addition, the day-by-day relationship of the professionals of the various agencies results in a less formal exchange of the manifold skills needed by those engaged in the human service enterprise.

Most human service agencies experience varying demands for their service, depending on their functions, the economic state of the community, and changes in the social structure of the community as a result of in or out-migration. The island in particular, based as it is on a seasonal economy, shows great variations in seasonal demand for social services. The needs of young people for a youth center are greatest during the fall, winter, and spring and are hardly needed at all during the summer when most island youngsters are employed at summer jobs and when recreational facilities are more than adequate. In contrast, there is each summer a great in-migration of young people in search of jobs, housing, and recreational experiences. They often come in flight from home, having planned to earn their own living and secure their own housing, in both of which efforts they may be thwarted. They come too with the currently common problems of young people, alienation, habituation to drugs, and a disenchantment with the political process, which they feel has wreaked havoc with their plans and dreams. Given these two different tides, it is possible to shift some of the personnel of the Youth Center to the organization designed to take care of the summer problems of young people, the Summer Project. Since much of the need for counseling of young people first makes itself evident at Summer Project rather than at the Mental Health Center, and since islanders now employed and stimulated by the summer environment decrease their demands for psychiatric service at that time, it is not difficult for some of the staff of the clinic to spend part of their time at Summer Project. These are a few examples of the many similar arrangements that are possible.

In addition to professional relationships with agencies under the same umbrella, members of the staff of the Mental Health Center have worked with other community human service programs either by means of contractual relationships, as with the school system, or by virtue of membership on committees and boards of those other community agencies (Fig. 2). Close functioning relationships have also been maintained with others in the community who provide human services. The probation office of the district court and the staff of the Mental Health Center often have collaborative functions with the same client. The present probation officer often sees his clients in the center's offices when he considers that site more suitable than his own office in the court house. He participates in some of the center's clinical conferences and has been a cotherapist in family therapy when the "labeled" individual is his probationer. He and others in the human service community—guidance counselors, social workers, and teachers—have all been co-therapists in the evening group programs.

An Informal Network

Encounters between human service workers on the island do not

Fig. 2. Mental Health Center Staff Affiliations, 1970

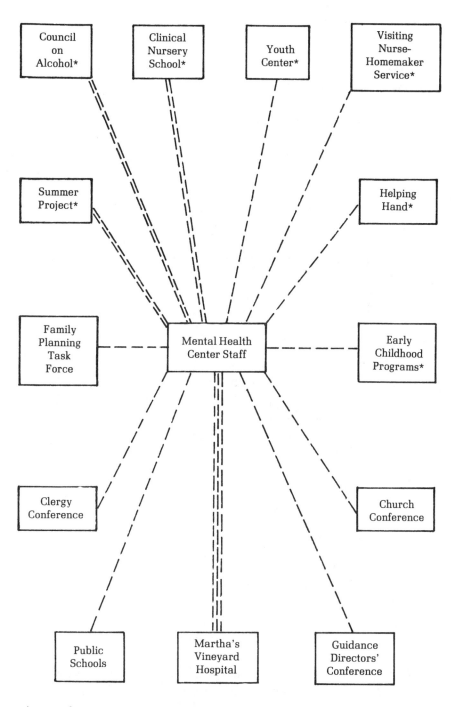

*Agency of Martha's Vineyard Community Services

differ from most other person-to-person contacts between islanders. They are frequent and informal. Face-to-face consultations between workers serving the same client take place as often in a corner of the post office, on the street, or in a dozen other places as they do in agency offices. A conference between a mental health worker and the probation officer or the clerk of the court may, if needed, occur on ten minutes' notice since their offices are within a two-minute walk of each other. As with most island relationships, the multiple roles in which people meet make for informality, and the use of first names is commonplace. The hierarchal structure of public position and office which in larger places limits person-to-person access is hardly noticeable. The judges of the island's courts, the superintendent of its schools, or the presidents of its banks are all readily accessible to social agency workers.

The high visibility of the island's caretakers serves to make them less fearsome of approach. The psychologist seen hauling his scallop drags out of the water on a frosty November morning, the psychiatrist carting his garbage to the dump on Sunday, or the social worker trying to manage her children as they frolic on the beach scattering sand into picnic baskets can no longer be seen as silent critics hidden beyond their therapeutic incognitos. The judge of the district court seen marketing in shirt sleeves at the supermarket on Saturday mornings is never again completely hidden by his judicial robes.

The Multi-Interest Board

Membership on the board of directors of each different human service agency naturally reflects a particular interest in that area. Those interested in mental health are found on the boards of mental health associations, and those interested in the problems of youth are found in associations dedicated to the needs of the young. This fragmentation of interest into separate and often competing agencies within the broad spectrum of human services has some unfortunate consequences.

Often it leads to an imbalance in the services offered. Each agency seeks to offer the maximum service to its clientele and at the same time is in competition for the same private and public funds. The allocation of funds for the various services that result from such competition is rarely rational, depending on the comparative skills of each agency in influencing the legislature for state funds or in appeals to the general public. In many communities, in order to avoid the competition for the public purse, agencies delegate their fund-raising task to nonprofit fund-raising agencies, such as the Red Feather, United Fund, and Community Chest. While this arrangement allows for the possibility of a rational allocation of funds, it puts the fund-raising organization in the position of an uneasy broker. In practice, the allocation of funds by such fund-raising collectives is often in proportion to that raised when the organization entered the collective, thus perpetuating whatever irrational system of allocation already existed.

The existence of a number of boards for those interested in providing human services may also make for a waste of human resources. The special skills and talents required for effective board membership are limited in number and may in small communities soon be exhausted by a multiplicity of boards. An expert in finance and budgeting may have too little to do on the board of one organization, while other agencies are in need of the skills he possesses. The public relations activities so necessary to organizations in public service and dependent on public funds are found to be fragmented and ineffective. If the eight agencies of Martha's Vineyard Community Services were independent of each other with only fifteen or twenty board members for each association, the limited number of people in its small community with the skills and interest required would be fragmented and underutilized.

While each member of a multi-interest board is likely to have a primary interest in one or another of its agencies, the very process of interagency cooperation which he observes is likely to widen his loyalty, for the fact is that none of the agencies of Martha's Vineyard Community Services is self-sufficient. Those board members primarily interested in the welfare of the young soon learn that the task cannot be assigned to one agency alone. For example, assistance to young people on the island is given by a significant proportion of the agencies of Community Services, among them the Youth

Center, Summer Project, Early Childhood Programs, the Pre-Start School, and the Mental Health Center. This situation has resulted in the gradual widening of interest on the part of board members, so that the competition among agencies for available resources which it was feared might occur has been of relatively small consequence.

One of the difficulties encountered, however, in maintaining the even-handed interest of board members in all of the agencies of Martha's Vineyard Community Services results from the nature of the services offered by each agency. The less technical the services offered by an agency, the more likely are board members to understand and be informed of its role. On the contrary, if the services offered are quite technical, such as those offered by a psychiatric clinic, and require total confidentiality, the board member is more likely to feel excluded from the decision-making processes that go on within the agency. This alienation often comes about because in the technical roles that require considerable training, as in the case of mental health workers, the executive of the agency is likely, by virtue of what he sees as the nature of his activities and his high level of training, to be less forthcoming in informing the board of his activities than are the directors of less technical agencies. Because of the need for confidentiality, board members may rarely have the opportunity even to see the physical plant in which a psychiatric clinic operates and may feel that their role in determining the purpose and function of the agency is minimal. When dependent only upon what the executive communicates, the members of a board are in danger of losing interest in that agency, because they feel they have little influence on it.

Funding the Multi-Service Organization

The experience with funding the agencies of Martha's Vineyard Community Services suggests certain advantages of the multi-service organization. By providing for a variety of interests among members of the community and ensuring the development of a board with many interests, the multi-service organization increases the acceptability of each of its component agencies, and those who contribute funds to the overall organization are by virtue of their contributions committed to it as a whole. Such commitments diminish competition among agencies and relieve the directors of the kind of public relations activities at which they may not be adept. When the Mental Health Center was the only agency of Martha's Vineyard Community Services, the first year's drive for funds resulted in contributions of approximately $11,000. The director of the center predicted in the annual report for that year that the community could not be expected to contribute as much in subsequent years. The fact is that in over fourteen years contributions from the public have more than quintupled, and there is evidence that the initiation of a new agency was generally followed by an increase in public contributions. Public contributions showed a gradual increase from 1962 to 1964. Then in 1964 the Youth Center was opened, and in 1965 the Visiting Nurse and Homemaker Services were founded. Public contributions for 1966 rose and have continued to increase since that time. In short, it appears likely that the introduction of each new agency appealed to the various interest groups in the community. Contributions have also kept pace with the rapidly mounting expenses of the organization. Income from other sources, the Commonwealth of Massachusetts, Dukes County, foundations, grants, third-party payments, and client fees grew rapidly as the organization increased its services and visibility. Between 1962 and 1975 the budget of the organization increased twenty-four fold.

Within the first year of its incorporation, Martha's Vineyard Community Services also established the Thrift Shop, a store which accepts either as gifts or by consignment new and used articles to be sold. The nature of the articles accepted is not limited, having included clothing, jewelry, silver, books, glassware, and furniture. The initial investment in starting the Thrift Shop was $150. The shop provides a substantial source of funds and at present earns a significant proportion of the amount required for the organization's budget.

The Thrift Shop has a secondary function which is of considerable importance. It gives to those members of the community who would like to support the entire enterprise by providing their skills and time the opportunity to do so. More than sixty islanders regularly contribute their time and skill, often for only a half-day a week, and once they have invested something of themselves, they are more likely to continue their support of the entire organization.

19

The Therapist in the Community

It was recognized at the outset that the role undertaken by the psychiatrist as therapist in a small community was a new one. At the time that the Mental Health Center was established, the practice of psychiatry was rare in rural communities. State and locally supported clinics were few in number in rural areas of the United States, but the increasing demand for comprehensive psychiatric service and the federal government's commitment to providing mental health facilities based on small mental health centers and satellite outpatient clinics made it evident that new roles and tasks for psychiatrists and other mental health workers would soon confront the profession.

If psychiatric services are to be made available to those who live in small communities or in areas of low population density, they must be geographically accessible as well as low in cost and promptly available. Studies have shown that admission rates to state hospitals from participating communities are inversely related to the distance of the community from the state hospital. If this is a fact for state hospital admissions, which are generally considered to be nonelective, it must certainly be even more true for outpatient admissions. In practice, therefore, even though mental health centers are generally designed to offer services to populations of 75,000 to 150,000 persons, it has been found desirable, when population density is low, to establish satellite clinics in order to put the service where the people are. Even in a state as urbanized as Massachusetts, it has been necessary in certain parts of the state to plan for mental health clinics to be supplemented by satellite units scattered throughout the area served by the clinic.

The changes in delivery of mental health services that have occurred over the past two decades have produced both new problems and new opportunities. A growing number of therapists live in or near the communities in which they practice; they therefore no longer treat only patients who extract themselves from the millions in urban centers to enter the office or clinic and disappear from it into *terra incognita* at the end of an hour. More and more often, therapists are also called upon to perform community functions and to act in roles that are new to them. Thus, the maintenance of the therapeutic incognito long advocated by psychiatrists for both technical and therapeutic reasons is less possible in rural areas. Such changes have produced situations of stress for psychiatrists, the results of which have been likened to culture shock (deSole et al 1967).

The new opportunities that have resulted from these changes in the delivery of psychiatric services are many. Although the opportunity to see the patient in other social roles, to understand and participate in his social interactions, certainly produces new stresses for the therapist, it also may increase his understanding of the patient as a social being. The new role of the therapist in the community may give him opportunities for anticipatory intervention in the lives of persons with psychiatric disorder in the making. His effect on community caretakers and on the community's climate of opinion is no longer limited to his participation in formal meetings. His presence in the community as both professional and citizen is, for good or bad, constant and pervasive.

Initial Anxieties

It is inevitable for all but the unrealistically overconfident that the entrance into a strange and intimate community, as the sole provider of a highly technical and personal service, will be associated with much anxiety. Will one be accepted as a person? Will the anxieties produced in the community by making the problems within it overt cause the community to turn against the mental health worker? Does the therapist have the training and experience that his new job as a general practitioner of psychiatry demands? Will his competence, until then supplemented by the skills of ever-present colleagues, suffice for the all-purpose role in which he is now placed?

These questions illustrate some of the sources of anxiety associated with entering a small community in order to introduce a new, often anxiety-provoking service. Since the concerns are to a significant degree based on realistic expectations, they should be called fears rather than anxieties, and it should be recognized that there are perhaps no means for eliminating them save by the experience gained with the passage of time.

Loss of Therapeutic Incognito

Most psychotherapists have long been accustomed to operating under the protection of a therapeutic incognito. Following Freud's dictum, they attempt to remain anonymous to the patient in order to facilitate the development of transference uncomplicated by the personality of the therapist. Maintenance of the incognito probably often has another function which has rarely been mentioned; it protects the therapist from the anxiety inherent in any vital human encounter.

At present, this technical device of the therapeutic incognito is limited largely to classical psychoanalytic therapy, and its usefulness has been severely questioned by a number of neo-Freudian analysts, particularly by H. S. Sullivan (1953), who described the position of the therapist in the therapeutic venture as that of a "participant-observer." Even if the incognito is a desirable stance for the therapist, it is doubtful that it can be maintained in a small community. If the therapist is to live and work in the community, to participate in its social and political life, to have a spouse doing the same and children studying in its schools, he can no longer retain the anonymity which such a stance requires.

Role Confusion

When the psychiatrist moves from a large to a small community, his experience involves another new change, role confusion. The means by which rural dwellers simplify the interactions of the moment in a small community is to segregate roles. The problem for the psychiatrist, however, is often more complex. The fact that he and his patients are likely to know each other in multiple roles often introduces serious difficulties into the interpersonal situation in general and the therapeutic one in particular.

If an acquaintance calls the therapist and says, "I'd like to come over to see you," the very ambiguity of the situation contains the seeds of difficulty. Is he coming as a patient, as a member of the committee on which they both serve, or as a friend? Such an ambiguous call is often, in fact, a device for seeking psychiatric help without identifying oneself as a patient. Both the putative patient and the therapist may therefore find themselves in a morass unless they become aware of and define the nature of the relationship at once.

Even after having defined it for both himself and the other person, the therapist must watch carefully during the session for shifts from one role relationship to another. If the person acting as patient makes reference to some problem in another role relationship they share, the seeds of difficulty are planted. The therapist has two choices. If he feels the material is actually part of the therapeutic session, he can so understand and interpret it. However, if a reference appears to be a diversionary maneuver, a possibility to which he must be ever alert, he can point this out or alternatively suggest that it be taken up after the session is over, when each can assume the role appropriate to the personal reference.

Social Interactions with Patients

A common concern for both patient and therapist even in urban centers is that somehow, someday, they may meet on a social occasion, and each is afraid that he will not know how to behave toward the other under the new circumstances. This concern stems from the fact that they have known each other in a single well-defined role relationship, and each is anxious lest a social encounter in another role strain the primary relationship.

In a small community, this possibility becomes a probability. On the island, it is almost impossible for the mental health worker to enter any social or other group of any size without meeting one or more persons who are or have been his patients. The fact is that in the first eight years the psychiatrist had already seen approximately 5 percent of the people living on the island, which meant that one of every twenty persons was likely to be or to have been a patient. In social groups that are selective in terms of social class, education, or other characteristics, the probabilities are even higher. In one year, of the fifty members of the community orchestra performing on the stage of an island school, seven were former patients. When the roster of those taking adult education courses in 1969 was tabulated, over 10 percent were or had been patients, and close to an additional 10 percent lived in the same household as a present or ex-patient. In short, one-fifth of the people taking the courses had had some direct or indirect experience with the psychiatrist. These figures do not include the adult education course on personality and psychiatric disorder which the psychiatrist himself taught that year. In this course, 12 of the 32 participants were or had been in treatment.

It is inevitable that friends and acquaintances of the therapist turn up as patients, and this results in stress on both sides. One of the problems for the therapist lies in his ability to tolerate the transient hostilities which his friends may experience in the therapeutic relationship and his fear that the knowledge he has gained may result in the alienation of his friends by embarrassment. The problem causes similar difficulties for the patient. The image he has labored to present to the world may now be altered for the therapist. Since the therapist already knows a great deal about him, the patient in a small community does not have as much control as does the anonymous patient concerning what he will reveal. He knows further that the therapist has other sources of data about him from friends and relatives who have been in treatment. Finally, the common fear that, after he reveals himself, he will not be accepted by the therapist becomes even more frightening if the therapist is actually an ever-present member of his community.

Public Failure and Public Success

Under most circumstances the entrance into psychiatric therapy is a private matter within the control of the patient. He may choose to tell others of the fact that he is in treatment, but this choice remains entirely his prerogative. On the island, the fact that a person is attending the Mental Health Center is less likely to be a private matter. The clinic building is in the community. The patient may be seen entering it, or his car may be seen parked in its vicinity. Just as membership in Alcoholics Anonymous is not accompanied by anonymity in this small community, the psychiatric patient cannot be assured that his visits to the clinic will not be noted.

The building in which the Mental Health Center first operated was situated on a main street in the town of Edgartown, directly across from a small restaurant. Patients could either enter by the front door, visible to all in the restaurant, or come in more anonymously by a side door reached by a footpath accessible from two streets. When the clinic was new to the community, most patients entered by the side door, but after a few years entrance to the clinic building by any but the front door was unusual. The clinic's mental health workers have been stopped on the street by patients who wished to pay their clinic fees then and there, and both the psychiatrist's wife and secretary have had money passed into their hands while shopping as payment for clinic services. It is not uncommon to be stopped in the street by a friend or an acquaintance of a patient to be given some bit of knowledge that the friend feels may add to the success of the treatment or to be asked by the friend or relative how he should act when the patient's behavior is odd. Under such circumstances, no response would seem unfriendly, unreasonable, and patently evasive. The practice adopted in such circumstances is to indicate that the mental health worker obviously cannot say anything but will be glad to listen, at least, when he feels that the communication is being made in good faith.

The fact that a significant number of people may know that a particular patient is in treatment may be a source of anxiety for the therapist. In large centers, his therapeutic failures are generally known only to the patient and his relatives; in the small community both his failures and his successes are relatively public. In addition, what he considers success may be interpreted publicly as failure, and he is subject to the probability that some patients may quote or misquote his comments or interpretations in ways that discredit him.

In situations of crisis the therapist may feel particularly threatened. He may be concerned that the need to hospitalize someone will be interpreted by the community as a failure. When treating a depressed patient, he may become disturbed at the possible effect that suicide would have on his professional position in the community. However, experience has shown that a reasonable proportion of failure is well tolerated. It is probably true that people living in small communities, students of lives in depth as they are, have a greater tolerance for human failure than do city dwellers. They are not as persuaded that men can solve all problems, and they do not share the belief in the omnipotence of the expert so common to the modern temper. On the contrary, the successful interventions of the therapist frequently become known and are sources of credit to him, and he is often embarrassed by being given credit for successes that he knows are not his.

The Patient in Power

The intense emotions often felt by patients toward the therapist, whether hostile or loving, are generally well tolerated by therapists if they recognize the distortions involved, if the feelings expressed do not resonate with some of their own problems, and if the patient does not in fact have any power over them. This last consideration is one that may become a problem for the therapist in the small community. Since patient and therapist may share other role relationships, some of those interactions may involve the possession of power by the patient over the therapist. The patient, for example, may be a schoolteacher who has the therapist's child as one of his pupils, or he may be a member of the school committee which must decide whether to appoint the therapist as consultant to the school system. Even more directly and powerfully, he may be a member of the board of directors of the mental health or other association that operates the clinic in which the therapist is employed. Under such circumstances, the patient may during periods of hostile transference or a paranoid state act to subvert one or another of the activities of the mental health enterprise. If the irrationality of the patient's behavior is not obvious, as is likely in view of the tolerance for deviation that often exists in small communities, what the patient says may be taken at face value for a long time.

The same problem arises when the teacher of one of the therapist's children comes for treatment. The dangers lie in two directions. If the transference is positive, the teacher may irrationally favor the therapist's child, or if negative, he may use his professional position to express his anger at the therapist through the child. The only way to ameliorate such a situation is by being alert to the events and by interpreting the meaning of the patient's behavior to him. The danger certainly cannot be eliminated entirely and represents one of the problems inherent in living closely with other human beings.

The Therapist in Power

The very nature of the therapeutic relationship and the assumption that patients bring to treatment of undergoing an experience bordering on magic place great power in the hands of the therapist. It is assumed that the ethical standards of the profession inculcated during training will operate to prevent conscious exploitation of the power of the office. It is further assumed that the self-understanding acquired during training, often through personal psychoanalysis, will tend to eliminate unconscious impulses on the therapist's part to exploit his patient. Avoiding these pitfalls is among the everyday problems of being a therapist.

However, the therapist practicing in the small community, where he may also have extra-therapeutic relationships with his patients, may find himself in positions of authority for which he has not been prepared. He may serve in roles in community organizations that give him the power of decision, and if the subject of a decision involves his patient or his patient's family, contamination of the normal patient-therapist relationship may occur. Although in the therapeutic meeting the therapist ordinarily puts no restraint on the words the patient may use, he may find himself in a quite different position if he chairs a meeting participated in by a number of his patients. For example, the island psychiatrist was once chairman of a meeting in which the husband of a patient made a personal attack on another citizen with charges bordering on slander. In the psychiatrist's role as chairman, it was necessary for him to ask the patient's husband either to withdraw the attack or to substantiate it, a stance which is quite different from that in the consultation room. It is not always possible to avoid such difficulties, and role segregation may not operate in every instance. After such an encounter the therapist should try to make clear to the patient involved the nature of his position in each role.

The Patient in His Environment

The therapist practicing on the island has sources of information about his patients other than the data that they or their relatives provide in the therapeutic conference. He may have heard them commented about by other patients or by friends. He may have observed gross character problems in their behavior in public situations and in social groups. The opportunity of seeing the patient in other than the sick role can be enlightening. The communication of difficulty and distress that comes within the therapeutic session may be illuminated by events in the patient's life. For example, a patient's description of the imperious attitude of her husband was difficult to give credence to, particularly after he had been interviewed, until he was observed as chairman at a small community meeting. And it is often enlightening to compare the patient's behavior in the sick role in the consulting room with his competent functioning in the community.

Home visits provide unique opportunities for therapeutic observation and intervention. Besides the fact that such visits can more readily be made in the small community, they can, because of the presence of the psychiatrist as an inhabitant, often be made in situations of crisis. The description of a paranoid woman and her effect on the family as related by her husband in the consulting room may be limited by the tempering effect of time and the anemia of his descriptive powers, but the therapist may get a far different impression when he visits the home during the paranoid crisis. A woman in paranoid panic, three frightened children huddled in the bedroom, the odor of rotting food, and the husband dashing between bedroom and living room, fatigued from lack of sleep, helpless to relieve his wife's fears and concerned about the effects of the situation on his children—this is quite a different picture from the one the therapist gets the next day from the patient in the aseptic atmosphere of the consulting room.

Such observations permit the therapist to decide more rationally whether the patient must be sent to a hospital or whether treatment at home is a tolerable alternative for the family. If he should decide on the latter, his observation of the household can tell him what kind of help—nursing, household, or other—is needed. He can observe the effect of crowding on the human personality. A mother's complaint, for example, that her child does poorly at school and does not finish his homework may be explained when the therapist observes the father, tired from the day's work, watching the television set with the sound turned up while the child sits eight feet away trying to study. If he sees in an otherwise impoverished household a new, hard-earned set of the Encyclopedia Britannica, he may get some notion of aspirations that transcend the family's position in the class structure of their community.

The Expression of Anger

The complex nature of human relationships in the small community imposes significant difficulties on the human interaction known as psychotherapy. The fact that dwellers in the small community habitually seek accommodation at the expense of resolution places a strain on human relationships in general and on the psychotherapeutic encounter in particular. The expression of anger by the neurotic patient, which often first occurs for him in the relative safety of the consulting room and which may be a landmark in his emotional development, is certainly made more difficult by the fact that his therapist is not an anonymous being who retreats to Larchmont, Newton, or Bethesda at the end of a session, but is someone he may encounter that evening or the next day in a relatively intimate setting. The training that dwellers in small communities have in seeking accommodation may simply reinforce the repression of anger learned in childhood.

Under the conditions in which psychotherapy is generally practiced, the patient knows little about the therapist. His irrational anger must therefore attach itself to what little data he has, usually something superficial about the therapist, his manner, his dress, or the furnishings of his office. Since these are generally not vital matters to the therapist, anger focused on such issues is the more readily recognized as transference, and it does not touch the core of the therapist's being or cause a shaking of his emotional foundations. The therapist practicing in the small community, where he, his spouse, and children are exposed daily, is not so protected. The patient in fact may have a great deal of real data for the expression of his negative transference. He may have seen his therapist perform poorly at a public meeting or behave badly at a cocktail party. In short, the patient's facts may be straight, and his attack may hit home. To say that therapists should by training be entirely immune from such onslaughts is to deny their humanity. The expression of hostility that appears to be based on fact can be particularly disturbing, and when it is so, the therapist may neglect to notice that the patient's reaction is in fact irrational.

In patients in whom transference phenomena are extremely intense, those with schizophrenic processes or in borderline states, chance encounters with the therapist outside of the consulting room may be quite disturbing for the patient. Since these are likely to occur in a small community, they impose a special problem, particularly at the beginning of treatment. The therapist may sense or be told explicitly by the patient of the disturbances that result from such meetings. This awareness may cause the patients to avoid encounters with the therapist, particularly during the early phase of treatment.

As does everyone, therapists too need friends and other intimates. They need to be able to cast aside the restraints of the role of healer. The development of such relationships may render the therapist incapable of the degree of detachment necessary for therapy with the persons involved. As the result of such experiences, the therapist must recognize that his own needs for friendship and the claims of friendship upon him may make it impossible for him to treat certain persons in his community, and in those instances he should refer them elsewhere.

The Varieties of Therapy

At first blush it would seem that there should be no difference between the varieties of therapy adaptable to the small community and methods used in large populations. However, two considerations have some bearing on the matter. The first relates to group therapy. Ordinarily in group therapy the participants in the group are introduced to each other rather anonymously; whether they choose to enter each other's lives outside of the therapeutic encounter is a matter of choice for them. If they do not, it is likely that they will not be identified, and they can therefore make revelations with some degree of confidence that anonymity will be preserved. The situation in the very small community is quite different. First, personal anonymity cannot be guaranteed. The knowledge of this fact may inhibit group communication. The concern is not with one's identification as a psychiatric patient but rather with the details about one's life, hopes, fears, and fantasies that will be revealed in a group situation, a consideration which led the clinic not to offer group therapy for its first six years (Mazer 1970b). Despite these concerns, the conduct of group therapy on the island has been found to be possible, particularly when focused on specific areas and for groups with common problems. One therapeutic group that has long functioned in this community is Alcoholics Anonymous. It functions, however, despite the lack of anonymity, because alcoholism itself is not a disorder that permits anonymity in the small community, and virtually all those in Alcoholics Anonymous are generally known to be or to have been alcoholics.

The second factor which is likely to operate in the small community in determining the kind of therapy that will be acceptable does not relate directly to the size of the community but rather to its value system. In general, the values of the people of the island operate against an interest in and desire for long-term reconstructive therapy. The search for happiness, the desire to live up to one's potentialities, or the striving for creative expression—concerns that are frequently presented as passports for entering psychoanalytic therapy in the large city—are generally not perceived on the island as psychiatric problems; they are seen rather as issues of fate or of God's design. Further, the people of this community have less faith in the omnipotence of the expert and more tolerance for the less-than-perfect than do the upper middle class dwellers of the cities.

The people of the island and other rural communities come for treatment for specific symptoms: depression, anxiety, phobic reactions, alcoholism, and occasionally behavior disorders and learning difficulties in their children. They seek relief of symptoms, not passports to the rich and creative life, and they are content with as much relief as they can get in the briefest time possible. Oriented as they are to the here-and-now and the practical, they expect not magic but a little help. This is not to say that long-term intensive therapy may not be used or is regularly rejected, but experience shows that intensive therapy is most resourcefully employed when timed to the immediate needs of the patient, not to a program worked out long in advance because large-city life requires fixed commitments in both patients' and therapists' schedules. Because distances are short and schedules are adaptable, it is possible in the small community to treat a patient once or twice a week for a while and then to see him every day during a period of crisis, as in a potentially suicidal depression.

A Community Resource

The professional who comes to live and work on the island is immediately seen as an all-purpose community resource. Although the therapist in the city may find his social life more or less limited to those in his own social class, even perhaps to his own profession, the therapist in the small community finds that his social life breaches these narrow boundaries. Because experts of any sort are scarce, he may find himself treated as a multipurpose expert and expected to function skillfully in areas where he feels he has no competence. This expectation is consistent with the multiple-role functions of most citizens in small communities. For example, of the five general practitioners on the island in 1970, two have served on school committees and hold a number of other posts. Shortly after the psychiatrist arrived on the island, he was asked by the superintendent of schools and the principal of the high school to advise them on the detention system of enforcing discipline. When a program of adult education was being planned, he was asked to serve on its planning committee. When the post of moderator in the town where he lives became vacant, he was asked by the selectmen to run for the office, and when an Economic Development Commission was formed, he was invited by his selectmen to become a member of that body. All these positions involve functions in which a psychiatrist as psychiatrist has no specific competence by training.

The question arises as to whether the functioning of the therapist as an expert in such areas is related to his role as a therapist. The answer to the question bears a relationship to the model of psychiatric disorder used. A strict adherence to the belief that psychiatric disorder is a consequence of the emotional vicissitudes of early life and remains largely intrapsychic, would argue against the utility of the psychiatrist's engaging in such extraprofessional activities. However, the view that, no matter how the substrate for psychiatric disorder was laid down, breakdown at some later time in life bears a direct relationship to current stress clearly allows for the so-called extraprofessional interventions of the therapist to be thought of as social therapy. This point was put in useful perspective by A. H. Leighton (1967a) in his concept of "salient cause." He pointed out that there are many factors which contribute to an episode of psychiatric breakdown and that some of these may be related to sociocultural disintegration in the community. The salient cause is not to be thought of as the essential cause or the main cause, but simply as one of the factors about which something effective might conceivably be done.

If the detention system for enforcing discipline in a school system seems to the mental health worker to be based on the view that man is essentially evil and must be restrained, and if the psychiatrist believes that this system incites counteraction on the part of students, then certainly his counsel to the authorities of the system may make a contribution to mental health. If there is an absence of productive activities during the winter months in a small community and if the therapist feels this may contribute to both alcoholism and a sense of social emptiness, then certainly his contribution to the development of a program of adult education may be considered preventive psychiatry. This view also emerged from the experience of a mental health worker in a rural area of Wyoming (Tranel 1970).

It should now be clear that psychiatric practice in the small community is quite different from that to which psychiatrists are accustomed by either training, experience, or inclination. The psychiatrist entering the small community must be prepared to become a generalist and to engage in the general practice of psychiatry. He must expect that the demands on him will be varied and many-faceted. He must be prepared to become more need-centered and less method-oriented. Although in large-city practice he can confine himself to the particular method that interests him and refer those not suitable for the method to his colleagues, in the small community he represents a public resource and must be prepared to respond to the manifold problems present in his community. This shift may involve a subtle change in his professional orientations. In a large community he need not feel himself a significant public resource, and his commitment remains to psychiatry as a profession providing a specialized service. In the small community he soon realizes that his commitments change; they attach less to his profession and more to the community, and all of the resources of his profession and any paraprofessional skills he acquires become instruments in the performance of his new roles.

Finally, the therapist in the small community finds that his customary entrenchment behind the facade of his profession and the distance that its prestigious position places between him and others may serve him poorly in his work. His many-faceted position constantly exposes him as a human being, and if he does not remain modest in his pretentions, he is likely to find himself humbled by events. The therapist in the small community, situated as he is on the interface where persons engage with social institutions, must be prepared to learn from both his inferiors and his betters, and he may often find it difficult to tell which are which. He must remain ever innovative and ever venturesome, for all the roads of his journey have not yet been charted. For his own benefit, both as person and as therapist, he needs to be often reminded of Kierkegaard's comment, "To venture causes dread but not to venture is to lose oneself."

20

The Human Uses of the Community

The community is the great arena in which human life is lived, and it is within this arena that psychological disorder can best be prevented, or treated when it occurs. The community is where we are shaped and made aware, where we learn or do not learn to engage with our fellows, where in distress we receive or do not receive the concerned support of those in our social network. While it is the individual who must attempt to cope with the stresses to which life subjects him, the outcome of the struggle is often determined by the characteristics of the community in which he lives. Certain qualities of communities are crucial in determining the burden of disorder their citizens bear and the help they may expect when the burdens become overwhelming.

As psychological disorder is recognized more and more clearly to result from many factors, it becomes useful to scrutinize more carefully both the stressful and the nurturing qualities of our various communities. The role of the members of the nuclear family of the individual labeled as mentally ill is coming to have greater importance and has led to the increasing interest in family therapy. The loss of the nurturing role of the extended family as we become a more migrating people has its unhappy consequences. With the progressive disappearance of the functioning extended family, it becomes important that communities take on new tasks, for responsive communities with a close-knit network of nurturing relationships and of community resources can aid the individual as he attempts to cope with his difficulties. In short, communities or subcommunities can act to some degree as extended nurturing families, and any dweller in rural communities knows that there are within them disturbed persons who manage only because of such support.

Human beings also live in groups that extend beyond the confines of their homes, and such communities have important effects upon their members, depending on whether they are coherent or not, well-integrated or disintegrated. The Stirling County study found that communities identified as disintegrated showed higher rates of disorder than those considered well integrated (A.H. Leighton 1959; Hughes et al 1960; D. C. Leighton et al 1963). More significant, a follow-up study in one community indicated that a change in the direction of better sociocultural integration was associated with a significant decrease in the rate of psychological disorder (A.H. Leighton 1965, 1967b).

The striking implications of these findings are perhaps best put in the words of the study's authors: "If you were to introduce a random sample of symptomatically unimpaired people into the Disintegrated Areas in numbers small enough that they produced no significant change in the sociocultural system, we think most of these individuals would become impaired. Conversely, if you were to take people out of the Disintegrated Areas and make a place for them in a well-integrated community, we believe that many of them would show marked reduction or disappearance of impairment" (D.C. Leighton et al 1963). Since steps for improving community integration may be taken deliberately by means generally included under the term *community development*, there exist possibilities of achieving significant decreases in the rates of mental disorder by such public action.

The approach taken in the attempt to decrease the frequency of psychiatric disorder on Martha's Vineyard was based on two premises. The first assumes that an increase in the coherence of life will be associated with a decrease in the rates of disorder, a premise arising from the Stirling County study. The second premise is that early supportive responses to stress can prevent the development of significant disorder, which is one of the premises of crisis theory (Lindemann 1941; Caplan 1964; Hirschowitz 1973).

The two functions of the community that were emphasized in the effort to decrease the incidence of psychiatric disorder on the island were thus coherence and responsiveness, concepts that parallel the terms *well-integrated* (D.C. Leighton et al 1963) and *competent* (Cottrell 1976). The term *coherence* refers to those qualities of a community that favor the preservation of mental health, and the term *responsiveness* refers to the capacity of a community to react to disruption in the psychological equilibrium of its citizens by a concerted, appropriate effort on the part of all of its community resources. Further, the hallmark of a responsive community is that it possesses the repertory of services that are required or, failing this, that it is responsive to the need for new services as the occasion arises. In brief, the coherence of the community life presumably prevents the occurrence of intolerable stress, while the responsiveness of the community tries to meet the needs of individuals experiencing stresses that may eventually lead to psychiatric disorder.

Toward a Coherent Community

A community is coherent when its institutions, class structure, system of values, and all of the other aspects of its life do not subject its members to intolerable stress. This definition implies that some degree of stress is unavoidable. Stress is unavoidable so long as people grow, move through the developmental process, and have strivings which alter their lives. Some degree of stress may be a consequence of the self-regenerating properties of the community in response to alterations in the composition of its population, to migration, to technological change, and to the impact of other forces that reach it from the larger society of which it is a part.

An examination of the stressful elements in island life reveals that they are associated with four of its characteristics. First, the small size of the island's population is responsible for the stresses associated with status inconsistency, with the repression of anger, with the clinging of stigmatization to an individual once it occurs, and with the conflict in roles. The stresses that arise from the community's small size cannot be prevented but are compensated for to some degree by its inhabitants' awareness of a common destiny, by their long tradition of mutual helpfulness, and by the nurturing bonds of its intricate social network.

The second characteristic of island life that produces stress is its relative poverty. For decades it has had the lowest median income of the fourteen counties of Massachusetts, and there is abundant evidence that rates of psychological impairment are highest at the lowest end of the socioeconomic scale.

The fact that it is an island dependent on a tourist economy is a third important characteristic of its life which produces significant stress. The sense and fact of the islanders' loss of power over their own lives to their summer visitors becomes more and more inescapable. In recent years, however, in response to the depredations of speculators in their land, islanders have gradually and contrary to tradition asserted their political power. While attempts at rational land use through zoning were almost invariably voted down a decade ago, each town has now passed zoning ordinances. Through the efforts of islanders, the Massachusetts legislature has enacted a law which gives islanders greater control over the shape of the island's future, and there is a likelihood that federal supporting legislation for the Vineyard along with the other islands of the region will be seriously considered by the Congress. But as important as the legislation on land use is to the future of the island's physical ecology, its effect on the psychosocial texture of the lives of islanders promises to be even greater, for the legislation represents nothing less than an attempt to regain a sense of control over their own lives and the destiny of their children for so long left to the wishes and whims of their summer visitors.

Although the conflict in values to which islanders are subjected each summer has its damaging effects, these have in recent years been mitigated to some degree by the signs that many Americans are beginning to yearn for what islanders already have, all that is included in the evocative term *rural life*. The significant number of young people, individuals, and new families who have moved to the island in the last six or seven years is an ever-present reminder of this trend. The migration of families and individuals, however, while often in pursuit of the Jeffersonian vision, is often, too, the result of familial crisis, and once on the island these in-migrants experience the stresses of accommodation to a community unlike any they have ever known.

Finally, islanders suffer stress because of the cultural confusion induced by the number of variant groups living together. Such confusion is probably less stressful for the two larger groups, the so-called "old Americans" and people of Portuguese origin, because it has been found that the stresses of belonging to an ethnic minority are less intense if the minority represents a significant part of the population (Mintz and Schwartz 1964). Probably the greatest stresses from cultural confusion are experienced by the two smaller culturally different groups on the island, the Gay Head Indians and the people of Portuguese descent whose ancestors migrated from the Cape Verde Islands. The members of the latter group in fact live with a crisis in identity, neither identifying themselves with the small black population nor being entirely accepted by the Portuguese-American community.

Any attempt to reduce the stresses impinging on islanders must be the work of many hands. The response to the rampant subdivision of their land for commercial gain by outside forces has resulted in a greater appreciation of what they already have and has caused them to take steps to influence the future of their island. The inmigration of young couples with children and changes in the administration of the schools have resulted in a reordering of educational priorities, and the island now has a school system which barely resembles that of a decade ago. The relative indifference of islanders to the quality of their schools has been replaced by pride as the citizens have engaged more actively in this most important of community enterprises.

Perhaps the most important task for community development is an effort to eliminate the poverty and uncertain income under which so many islanders live. But improvement is unlikely so long as the livelihood of islanders remains largely dependent on a seasonal tourist economy. Although small-scale industrialization has proven feasible for other rural, relatively isolated communities, there is on the island no tradition which supports such efforts. The local business community consists almost entirely of two groups, those who provide services and the merchants who are accustomed to enterprises involving distribution rather than production. As a result, there has been virtually no effort to acquire the kind of industry that might be feasibly located on the island, and this represents a failure in island leadership. Two arguments are usually given for the absence of small-scale industry, the lack of a skilled labor force and the cost of shipping finished products to the mainland. But problems of this sort have been solved in other communities by a concentration on small-scale industry whose products require easily taught skills, have a high labor input, and are small in bulk so that shipping costs are a small fraction of final costs, particularly when, as in the island's case, the community is within a large market. The problem is not industrial but cultural, a long-held aversion to cooperative enterprises in favor of independent initiative. But this cultural aversion is simply part of the history of all preindustrial communities, and it is probable that islanders will respond to the opportunity to escape from the cycle of poverty as readily as have other less favored communities when the proper means and suitable leadership converge.

Since there is evidence that migration is associated with high predicament rates, a fruitful challenge to the community is an effort to assist those coming to live in it (Heller 1975). In this effort, the school system is in a strategic position, since it has the opportunity to diminish stress for those at the most vulnerable period of their lives. It needs to be responsive both to the children who enter the schools from other systems and to its teachers often new both to profession and community.

Whether or not community development is a legitimate and possible role for mental health workers is much debated. It has been argued that the mental health specialist can have a role in designing community action programs which foster mental health, and that by consulting with legislators and administrators, he can influence governmental agencies in modifying laws and regulations which directly affect the welfare of high-rate groups (Caplan 1964). But this point of view has also been criticized as being based on a theory of primary prevention which has not been sufficiently validated and beyond the capacities of the psychiatrist (Mechanic 1969).

The issue, however, does not arise in the small community either as deliberately or as hopelessly as suggested. Those in the community who are in charge of shaping social policy often do not formulate the issues in yes or no terms, nor do they directly ask for consultation with the mental health specialist as such. Whatever influence mental health workers may have upon the rural community's decision makers in the realm of social policy often occurs by indirection. What the mental health worker conveys is often transmitted not in a meeting called to discuss a particular issue but in a series of encounters over a longer period during which something of his general outlook on human life and human problems may help the decision maker to become aware of another climate of opinion. In fact, it may be argued that the mental health worker must avoid making decisions for the decision makers, because as important as the decision itself is the climate in which it is carried out.

What the mental health specialist can effectively do is to ask the right questions when his opinion is invited, so as to shake the taken-for-granteds of the administrator. Suppose, for example, a school official operates as though human beings are basically aggressive and brutish and that in consequence a sufficient degree of coercive control must be imposed before education can begin. The questions asked by the mental health worker, his attitudes as displayed in consultations on other issues, and his demeanor in his encounters with young people may do much to weaken the value that leads to the coercive atmosphere in the school. A change in policy applied tenderly and hesitantly may then occur, but it will be based on a decision made by the administrator with which he has come to feel comfortable, and its implementation is therefore likely to be far more realistic and effective. In short, the mental health specialist as a rule does not have the means for taking direct action in altering community values, attitudes, and actions. If, however, he makes himself available to those who are confronted with such decisions, if he understands the anxieties which confront them in making decisions, and if he is prepared to see his influence felt slowly, he may find that he can be one of the agents for beneficent change.

Toward a Responsive Community

The attempt to establish preventive programs for a community at large is a formidable task. While educational programs on the problems of human relations may be offered for the entire community, it is perhaps more economical to concentrate the efforts of human service agencies on groups which both experience and research have shown to be either at high risk of developing psychological difficulties or strategic in the lives of others. There are some who fall into both groups, at high risk themselves and strategic to the lives of others. For both high risk and strategic groups the Mental Health Center provides group work designed to enhance their capacities to cope with the stresses that life has imposed upon them. Since stress is part of life, with no one immune to it, neither the mental health clinic nor the human service network can do the job alone. To this end, the clinic attempts to make each preventive enterprise self-perpetuating, by using the inherent skills of the citizens, given support and sanction by training, and by marshaling every community agency or institution which has the capacity to or can learn to support such an enterprise.

Of importance in the effort to make communities both coherent and responsive is the relation between the mental health or other human services workers and the communities they serve. The commonest arrangement is that the human service worker enters the community each day to do his job and leaves it each evening to return to another community which is invariably more coherent and responsive to human needs. A total commitment to community life can hardly exist under these circumstances, for the worker is absent when a good proportion of the community crises occur. Further, since his life and that of his family are not contaminated by the noxious elements of community life, there is less commitment to changing them. To live in a community is to have a personal stake in its development, a common destiny with its members (Howe 1964).

The model of disorder on which the agencies of Martha's Vineyard Community Services have based their efforts to be responsive to human needs is a frugal one. It takes note of three factors which are involved in the individual's encounters with life. The first is his repertory of coping techniques acquired during early life but refined and made more competent in response to later events. The second is the magnitude and duration of the individual's encounters with stress, some of which are inevitable and others of which occur by chance. The third factor, important in determining whether or not psychiatric disorder occurs in a potentially vulnerable person under stress, is the support system available to him. Included in this system are his relatives, his friends, and perhaps more important for significant disorder, the network of agencies the community has seen fit to provide. The presence of an effective support system may permit an individual burdened by excessive stress to cope with it without the occurrence of frank psychiatric disorder. And in so doing, he may have increased his repertory of coping techniques, which will prove useful to him when again under stress. The coping-stress-support model is not the only possible model, and others may be useful for other specific problems (Scott and Howard 1970).

The experience of attempting to cope with the overt and covert burden of mental illness in the small population of the island of Martha's Vineyard, the commitment on the part of its human service workers to make a common destiny with their fellow inhabitants, the findings of the epidemiological studies, and the promising efforts to involve the community itself in the entire enterprise leads to one overriding conclusion. It is that the job of coping with mental disorder in the community cannot be reserved for the mental health professions alone. Since the frequency of occurrence of mental disorder is related to every aspect of life, biological, cultural, social, economic, moral, to name a few, an effective approach requires the help of many hands and many skills. This help is also made necessary by the fact that what mental health workers consider to be clear instances of psychiatric disorder are felt and experienced in other ways by those who suffer from them. It is even probable that mental health workers play a relatively small though important role in coping with psychological disorder and in preventing its occurrence. The fact is that political and social action to decrease the amount of poverty in modern society may do more for the mental health of citizens than can the entire mental health enterprise. These considerations suggest that mental health workers, particularly in the small community, may have important catalytic functions in a variety of activities designed to produce beneficent social change. It is much as James Jeans, the British astronomer, put it in attempting to illustrate the phenomenon of universal gravitation. "You cannot crook your little finger," he said, "without moving the most distant star."

Appendices
Bibliography
Index

Appendices

Population Characteristics, Research Methods,
and Tabular Data for Martha's Vineyard Studies

The use of decimals in rates or percentages in the tables is not intended to
suggest that the data are accurate to three or four significant figures, but
rather to permit whole numbers denoting persons to be readily distinguished from rates or percentages. Wherever percentage figures do not
add up to 100 percent, the difference is due to rounding-off.

1. Demographic Characteristics of the Population

The population under study was the entire resident population of the island
of Martha's Vineyard. Since the island has a large seasonal in- and out-
migration, because of its preeminence as a summer resort, the definition of
a resident was crucial. A resident or islander was defined as one who
makes the island the site of his residence or, if he has more than one, the
house in which he lives more than six months of each year.

The basic source of the census of population was the Massachusetts
Census (1965), a decennial census conducted by each town of the Commonwealth midway between the federal census enumerations. The census data
secured were for January 1, 1965. Since the data collection for most of the
epidemiological studies was done during the calender years 1964-1968, the
state's 1965 census was closer in time to the midpoint of the research than
were either the 1960 or 1970 federal censuses.

The use of the state census had other advantages. Because of the
relatively small population of the island in 1965 (circa 6,000) a total count
had an obvious advantage over the sample used in the U.S. Census.
Another important advantage of the state over the federal census was that
the state census cards identified each islander by name, sex, age, household, and place of residence. The data on household composition was used
for the study of familial clustering of predicaments. The roster of names of

each inhabitant permitted the census to be validated by various informants, town clerks, clergymen and others in order to delete those who,
though legally resident of the community, were not at risk within it since
they were away at school, in the armed services, or the like. It permitted,
too, the inclusion of those who were living on the island but were somehow
missed by the enumerators. During the process of validating the state
census, the occupation of each adult islander was recorded for use in the
studies of social class position.

There were no gross alterations in population between censuses, both
federal and state, taken during 1960, 1965, and 1970, nor were any observ-
able within briefer time spans. The only selective change in population
before 1970 began during the fall of 1968 when young people in their twen-
ties began to remain on the island over the winter.

For some studies, it was considered desirable to deal with a stable
population, those at risk over the entire five-year period of the study. This
stable population was secured by deleting from the file those who were not
in the community for the entire five-year period, namely, those who were
born, died, or moved in or out during that period.

The population of the Vineyard has changed over time far less than that
of Massachusetts or the United States. The first recorded count made in
1765 gave the population as 2,719 whites (Greene and Harrington 1932). A
count in 1776 which included 59 blacks recorded the presence of 2,828 persons. By the first federal census of 1790 the island had a population of
3,265. From 1790 to 1970 the growth of population was slow, averaging less
than one-half of one percent per year. From 1970 to 1975 the population
grew rapidly, 28 percent in five years (Mass. Census 1975).

Sex and Age. The population by sex and age in 1965 is shown in Appendix
2. The number of males in each age group exceeds the number of females
until age 24, after which the proportion of males to females steadily decreases, until at age 65 and over males make up 35 percent and females 65
percent of that age group.

The number of persons in each sex drops for the 25-34 age decade. The
decrease is actually first seen in the 20-24 age group, with the 25-29 age
group containing the smallest number for any five-year period until 75+.
This deficiency of young persons was due to their out-migration upon or
soon after graduation from high school.

Marital Status. Data on marital status for the population age 15 and over
are shown in Appendix 3. Particularly notable is the large excess of
widowed females over males owing to the higher male death rate in the
advanced years. The excess of females over males among the separated-
divorced group is due in part to the out-migration of males in those marital
categories. Females charged with the care of children are less likely than

are males to move after divorce. Data on marital status by age group were also available for special analyses.

Social Class Position. The occupation categories of Hollingshead (1957) were used as a measure of social class position. The scale divides occupations into seven categories, using roman numerals to designate ranks, with I as the highest and VII as the lowest. The occupation was always that of the head of the household, almost always that of the husband or father, but that of the mother or wife when she was the major source of income, and was assigned to each member of the nuclear family dependent on the head. The seven occupational categories are:

   I Higher executives, proprietors of large concerns, and major professionals
  II Business managers, proprietors of medium size businesses, and lesser professionals
 III Administrative personnel, proprietors of small independent businesses, and minor professionals
 IV Clerical and sales workers, technicians, and owners of small businesses
  V Skilled manual employees
 VI Machine operators and semiskilled employees
VII Unskilled employees

Appendix 4 gives the occupational classification of the population by sex. In some studies the seven categories were used. In others, where the use of seven categories would have placed few cases in each cell, the categories were collapsed and used to form occupational groupings.

Households. The size of island households is shown in Appendix 5. Almost 85 percent of households had four or fewer persons and 60 percent had only one or two persons. The commonest household size was two, with more people living in two-person households than in any other size. About half of the 10 percent of the population living alone consisted of widows and widowers.

The composition of households is given in Appendix 6. Thirty-five percent were husband-wife households, and thirty-four percent were husband-wife-children households. In 70 of the 115 mother-children households, the children were all below age 20. Of the 515 single-person households, female households were more than double the number of male households, largely owing to the differential death rate favoring women and to selective in- and out-migration differences between the sexes.

Religion. The religious composition of the population was determined by a house-to-house census conducted by the island's churches in 1962. The survey reached approximately 75 percent of island households and 85 percent of the population, since larger households were more likely than smaller households to have someone at home when the enumerator called. It is probable that households missed in the count were those with fewer members, which would result in an overestimate of the Roman Catholic population since Catholic households are larger on the average than those of the other faiths. Since the survey was done by church-goers, it is also probable that among those enumerated there was some inhibition in professing no religion; very few persons in fact were recorded as unaffiliated. The census gave the following religious make-up: Roman Catholic, 47 percent; Protestant, 49 percent; Jewish, 1 percent; "other" and unaffiliated, 3 percent.

2. Population by Sex and Age, 1965

Age	Males		Females	
	No.	%	No.	%
0 – 14	802	28.8	744	23.4
15 – 24	333	12.0	331	10.4
25 – 34	249	8.9	263	8.3
35 – 44	326	11.7	361	11.4
45 – 54	329	11.8	408	12.9
55 – 64	351	12.6	396	12.5
65 – 74	242	8.7	381	12.0
75 +	154	5.5	289	9.1
Total	2786	100.0	3173	100.0

3. Population by Sex and Marital Status, Age 15 and Over, 1965

Current marital status	Males		Females		Both sexes	
	No.	%	No.	%	No.	%
Never married	401	20.2	414	17.0	815	18.5
Married	1430	72.1	1427	58.7	2857	64.7
Widowed	79	4.0	450	18.5	529	12.0
Separated	14	0.7	27	1.1	41	0.9
Divorced	60	3.0	111	4.6	171	3.9
Total	1984	100.0	2429	99.9	4413	100.0

4. Population by Sex and Occupation of Head of Household (Hollingshead), 1965

Occupational position	Males		Females		Both sexes
	No.	%	No.	%	%
I	162	5.8	227	7.2	6.5
II	214	7.8	296	9.3	8.6
III	615	22.1	746	23.5	22.8
IV	249	8.9	330	10.4	9.7
V	1029	36.9	963	30.3	33.4
VI	392	14.1	440	13.9	14.0
VII	125	4.5	171	5.4	5.0
Total	2786	100.1	3173	100.0	100.0

5. Households by Size and Population by Size of Household, 1965

Size of household	Households		Persons	
	No.	%	No.	%
1	591	26.6	591	9.9
2	755	34.0	1510	25.3
3	286	12.9	858	14.4
4	243	11.0	972	16.3
5	172	7.8	860	14.4
6	93	4.2	558	9.4
7	46	2.1	322	5.4
8	16	0.7	128	2.1
9	8	0.4	72	1.2
10-15	8	0.4	88	1.5
Total	2218	100.1	5959	99.9

6. Household Types, 1965 (Based on 20% Sample)

Household type	No.	%
Husband-wife	770	34.6
Husband-wife-children	750	33.7
Mother-children	115	5.2
Father-children	20	0.9
Female alone	365	16.4
Male alone	150	6.7
Adults, not husband-wife	55	2.5
Total	2225	100.0

7. The Study of Values

The Kluckhohn-Strodtbeck (1961) instrument used for testing the values of high school students and teachers is a schedule of 22 human situations which determines the subject's attitude toward each of four orientations. Each item of the schedule first describes a life situation common to rural or folk societies and then gives alternative solutions for the subjects to choose from. A test of the human nature orientation was not given by Kluckholn and Strodtbeck.

In order to apply the instrument to the high school population on the Vineyard, it was necessary to decrease the time of administering the test so that it could be given within a class session. This was done by using only three stories for each of the four orientations, thereby cutting the number of stories from 22 to 12. Thus, each subject had three chances to react to his choice of value within each orientation. If he chose two or three solutions indicating the same attitude, this was recorded as his value for that orientation. If he chose solutions indicating no clear preference, no dominant value for that orientation was recorded.

8. Values of American Middle Class and Martha's Vineyard Adults

Orientation	American middle class[a]	Martha's Vineyard adults[b] (estimated)	Fifteen island teachers (tested)
Relational	Ind > Coll > Lin	Coll > Ind > Lin	Ind > Coll > Lin
Time	Fut > Pres > Past	Pres > Past > Fut	Fut > Pres > Past
Man-nature	Over > Subj > With	Subj > With > Over	Over > With > Subj
Activity	Doing > Being	Being = Doing	Doing > Being
Human nature	Mixed > Evil > Good	Evil > Mixed > Good	

a. GAP (1970).

b. Censensus of estimates of 18 observers: 16 teachers, 1 public health nurse, 1 psychiatrist.

9. Values of Martha's Vineyard High School Seniors

Orientation	Males (tested)	Females (tested)	Both sexes (tested)
Relational	Coll > Ind > Lin	Coll > Ind > Lin	Coll > Ind > Lin
Time	Fut ≥ Pres > Past	Pres ≥ Fut > Past	Pres = Fut > Past
Man-nature	Over > With > Subj	Over > With > Subj	Over > With > Subj
Activity	Doing ≥ Being	Being = Doing	Doing = Being

Statistical method was that of total item patterning using rank correlation technique (Kluckhohn and Strodtbeck 1961).
= equal preference
> preference at probability of 0.05 or less
≥ more frequent response but not at 0.05 level
Example: "Fut ≥ Pres > Past" means Future a more frequent response than Present, but not at 0.05 level; Future and Present both more frequent than Past at 0.05 level or less.

10. Values of Young and Adult Islanders

Orientation	High school students (tested)	Adults[a] (estimated)
Relational	Coll > Ind > Lin	Coll > Ind > Lin
Time	Pres = Fut > Past	Pres > Past > Fut
Man-nature	Over > With > Subj	Subj > With > Over
Activity	Doing = Being	Being = Doing

a. Consensus of estimates of 18 observers: 16 teachers, 1 public health nurse, 1 psychiatrist.

11. The Prevalence of Psychiatric Disorder in General Practice

The two studies of psychiatric disorder in general practice reported were based on records of the practices of five of the six practitioners practicing on the island when the studies were done. Their cooperation was readily secured. That of the sixth practitioner, who was then also the local surgeon, was not sought for reasons given in Chapter 8.

During each study, the practitioners reported at monthly intervals both demographic data and the psychiatric diagnoses for all those seen for significant psychiatric disorder. A patient was considered to be a psychiatric patient when the primary condition for which he consulted his practitioner was psychiatric. That there can be congruence between psychiatrists and general practitioners as to what is or is not psychiatric morbidity has been demonstrated (Rawnsley 1966), and such congruence was assured in this study by the data collection method used.

To avoid bias for a particular diagnosis and to indicate the wide variety of possibilities, the checklist on which the physician noted the diagnosis of his patient contained a list of possibilities. Despite this precaution, it can hardly be hoped that diagnostic bias on the part of individual practitioners was entirely avoided. A tendency to use a particular diagnostic entity may be related to the physician's training, to his unconscious attitudes toward persons with psychiatric disorder, and presumably to many other factors of which we are not aware.

The second device for attempting to avoid diagnostic bias was the face-to-face interview between the general practitioner and the psychiatrist conducting the study. In each case they briefly discussed the patient's symptom pattern, with the psychiatrist the final arbiter as to the diagnosis recorded. Only occasionally did the psychiatrist find it necessary to alter the diagnosis made by the general practitioner. While this technique encouraged a standardization of diagnoses among the five general practitioners taking part in the study, it could not eliminate diagnostic bias on the part of the psychiatrist.

It is likely that the very participation of a practitioner in such a survey will increase his alertness to the presence of psychiatric problems in his patients. This would tend to assure more complete reporting. The danger of overreporting, of identifying nonpsychiatric problems as psychiatric, was guarded against in these studies by the face-to-face psychiatrist-practi-

250
APPENDICES 11-13

tioner meetings. Further, the enlistment of interest in psychiatric problems on the part of the general practitioners was not begun with the initiation of this study; the practitioners and psychiatrist had shared a professional working relationship for two and one-half years before the first study began and had participated in seminars on psychiatric problems in general practice.

12. Psychiatric Disorder in General Practice by Diagnosis and Sex

Diagnosis	Males		Females		Both sexes
	No.	%	No.	%	%
Psychoneurotic disorder	43	32.3	70	40.2	36.8
Personality disorder[a]	54	40.6	36	20.7	29.3
Psychophysiological disorder	25	18.8	49	28.2	24.1
Chronic brain disease	8	6.0	8	4.6	5.2
Psychotic disorder	3	2.3	10	5.7	4.2
Mental deficiency	0	—	1	0.6	0.3
Total	133	100.0	174	100.0	99.9

a. Includes transient situational personality disorders: 37 males and 15 females had alcohol addiction (28 percent of all males and 9 percent of all females).

13. Psychiatric Disorder in General Practice by Age and Sex (Rates per 1000 Population)

Age	Males (n=133)	Females (n=174)	Both sexes[a] (n=307)
0 - 14	8.7	4.0	6.5
15 - 24	48.0	39.3	43.7
25 - 34	76.3	68.4	72.2
35 - 44	76.6	91.4	84.3
45 - 54	63.8	90.7	78.7
55 - 64	65.5	53.0	58.9
65 - 74	62.0	84.0	75.5
75 +	45.5	58.8	54.2
Total	47.7	54.8	51.5

a. Adjusted for sex distribution at each age group.

14. Psychiatric Disorder in General Practice by Current Marital Status, Adults Age 25 and Over (Rates per 1,000 Population)

Current marital status	All persons	Psychiatric patients	Rate/1,000
Never married	360	33	91.7
Married	2763	169	61.2
Separated, divorced, widowed	726	65	89.5

15. Psychiatric Disorder in General Practice by Occupation of Head of Household (Hollingshead; Rates per 1,000 Population in Each Class Position)

Occupational position	Males	Females
I - II	90.4	59.3
III - V	38.6	52.0
VI - VII	62.2	60.6

16. Primary Psychiatric Admissions by Diagnosis

Diagnosis	Period		
	1962-1966 %	1967-1971 %	1972-1973 %
Alcoholic disorder	12.2	12.1	8.5
Psychotic disorder	10.3	7.1	6.4
Psychoneurotic disorder	33.3	23.0	29.7
Personality disorder	17.1	13.2	19.5
Transient situational personality disorder	21.7	31.5	30.0
Organic brain disorder	4.3	2.7	2.1
Mental deficiency	1.1	1.1	1.7
Drug dependency	—	9.3	2.1
Total	100.0	100.0	100.0

17. Average Number of Psychiatric Patients per Year for Two Conditions

Diagnosis	1962-1966	1967-1971	1972-1973
Transient situational personality disorder	15	23	35
Marital maladjustment	3	18	39

18. Primary Psychiatric Admissions by Age (Mean Yearly Rates per 1,000 Population)

Age	1962-1966		1967-1971		1972-1973	
	Males	Females	Males	Females	Males	Females
0 - 14	9.1	4.4	13.4	6.1	20.8	15.1
15 - 24	13.7	13.2	55.1	48.2	57.3	94.9
25 - 34	21.9	33.2	31.9	29.8	74.9	92.1
35 - 44	15.1	11.6	18.5	15.8	21.5	24.2
45 - 54	14.4	12.0	10.5	14.5	17.4	17.5
55 - 64	6.2	8.7	6.0	9.3	6.0	4.6
65 - 74	4.5	5.2	5.1	5.0	5.5	10.1
75 +	4.7	6.9	2.6	4.6	3.3	5.0

19. Primary Psychiatric Admissions by Occupation of Head of Household (Hollingshead) 1967-1971 (Mean Yearly Rates per 1,000 Population)

Occupational position	Males	Females	Both sexes
I - III	19.9	15.9	17.2
IV - V	18.4	17.0	19.9
VI - VII	23.2	15.9	17.8

20. Primary Psychiatric Admissions by Occupational Mobility for Selected Conditions, 1967-1971

Diagnosis	No change	Up	Down	Up	Down
		No.		%/o	
Psychotic disorder	6	5	14	20.0	56.0
Psychoneurotic disorder	22	26	25	35.7	34.2
Personality disorder	16	6	18	15.0	45.1
Alcoholic disorder	13	10	16	25.6	41.0
Marital maladjustment	23	22	34	27.9	43.0

21. Primary Psychiatric Admissions by Current Marital Status, Ages 15-54, 1967-1971 (Mean Yearly Rates per 1,000 Population)

Current marital status[a]	Rate/1,000
Never married	61.2
Married	18.7
Separated	135.7
Divorced	31.6

a. Too few admissions of widows or widowers for meaningful rates.

22. Primary Psychiatric Admissions by Place of Residence Five Years before Admission, 1967-1971 (Mean Yearly Rates per 1,000 Population)

Residence five years before admission	Rate/1,000
Same house on island	12.4
Other house on island	17.0
Same state	27.8
Different state	52.8

23. Psychiatric Disorder in Psychiatric and General Practice by Sex and Age

Age	Males[a]		Females[b]	
	Psychiatric practice	General practice	Psychiatric practice	General practice
0 - 14	59	7	24	3
15 - 24	40	16	44	13
25 - 34	40	19	70	18
35 - 44	39	25	38	33
45 - 54	34	21	39	37
55 - 64	18	23	25	21
65 +	14	22	30	49
Total	244	133	270	174

a. Males: $X^2 = 37.8$; df, 6; P <.001
b. Females: $X^2 = 50.8$; df, 6; P < .001

24. Psychiatric Disorder in Psychiatric and General Practice by Diagnosis

Diagnosis	Psychiatrist		General practitioner	
	No.	%	No.	%
Alcoholic disorder	43	12.3	52	16.9
Psychotic disorder	36	10.2	13	4.2
Psychoneurotic disorder	117	33.4	113	36.8
Personality disorder	136	38.8	38	12.4
Organic brain disorder	15	4.3	16	5.2
Mental deficiency	4	1.1	1	0.3
Psychophysiological disorder	—	—	74	24.1
Total	351	100.1	307	99.9

25. Psychiatric and Parapsychiatric Events by Type and Sex, with Sex Ratio, 1964-1968 (Rates per 1,000 Population)[a]

Predicament	Males		Females		Both sexes		Sex Ratio Male rate ÷ female rate
	No.	Rate	No.	Rate	No.	Rate	
Jail	13	4.7	1	0.3	14	2.3	15.7
Probation	110	39.5	11	3.5	121	20.3	11.3
Acute public alcoholism	91	32.7	11	3.5	102	17.1	9.3
Fine	249	89.4	36	11.3	285	47.8	7.9
Juvenile delinquency	26	9.3	4	1.3	30	5.0	7.2
Single-car accident	83	29.8	19	6.0	102	17.1	5.0
Auto license suspension	33	11.8	8	2.5	41	6.9	4.7
School disciplinary problem	124	44.5	36	11.3	160	26.9	3.9
Suicide	6	2.2	2	0.6	8	1.3	3.7
Chronic alcoholism	81	29.1	36	11.3	117	19.6	2.6
Mental hospitalization	49	17.6	47	14.8	96	16.1	1.2
Premarital pregnancy	39	14.0	37	11.7	76	12.8	1.2
School under- achievement	78	28.0	89	28.0	167	28.0	1.0
Marital dissolution	54	19.4	63	19.9	117	19.6	1.0
Suicide attempt	8	2.9	10	3.2	18	3.0	0.9
Psychiatric episode	144	51.7	216	68.1	360	60.4	0.8
General population		2786		3173		5959	

a. Number of predicaments total 1,814, since some of the 1,317 persons experienced more than one event over the five-year period of the study.

26. Males Experiencing Psychiatric and Parapsychiatric Events by Age, 1964-1968 (Rates per 1,000 Population for Each Age Group)[a]

Predicament	0-14	15-24	25-34	35-44	45-54	55-64	65+
Jail	—	**30.0**	—	6.1	3.0	—	—
Probation	—	**126.1**	76.3	42.9	54.7	34.2	12.6
Acute public alcoholism	—	63.1	52.2	**67.5**	60.8	25.6	15.2
Fine	—	**366.4**	188.8	79.8	72.9	34.2	45.5
Juvenile delinquency	16.2	**36.0**	—	—	—	—	—
Single-car accident	—	**117.1**	68.3	33.7	12.2	8.5	15.2
Auto license suspension	—	**57.1**	12.0	18.4	9.1	—	5.1
School disciplinary problem	22.4	**318.3**	—	—	—	—	—
Suicide	—	3.0	—	3.1	3.0	5.7	2.5
Chronic alcoholism	—	—	20.0	58.3	72.9	**74.1**	17.7
Mental hospitalization	1.2	9.0	24.1	**39.9**	30.4	31.3	12.6
Premarital pregnancy	—	**90.1**	32.1	3.1	—	—	—
School under-achievement	6.2	**219.2**	—	—	—	—	—
Marital dissolution	—	21.0	**52.2**	49.1	33.4	17.1	2.5
Suicide attempt	—	**15.0**	—	9.2	—	—	—
Psychiatric episode	42.4	66.1	64.3	**82.8**	63.8	39.9	25.5
General population	802	333	249	326	329	351	396

a. Peak rate for a predicament is show in boldface. If peak rate is based on five or fewer events, a rate is not shown.

27. Females Experiencing Psychiatric and Parapsychiatric Events by Age, 1964-1968 (Rates per 1,000 Population for Each Age Group)[a]

Predicament	0-14	15-24	25-34	35-44	45-54	55-64	65 +
Jail	—	—	3.8	—	—	—	—
Probation	—	9.1	7.6	5.5	9.8	—	—
Acute public alcoholism	—	6.0	3.8	5.5	**14.7**	—	—
Fine	—	**39.3**	26.6	16.6	17.2	—	4.5
Juvenile delinquency	—	12.1	—	—	—	—	—
Single-car accident	—	**30.2**	26.6	2.8	2.5	—	—
Auto license suspension	—	9.1	7.6	5.5	—	—	1.5
School disciplinary problem	18.8	**66.5**	—	—	—	—	—
Suicide	—	—	—	2.8	—	2.5	—
Chronic alcoholism	—	—	7.6	22.2	**36.8**	20.2	4.5
Mental hospitalization	—	9.1	15.2	19.4	**39.2**	15.2	16.4
Premarital pregnancy	—	**102.7**	7.6	2.8	—	—	—
School under-achievement	9.4	**247.7**	—	—	—	—	—
Marital dissolution	—	36.3	**72.2**	36.0	34.3	10.1	1.5
Suicide attempt	—	12.1	15.2	2.8	2.5	—	—
Psychiatric episode	21.5	120.8	**186.5**	85.9	93.1	45.5	35.8
General population	744	331	263	361	408	396	670

a. Peak rate for each predicament is shown in boldface. If peak rate is based on five or fewer events, a rate is not shown.

28. Persons with Psychiatric and Parapsychiatric Events by Occupation of Head of Household (Hollingshead) and Test of Significance, 1964-1968 (Rates per 1,000 Population)

Predicament	Occupational position						Chi-square test P
	I-II		IV-V		VI-VII		
	No.	Rate	No.	Rate	No.	Rate	
Probation	15	6.6	60	23.3	46	40.8	.001
Acute public alcoholism	15	6.6	54	21.0	33	29.3	.001
Fines	72	31.9	128	49.8	78	69.1	.001
Marital dissolution	23	10.2	58	22.6	34	30.1	.001
Premarital pregnancy	11	4.9	43	16.7	19	16.8	.001
Auto accident	24	10.6	46	17.9	30	26.6	.01
Auto license suspension[a]	7	3.1	20	7.8	13	11.5	.02
Jail	—	—	7	2.7	7	6.2	.05
Mental hospitalization	29	12.8	39	15.1	27	23.9	.05
Juvenile delinquency	6	2.7	14	5.4	10	8.9	.05
Psychiatric treatment	155	68.6	133	51.7	72	63.8	.05
School underachievement	46	20.4	74	28.8	35	31.0	.10
Suicide attempt	5	2.2	11	4.3	2	1.8	.5-.3
School disciplinary problem	55	24.3	75	29.2	27	23.9	.7-.5
Chronic alcoholism	40	17.7	56	21.8	21	18.6	.8-.7
Suicide	3	1.3	3	1.2	2	1.8	—
General population	2260		2571		1128		

a. One-year prevalence rate; all others are five-year rates.

29. Psychiatric Patients, Population at Risk, and Their Parapsychiatric Events, 1964-1968

Subject groups	All subjects[a] No.	With para-psychiatric events[a] %	Parapsy-chiatric events No.	Mean para-psychiatric score
Psychiatric patients	285	33.0	277	0.97
Population at risk	4519	15.0	1290	0.29

a. $X^2 = 56.0$; df = 1; P < .001

30. Parapsychiatric Scores for Persons with and without Psychiatric Consultation by Sex

Predicaments	Subjects No.	Mean parapsychiatric score
Both sexes[a]		
Psychiatric	94	2.86
Nonpsychiatric	572	1.67
Men[b]		
Psychiatric	51	3.86
Nonpsychiatric	405	1.84
Women[c]		
Psychiatric	43	1.67
Nonpsychiatric	167	1.27

a. Both Sexes: z = 3.165; P < .002.
b. Men: z = 3.45; P < .0005
c. Women: z = 1.21; P = ns.

31. Parapsychiatric Scores by Psychiatric Diagnosis

Predicaments	Subjects No.	Mean parapsychiatric score
Psychiatric		
Organic brain disorder	2	1.00
Psychotic disorder	6	2.00
Psychophysiological disorder	2	2.00
Psychoneurotic disorder	25	1.80
Personality disorder	7	1.57
Sociopathic disorder	35	4.83
Transient situational personality disorder	17	1.53
Nonpsychiatric	572	1.67

32. Persons in Predicament, Parapsychiatric Scores and Psychiatric Subjects by Sex

Sex	All predicament subjects[a]		Psychiatric subjects only[b]	
	No.	Parapsychiatric score	No.	% of all predicament subjects
Males	544	1.80	141	25.9
Females	320	0.97	144	45.0
Total	864		285	

a. $z = 6.77$; $P < .0001$
b. $X^2 = 31.5$; $df = 1$; $P < .0001$

33. Persons in Predicament, Parapsychiatric Scores and Psychiatric Subjects by Age

Age	All predicament subjects[a]		Psychiatric subjects only[b]	
	No.	Parapsychiatric score	No.	% of all predicament subjects
5 - 14	74	0.62	36	48.6
15 - 24	307	1.75	33	10.7
25 - 34	136	1.30	54	39.7
35 - 44	108	1.52	48	44.4
45 - 54	103	1.54	53	51.5
55 - 64	79	1.99	36	45.6
65 - 74	42	0.88	18	42.9
75 +	15	0.81	7	46.7
Total	864		285	

a. $F = 4.29$, df 7,857; P   .001
b. $X^2 = 110.8$; df = 7; P   .0001

34. Persons in Predicament, Parapsychiatric Scores, and Psychiatric Subjects by Occupational Position (Hollingshead)

Occupational position	All predicament subjects[a]		Psychiatric subjects only[b]	
	No.	Parapsychiatric score	No.	% of all predicament subjects
I	40	1.10	17	42.5
II	55	0.69	33	60.0
III	169	1.04	68	40.2
IV	78	1.43	22	28.2
V	287	1.92	83	28.9
VI	155	1.41	40	25.8
VII	71	1.99	21	29.6
Total	855		284	

a. $F = 7.20$; df 6,848; P < .0001
b. $X^2 = 30.6$; df = 6; P < .001

35. Selection of Control Samples for Multipredicament Family Study

Systematically Sampled Households. In order to determine the demographic characteristics peculiar to multiproblem families, a systematic
sample of 63 nonpredicament households was drawn from the file of all
island households for comparison. The 2,218 household cards were first
segregated by town, with the towns arranged in alphabetical order. Within
each town, the household cards were arranged in alphabetical order by
family name of head of household. From a random start, every fourteenth
card was scrutinized. If the card was one of either a single-person household or a multiple household in which one or more of the subjects had
experienced a predicament during the five-year period of the study, it was
returned to the file and the next card scrutinized until one meeting the
criteria was reached. The fourteenth card after that one was again subjected to the same procedure.

This procedure is equivalent to having removed from the file the cards of
all single-person households and all predicament households before the
systematic selection process was begun. It was estimated that, with these
two disqualifications, the use of every fourteenth card would yield 63
appropriate households close to the end of the file. This proved to be the
case. The procedure made certain that the families selected would be a
fair geographic and ethnic representation of the population at large. The
two large segments of the population, Portuguese and "old American,"
each contain a great many individuals bearing the same family name,
Portuguese in one case and old American in the other. The systematic
selection procedure therefore assured, to a greater degree than might a
random sample, that one common Portuguese or old American name would
not be overly represented. Thus, the two groups chosen were as far as
possible selected only with respect to the presence of predicaments in one
group and not in the other, and any significant differences between the two
should be related to this distinction.

Matched Control Households. The systematically selected households
and the multiproblem households were likely to be different in size of
household, age, and social class position. In fact, the systematically
selected sample was designed to determine to what extent the two groups
differed in these respects. The use of such a control sample, however, may
fail to give equitable comparative information with respect to social class
position. In the present study, the index of social class position used was
the occupation of the head of the household by Hollingshead's classification. Yet occupational position is significantly influenced by the sex of the
head of the house. Further, occupational level often increases with age. As
a result, two samples that differ with respect to the sex and age of the

heads of household might show significant social class differences due to those variables alone rather than to the one at issue—in this case, whether a household has a high rate of predicaments or none at all.

In order to eliminate the possible hidden effects of differences in sex and age between the multiproblem and the systematically selected households, a second control sample was chosen to match the multiproblem household with respect to family composition and ages of its members. A pilot review made clear that precise matches of age and sex for each family would be impossible because of the great number of possible combinations of ages and sexes of those in any one household. Instead, each multiproblem household was matched with another, whose two oldest members, usually the parents, had ages within three years of those of the multiproblem household, and which had the same number of children. It was assumed that by matching adult age and the number of children, the composition of the two groups would turn out to be similar with respect to age and sex of siblings. This proved to be the case.

The actual process of selecting a matched family for each multiproblem family was begun at the site in the file of the multiproblem family's card. From that point on, the first following card with two adults whose ages were within three years of those of the multiproblem household and with the same number of chidren was chosen, with the further condition that none of the matched family members had had predicaments during the five-year period of study.

ℬ𝒾𝒷𝓁𝒾ℴℊ𝓇𝒶𝓅𝒽𝓎

Abramson, J. H. 1966. Emotional Disorder, Status Inconsistency, and Migration. *Milbank Mem. Fund Quart.* 44: Part 1, 23-48.

Allodi, F. A., and Coates, D. B. 1971. Social Stress, Psychiatric Symptoms, and Help-Seeking Patterns. *Canad. Psychiat. Assoc. J.* 18:153-158.

Anderson, O. W., and Feldman, J. J. 1956. *Family Medical Costs and Voluntary Health Insurance: A Nationwide Survey.* New York: McGraw-Hill.

Arensberg, Conrad M. 1937. *The Irish Countryman: An Anthropological Study.* New York: Macmillan.

Bahn, Anita K. 1962. Psychiatric Case Register Conference. *Public Health Rep.* 77:1071-1076.

Bahn, A. K., Gardner, E. A., Alltop, F., Knatterud, G. L., and Solomon, M. 1966. Admission and Prevalence Rates for Psychiatric Facilities in Four Register Areas. *Am. J. Public Health* 56:2033-2055.

Baldwin, J. A. 1971. Five-Year Incidence of Reported Psychiatric Disorder, in Baldwin, J. A., ed. *Aspects of the Epidemiology of Mental Illness: Studies in Record Linkage.* Boston: Little, Brown.

Baldwin, J. A., Innes G., Millar, W. M., Sharp, G. A., and Dorricott, N. A. 1965. A Psychiatric Case Register in North-East Scotland. *Brit. J. Prev. Soc. Med.* 19:38-42.

Bellak, Leopold. 1964. Community Psychiatry: The Third Psychiatric Revolution, in Bellak, L., ed. *Handbook of Community Psychiatry and Community Mental Health.* New York: Grune and Stratton.

Bentsen, Bent G. 1970. *Illness and General Practice.* Oslo: Universitetsförlaget.

Bentz, W. K., Edgerton, J. W., and Kherlopian, M. 1969. Perceptions of Mental Illness among People in a Rural Area. *Ment. Hygiene* 53:459-465

265

Bille, Mogens. 1963. The Influence of Distance on Admissions to Mental Hospitals. *Acta Psychiat. Scand.*, Suppl. 169, 39:226-233.

Bing, S. R., and Roosevelt, S. S. 1970. *The Quality of Justice in the Lower Criminal Courts of Metropolitan Boston.* Boston: Lawyers Committee of Civil Rights Under Law.

Briggs, L. Vernon. 1928. Mental Ills Appearing in Barnstable, Dukes, and Nantucket Counties, Massachusetts 1850-1917. *Am. J. Psychiat.* 7:607-627.

Brown, A. B. 1962. Multi-Problem Families. Mimeo. Berkeley, Cal.: Council of Social Planning.

Bruhn, J. G., Brandt, E. N., and Shackelford, M. 1966. Incidence of Treated Mental Illness in Three Pennsylvania Communities. *Am. J. Public Health* 56:871-883.

Buber, Martin. 1965. *Between Man and Man.* New York: Macmillan.

Buck, C., and Laughton, K. B. 1959. Family Patterns of Illness: The Effect of Psychoneurosis in the Parent upon Illness in the Child. *Acta Psychiat. Scand.* 34:165-175.

Caplan, Gerald. 1964. *Principles of Preventive Psychiatry.* New York: Basic Books.

Cardoza, V. G., Ackerly, W. C., and Leighton, A. H. 1975. Improving Mental Health Through Community Action. *Comm. Mental Health J.* 11:215-227.

Carstairs, G. M., and Brown, G. W. 1958. A Census of Psychiatric Cases in Two Contrasting Communities. *J. Ment. Sci.* 104:72-81.

Chen, E., and Cobb, S. 1960. Family Structure in Relation to Health and Disease. *J. Chronic Dis.* 12:544-567.

CMF (Council on Multi-Problem Families). 1960. *Multi-Problem Families: A New Name or a New Problem?* New York: State Charities Aid Association.

Cooley, Chas. H. 1956. *Social Organization and Human Nature and the Social Order.* Glencoe, Ill.: The Free Press.

Cooper, B., and Brown, A. C. 1967. Psychiatric Practice in Great Britian and America: A Comparative Study. *Brit. J. Psychiat.* 113:625-636.

Cooper, B., and Morgan, H. G. 1973. *Epidemiological Psychiatry.* Springfield, Ill.: Charles C Thomas.

Cottrell, Leonard S. 1976. The Competent Community, in Kaplan, B. H., Wilson, R. N., and Leighton, A. H., eds. *Further Explorations in Social Psychiatry.* New York: Basic Books.

Crèvecoeur, J. Hector St. John de. 1912. *Letters from an American Farmer.* New York: E. P. Dutton.

Cummings, E., and Cummings, J. 1957. *Closed Ranks.* Cambridge: Harvard University Press.

Curtis, J. L., Simon, M., Boykin, F. L., and Noe, E. R. 1964. Observations on

Twenty-nine Multi-problem Families. *Amer. J. Orthopsychiat.*
34:510-516.

Curtis, W. Robert. 1973. Community Human Service Networks: New Roles
for Mental Health Workers. *Psychiat. Annals* 3:23-42

Davies, Vernon. 1945. The Development of a Scale to Rate Attitudes of
Community Satisfaction. *Rural Sociol.* 10:246-255.

DCPEDC (Dukes County Planning and Economic Development Commission).
1972. An Analysis of Local Housing Problems. Mimeo. Oak Bluffs,
Mass.: Dukes County Planning and Economic Development Commission.

deSole, D. E., Singer, P., and Roseman, J. 1967. Community Psychiatry and
the Syndrome of Psychiatric Culture Shock—The Emergence of a New
Functional Disorder. *Soc. Sci. and Med.* 1:401-418.

Devens, Samuel Adams, 1838. Sketches of Martha's Vineyard and Other
Reminiscences of Travel at Home, Etc. Boston: James Munroe and Co.

Devitt, M., et al. 1953. The Predicament Study: Survey of Mental Health
Problems Encountered in Wellesley by the Various Professions and
Agencies in the Month of March 1953. Mimeo. Wellesley Hills, Mass.:
Human Relations Service of Wellesley.

Dohrenwend, B. P., and Dohrenwend, B. S. 1969. *Social Status and Psychological Disorder: A Causal Inquiry.* New York: John Wiley and
Sons.

DSM (*Diagnostic and Statistical Manual, Mental Disorders*). 1952. 1st ed.
Washington, D.C.: American Psychiatric Assn.

Duane, E., Thomas, T., Logothetti, T., and Cox, S. 1974. *City Size and the
Quality of Life.* Washington, D.C.: U. S. Government Printing Office.

Durkheim, Emile. 1951. *Suicide.* Glencoe, Ill.: The Free Press.

Eaton, J. W., and Weil, R. J. 1955. *Culture and Mental Disorders: A Comparative Study of the Hutterites and Other Populations.* Glencoe, Ill.:
The Free Press.

Edgerton, Robert B. 1969. On the "Recognition" of Mental Illness, in Plog,
S. C., and Edgerton, R. B., eds. *Changing Perspectives in Mental Illness.* New York: Holt, Rinehart and Winston.

Eelkema, R. C., Brosseau, J., Koshnick, B. S., and McGee, C. 1970. A
Statistical Study of the Relationship Between Mental Illness and
Traffic Accidents: A Pilot Study. *Am. J. Public Health* 60:459-469.

Eisdorfer, C., Albrocchi, J., and Young, R. F. 1968. Principles of Community
Mental Health in a Rural Setting: The Halifax County Program. *Comm.
Ment. Health J.* 41:211-220.

Fink, R., Shapiro, S., Goldensohn, S. S., and Daily, E. F. 1969. The "Filter
Down" Process to Psychotherapy in a Group Practice Medical Care
Program. *Am. J. Public Health* 59:245-260.

Finn, R., and Huston, P. E. 1966. Emotional and Mental Symptoms in Private Medical Practice. *J. Iowa Med. Soc.* 56:138-143.

Frankenberg, Ronald. 1966. *Communities in Britain.* London: Penguin Books.

Fromm, Erich. 1941. *Escape from Freedom.* New York: Rinehart.

————. 1955. *The Sane Society.* New York: Holt, Rinehart and Winston.

GAP (Group for the Advancement of Psychiatry). 1970. *Treatment of Families in Conflict.* New York: Science House.

Gardner, E. A., Miles, H. C., Iker, J., and Romano, J. 1963. A Cumulative Register of Psychiatric Services in a Community. *Am. J. Public Health* 53:1269-1277.

Goldhamer, H., and Marshall, A. W. 1953. *Psychosis and Civilization.* Glencoe, Ill.: The Free Press.

Gottman, Jean. 1961. *Megalopolis: The Urbanized Seaboard of the United States.* New York: Twentieth Century Fund.

Greene, E. B., and Harrington, V. D. 1932. *American Population Before the Federal Census of 1790.* New York: Columbia University Press.

Grinker, R. R., and Spiegel, J. P. 1945. *Men under Stress.* Philadelphia: Blakiston.

Gurin, G., Veroff, J., and Field, S. 1960. *Americans View Their Mental Health.* New York: Basic Books.

Hagnell, Olle. 1966. *A Prospective Study of the Incidence of Mental Disorder.* Stockholm: Svenska Bokförlaget.

Hallock, A. C. K., and Vaughan, W. T., Jr. 1956. A Dynamic Component of Community Mental Health Practice. *Am. J. Orthopsychiat.* 26:691-708.

Halpert, H. P., and Silverman, C. 1967. Approaches to Interagency Cooperation. *Hosp. and Comm. Psychiat.* 18:84-87.

Hamilton, Edith. 1930. *The Greek Way to Western Civilization.* New York: W. W. Norton.

Haug, M. B., and Sussman, M. B. 1971. The Indiscriminate State of Social Class Measurement. *Social Forces* 49:549-663.

Helgason, Tómas. 1964. *Epidemiology of Mental Disorders in Iceland.* Copenhagen: Munksgaard.

Heller, Mary. 1975. Mental Health Services for Families New to the Community. *Hosp. and Comm. Psychiat.* 26:493-495.

Hirschowitz, Ralph G. 1973. Crisis Theory: A Formulation. *Psychiat. Annals* 3:33-47.

Hollingshead, August B. 1957. Two Factor Index of Social Position. Mimeo. New Haven: A. B. Hollingshead.

Hollingshead, A. B., and Redlich, F. C. 1958. *Social Class and Mental Illness: A Community Study.* New York: John Wiley and Sons.

Horney, Karen. 1939. *New Ways In Psychoanalysis.* New York: W. W. Norton.

Howe, Louisa P. 1964. The Concept of the Community: Some Implications for the Development of Community Psychiatry, in Bellak, L., ed. *Handbook of Community Psychiatry and Community Mental Health.* New York: Grune and Stratton.

Hughes, C. C., Tremblay, M-A., Rapoport, R. N., and Leighton, A. H. 1960. People of Cove and Woodlot. New York: Basic Books.

Jackson, Elton F. 1962. Status Consistency and Symptoms of Stress. *Amer. Sociol. Review* 27:469-480.

Jahoda, Marie. 1958. *Current Concepts of Positive Mental Health.* New York: Basic Books.

Jarvis, Edward. 1971. *Insanity and Idiocy in Massachusetts: Report of the Commission on Lunacy, 1855.* Cambridge: Harvard University Press.

Jesser, Clinton, 1963. Community Satisfaction Patterns of Professionals in Rural Areas. *Rural Sociol.* 32:56-69.

Johnson, R. L., and Knop, E. 1970. Rural-Urban Differentials in Community Satisfaction. *Rural Sociol.* 35:544-548.

Kaplan, H. B., and Pokorny, A. D. 1969. Self-Derogation and Psychosocial Adjustment. *J. Nerv. Ment. Dis.* 149:421-434.

Kellert, S. R. 1971. The Lost Community in Community Psychiatry. *Psychiat.* 34:168-179.

Kellner, Robert. 1963. *Family Ill Health.* Springfield, Ill.: Charles C Thomas.

Kessel, W. I. N. 1960. Psychiatric Morbidity in a London General Practice. *Brit. J. Prev. Soc. Med.* 14:16-22.

————. 1962. Conducting a Psychiatric Survey in General Practice, in *The Burden on the Community.* London: Oxford University Press.

Kessel, N., and Hassall, C. 1965. Psychiatric Outpatients in Plymouth: An Area Service Analyzed. *Brit. J. Psychiat.* 111:10-17.

Kleiner, R. J., and Dalgard, D. S. 1975. Social Mobility and Psychiatric Disorder: A Re-evaluation and Interpretation. *Am. J. Psychother.* 29:150-165.

Kluckhohn, Florence. 1950. Dominant and Substitute Profiles of Cultural Orientations: Their Significance for the Analysis of Social Stratification. *Social Forces* 28:376-394.

Kluckhohn, F. R., and Strodtbeck, F. L. 1961. *Variations in Value Orientations.* Evanston, Ill.: Row, Peterson.

Kramer, M. 1966. Some Implications of Trends in the Usage of Psychiatric Facilities for Community Mental Health Programs and Related Research. U. S. Public Health Service Publication No. 1434. Washington, D. C.: U. S. Government Printing Office.

Kreitman, N., Collins, J., Nelson, B., and Troop, J. 1970a. Neurosis and Marital Interaction: I. Personality and Symptoms. *Brit. J. Psychiat.* 117:33-46.

————. 1970b. Neurosis and Marital Interaction: II. Time Sharing and

Social Activity. *Brit. J. Psychiat.* 117:47-58.

Labov, William. 1963. The Social Motivation of a Sound Change. *Word* 19:273-309.

_____. 1972. On the Mechanism of Linguistic Change, in Labov, Wm., ed. *Sociolinguistic Patterns*. Philadelphia: University of Pennsylvania Press.

Langner, Thomas S. 1962. A Twenty-two Item Screening Score of Psychiatric Symptoms Indicating Impairment. *J. Health and Hum. Behav.* 3:269-276.

Langner, T. S., and Michael, S. T. 1963. *Life Stress and Mental Health*. Vol. II of *The Midtown Manhattan Study*. New York: The Free Press.

Leighton, Alexander H. 1959. *My Name Is Legion*. New York: Basic Books.

_____. 1965. Poverty and Social Change. *Scientific American* 212:21-27.

_____. 1967a. Is Social Environment a Cause of Psychiatric Disorder? in Monroe, R. R., Klee, G. D., and Brody, E. B., eds. *Psychiatric Epidemiology and Mental Health Planning*. Psychiatric Research Report 22. Washington, D.C.: American Psychiatric Association.

_____. 1967b. Some Notes on Preventive Psychiatry. *Canad. Psychiat. Assn. J.* 12:Suppl. 43-50.

Leighton, A. H., and Longaker, A. L. 1957. The Psychiatric Clinic as a Community Innovation, in Leighton, A. H., Clauson, J. A., and Wilson, R. N., eds. *Explorations in Social Psychiatry*. New York: Basic Books.

Leighton, Dorothea C. 1956. The Distribution of Psychiatric Symptoms in a Small Town. *Am. J. Psychiat.* 112:716-723.

Leighton, D. C., Harding, J. S., Macklin, D. B., Macmillan, A. M., and Leighton, A. H. 1963. *The Character of Danger*. New York: Basic Books.

Lindemann, Erich. 1941. Symptomatology and Management of Acute Grief. *Am. J. Psychiat.* 101:141-148.

Lindenthal, J. J., Claudewell, S. T., and Myers, J. K. 1971. Psychological Status and the Perception of Primary and Secondary Support from the Social Milieu in Time of Crisis. *J. Nerv. Ment. Dis.* 153:92-98.

Lippmann, Walter. 1955. *The Public Philosphy*. Boston: Little, Brown.

Llewellyn-Thomas, E. 1960. The Prevalence of Psychiatric Symptoms Within an Island Fishing Village. *Canad. Med. Assn. J.* 83:197-204.

Locke, B. Z., Finucane, D. L., and Hassler, F. 1967. *Emotionally Disturbed Patients under Care of Private Non-psychiatric Physicians*. Psychiatric Research Report 22. Washington, D.C.: American Psychiatric Association.

Locke, B. Z., and Gardner, E. A. 1969. Psychiatric Disorders in Medical Practice: A Survey of General Practitioners and Internists in a Community. *Public Health Rep.* 84:167-173.

Locke, B. Z., Krantz, G., and Kramer, M. 1966. Psychiatric Need and

Demand in a Prepaid Group Practice Program. *Am. J. Public Health* 56:895-904.

Macmillian, Allister M. 1957. The Health Opinion Survey: Technique for Estimating Prevalence of Psychoneurotic and Related Types of Disorder in Communities. *Psychol. Reports, Monograph Suppl.* 7, 3:325-339.

Malzberg, B., and Lee, E. 1956. *Migration and Mental Disease.* New York: Social Sciences Research Council.

Mangus, A. R., and Seeley, J. R. 1955. Mental Health Needs in a Rural and Semi-rural Area of Ohio, in Rose, A. M., ed. *Mental Health and Mental Disorder.* New York: W. W. Norton.

Mannheim, Karl. 1936. *Ideology and Utopia: An Introduction to the Sociology of Knowledge.* New York: Harcourt, Brace.

Maritan, Jacques. 1966. *The Person and the Common Good.* Notre Dame, Ind.: University of Notre Dame Press.

Mass. Census. 1965. The State Census of 1965. Boston: Commonwealth of Massachusetts.

———. 1975. The State Census of 1975. Personal communication. Boston: Commonwealth of Massachusetts.

Mazer, Milton. 1965. The Human Predicaments of an Island Population, in Masserman, J., ed. *Communication and Community.* Vol. VIII of *Science and Psychoanalysis.* New York: Grune and Stratton.

———. 1966. A Psychiatric and Parapsychiatric Register for an Island Community. *Arch. Gen. Psychiat.* 14:366-371.

———. 1967a. Psychiatric Disorder in General Practice: The Experience of an Island Community. *Am. J. Psychiat.* 124:609-615.

———. 1967b. Premarital Pregnancy in an Island Community. Mimeo. Edgartown, Mass.: Martha's Vineyard Mental Health Center.

———. 1969a. The Total Demand for Psychiatric Service in an Island Community. *Comm. Mental Health J.* 5:320-330.

———. 1969b. Psychiatric Disorders in the General Practices of an Island. *Medical Care* 7:372-378.

———. 1970a. Psychiatric Disorders in Young Women: The Public Health Implications. *Ment. Hygiene* 54:436-439.

———. 1970b. The Therapist in the Community, in Grunebaum, H., ed. *The Practice of Community Mental Health.* Boston: Little, Brown.

———. 1970c. Predicting the Demand for Psychiatric Services. *Mass. Ment. Health J.* 1:25-31.

———. 1972a. Two Ways of Expressing Psychological Disorder: The Experience of a Demarcated Population. *Am. J. Psychiat.* 128:933-938.

———. 1972b. Parapsychiatric Events as Expressions of Psychiatric Disorder. *Arch. Gen. Psychiat.* 27:270-273.

———. 1972c. Characteristics of Multi-problem Households: A Study in

Psychosocial Epidemiology. *Amer. J. Orthopsychiat.* 42:792-802.

_____. 1974. People in Predicament: A Study in Psychiatric and Psychosocial Epidemiology. *Soc. Psychiat.* 9:85-90.

Mazer, M., and Ahern, J. J. 1969. Personality and Social Class Position in Migration from an Island: The Implications for Psychiatric Illness. *Int. J. Soc. Psychiat.* 15:203-208.

McPartland, T. S., and Richart, R. H. 1966. Analysis of Readmissions to a Community Mental Health Center. *Comm. Ment. Health J.* 2:22-26.

Mead, George H. 1934. *Mind, Self, and Society.* Chicago: University of Chicago Press.

Mechanic, David. 1969. *Mental Health and Social Policy.* Englewood Cliffs, N. J.: Prentice-Hall.

Menninger, Karl A. 1952. *A Manual for Psychiatric Case Study.* New York: Grune and Stratton.

Merton, Robert K. 1957. *Social Theory and Social Structure.* New York: The Free Press.

Meyer, Adolf. 1948. *The Commonsense Psychiatry of Dr. Adolf Meyer.* Alfred Lief, ed. New York: McGraw-Hill.

Mezey, A. G. 1960. Psychiatric Aspects of Human Migrations. *Int. J. Soc. Psychiat.* 5:245-260.

Mintz, N. L., and Schwartz, D. T. 1964. Urban Ecology and Psychosis: Community Factors in the Incidence of Schizophrenia and Manic-Depression among Italians in Greater Boston. *Int. J. Soc. Psychiat.* 10:101-118.

Monahan, T. P. 1957. Family Status and the Delinquent Child: A Reappraisal and Some New Findings. *Social Forces* 35:250-258.

Murphy, H. B. M. 1965. Migration and the Major Mental Disorders: A Reappraisal, in Kantor, M. B., ed. *Mobility and Mental Health.* Springfield, Ill.: Charles C Thomas.

Nathanson, Constance A. 1975. Illness and the Feminine Role: A Theoretical Review. *Soc. Sci. and Med.* 9:57-62.

Nielsen, J., Juel-Nielsen, N., and Strömgren, E. 1965. A Five-Year Survey of a Psychiatric Service in a Geographically Demarcated Rural Population Given Easy Access to This Service. *Compreh. Psychiat.* 6:139-165.

NHS (National Health Survey). 1972. Vital and Health Statistics. Series 10, No. 75. Physician Visits: Volume and Interval since Last Visit. DHEW Publication No. (HSD) 72-1064. Washington, D.C.: U. S. Government Printing Office.

NYT (The New York Times), 1973. The Small Town: They Didn't Disappear After All. Nov. 11, 1973.

Ødegaard, Ørnulu. 1932. Emigration and Insanity: A Study of Mental Disease among the Norwegian-born Population of Minnesota. *Acta Psychiat. et Neurol.* Suppl. 4.

_____. 1946. Marriage and Mental Disease: A Study in Social Psychopathology. *J. Ment. Science* 92:35-59.

_____. 1975. Morbidity and Social Mobility in an Upper Class Educational Group. *Acta Psychiat. Scand.* 52:36-48.

Panum, Peter Ludwig. 1940. *Observations Made During the Epidemic of Measles on the Faroe Islands in the Year 1846.* New York: Delta Omega Society, American Public Health Association.

Parkes, C. M. 1964. Effects of Bereavement on Physical and Mental Health: A Study of the Medical Records of Widows. *Brit. Med. J.* 2:274-279.

Peterson, O. L., Andrews, L. P., Spain, R. G., and Greenberg, B. G. 1956. An Analytic Study of North Carolina General Practice, 1953-1954. *J. Med. Educ.* 31:1-165.

Phillips, D. L., and Segal, B. E. 1969. Sexual Status and Psychiatric Symptoms. *Am. Sociol. Rev.* 34:58-72.

Pickles, W. N. 1968. Epidemiology in Country Practice, in Pemberton, J., and Willard, H., eds. *Recent Studies in Epidemiology.* Oxford: Blackwell Scientific Publications.

Plunkett, R. J., and Gordon, J. E. 1960. *Epidemiology and Mental Illness.* New York: Basic Books.

Rawnsley, Kenneth. 1966. Congruence of Independent Measures of Psychiatric Morbidity. *J. Psychosom. Res.* 10:84-93.

Rogoff, Natalie. 1953. Recent Trends in Urban Occupational Mobility, in Bendix, R., and Lipset, S. M., eds. *Class, Status, and Power.* Glencoe, Ill.: The Free Press.

Rosanoff, A. J. 1917. Survey of Mental Disorders in Nassau County, New York, July-October, 1916. *Psychiat. Bull.* 2:109-231.

Roth, W. F., and Luton, F. W. 1943. The Mental Health Program in Tennessee. *Am. J. Psychiat.* 99:662-675.

Ryan, William. 1969. *Distress in the City: Essays on the Design and Administration of Urban Mental Health Services.* Cleveland, Ohio: Press of Case Western Reserve University.

Schlesinger, B. 1963. *The Multi-Problem Family.* Toronto: University of Toronto Press.

Scott, R., and Howard, A. 1970. Models of Stress, in Levine, S., and Scotch, N. A., eds. *Social Stress.* Chicago: Aldine.

Selzer, M. L., and Vinokur, A. 1974. Life Events, Subjective Stress, and Traffic Accidents. *Am. J. Psychiat.* 131:903-906.

Shaffer, J. W., Towns, W., Schmidt, C. W., Fisher, R. S., and Zlotowitz, H. I. 1974. Social Adjustment Profiles of Fatally Injured Drivers. *Arch. Gen. Psychiat.* 30:508-511.

Shepherd, M., and Gruenberg, E. M. 1957. The Age for Neuroses. *Milbank Mem. Fund Quart.* 35:258-265.

Shepherd, M., Cooper, B., Brown, A. C., and Kalton, G. W. 1966. *Psychiat-

ric Illness in General Practice. London: Oxford University Press.

Smith, Page. 1968. *As a City upon a Hill: The Town in American History.* New York: Alfred A. Knopf.

Sobel, Raymond. 1970. The Psychiatric Implications of Accidental Poisoning in Childhood. *Pediat. Clin. of North Am.* 17:653-685.

———. 1975. Personal communication.

Sohler, K. B., and Thompson, J. D. 1970. Jarvis' Law and the Planning of Mental Health Services: Influence of Accessibility, Poverty, and Urbanization on First Admissions to Connecticut State Hospitals. *Public Health Rep.* 85:503-510.

Spiegel, John P. 1959. Some Cultural Aspects of Transference and Counter Transference, in Masserman, J. H., ed. *Individual and Family Dynamics.* Vol. II of *Science and Psychoanalysis.* New York: Grune and Stratton.

Srole, L., Langner, T. S., Michael, S., Opler, M. K., and Rennie, T.A.C. 1962. *Mental Health in the Metropolis.* Vol. I of *The Midtown Manhattan Study.* New York: McGraw-Hill.

Stacey, Margaret. 1960. *Tradition and Change: A Study of Banbury.* London: Oxford University Press.

Sullivan, H. S. 1953. *The Interpersonal Theory of Psychiatry.* Perry, H. S., and Gawel, M. L, eds. New York: W. W. Norton.

Susser, Mervyn. 1968. *Community Psychiatry: Epidemiologic and Social Themes.* New York: Random House.

Susser, M. W., and Watson, W. 1971. *Sociology in Medicine.* London: Oxford University Press.

Sussman, M. B. 1959. The Isolated Nuclear Family: Fact or Fiction. *Social Problems* 6:333-340.

Taylor, James B. 1960. The General Practioner and the Emotionally Disturbed Patient: A Report on Five Washington Counties. Seattle, Wash.: Public Opinion Laboratory, University of Washington.

Thompson, Clara M. 1950. *Psychoanalysis: Evolution and Development.* New York: Hermitage House.

Tietze, C., Lemkau, P., and Cooper, M. 1942. Personality Disorder and Spatial Mobility. *Am. J. Sociol.* 48:29-39.

Tillich, Paul. 1952. *The Courage To Be.* New Haven: Yale University Press.

Tischler, G. L., Henisz, J. E., Myers, J. K., and Boswell, P. C. 1975a. Utilization of Mental Health Services: I. Patienthood and the Prevalence of Symptomatology in the Community. *Arch. Gen. Psychiat.* 32:411-415.

———. 1975b. Utilization of Mental Health Services: II. Mediators of Service Allocation. *Arch. Gen. Psychiat.* 32:416-418.

Tonge, W. L., Cammock, D. W., Winchester, J. S., and Winchester, E.N.M. 1961. Prevalence of Neuroses in Women. *Brit. J. Prev. Soc. Med.* 15:177-179.

Tranel, Ned. 1970. Rural Program Development, in Grunebaum, H., ed. *The Practice of Community Mental Health*. Boston: Little, Brown.

Uhlenhuth, E. H., Lipman, R. S., Balter, M. B., and Stern, M. 1974. Symptom Intensity and Life Stress in the City. *Arch. Gen Psychiat.* 31:759-764.

U. S. Bureau of the Census. 1961. Census of Population: 1960, General Population Characteristics, Massachusetts. Final Report PC (1)-23B. Washington, D.C.: U. S. Government Printing Office.

_____. 1961a. Census of Population: 1960, General Social and Economic Characteristics, Massachusetts. Final Report PC (1)-23C. Washington, D.C.: U. S. Government Printing Office.

_____. 1971. Census of Population: 1970, General Population Characteristics, Massachusetts. Final Report PC (1)-B23. Washington, D.C.: U. S. Government Printing Office.

_____. 1972. Census of Population: 1970, General Social and Economic Characteristics, Massachusetts. Final Report PC (1)-C23. Washington, D.C.: U. S. Government Printing Office.

_____. 1973. Statistical Abstract of the United States. 94th ed. Washington, D.C.: U. S. Government Printing Office.

Vobecky, J., Kelly, A., and Munan, L. 1972. Population Health Care Practices: An Epidemiology Study of Physician Visits, Hospital Admissions, and Drug Consumption. *Canad. J. Pub. Health* 63:304-310.

Warner, W. Lloyd. 1960. *Social Class in America*. New York: Harper and Brothers.

Waterston, J. F. C. 1965. Morbidity in a Country Practice. *J. Coll. Gen Practit.* 10:18-39.

Watts, C. A. H., Cawte, E. C., and Kuensberg, E. H. 1964. Survey of Mental Illness in General Practice. *Brit. Med. J.* 2:1351-1359.

Weil, Simone. 1955. *The Need for Roots*. Boston: Beacon Press.

West, James. 1945. *Plainville, U. S. A.* New York: Columbia University Press.

Willie, C. V., and Weinandy, J. 1963. The Structure and Composition of "Problem" and "Stable" Families in a Low Income Population. *Marr. and Fam. Living* 25:439-447.

Wing, L., Bramley, C., Hailey, A., and Wing, J. L. 1968. Camberwell Cumulative Case Register. Part I: Aims and Methods. *Soc. Psychiat.* 3:116-123.

WTI (*Webster's Third New International Dictionary of the English Language*). 1961. Unabridged. Springfield, Mass.: G. and C. Merriam.

Young, M., and Willmott, P. 1957. *Family and Kinship in East London*. London: Routledge and Kegan Paul.

Index

Einstein, Albert, 43
Elderly people, 185, 199
Employment, 18-19, 53-54
Epidemiology, 88, 89, 95

Familial clustering of predicaments,
100, 156-161
Families: broken homes, 68; dysfunctional, 69; income of, in 1969, 76-77;
multiproblem or predicament, 156-161
Family life, 68-72, 77
Family network study, 70-72
Family practice. *See* General practice
Family size, "old American" and Portuguese, 72
Family types, 69-70, 246
Females: awareness of distress, 93, 95,
152, 153, 154; migration and disorder,
124, 125; psychiatric treatment of,
124-127; premarital pregnancy, 127;
children in care of, 127-128; parapsychiatric experiences, 140,
152-153, 255, 256, 257, 260; social
class and predicaments, 143-146;
rates of disorder, 250, 252, 254, 259
Fines by court, 144, 145, 146, 157, 255-
258
Freud, Sigmund, 121
Funding of services, 191, 208-211

General practice, psychiatric disorder
in, 111-120, 249-251; by estimate, 115;
by age, diagnosis, and sex, 117, 250;
by marital status and social class
position, 118, 251; compared with
psychiatric practice, 138-141; referrals from, 139; research method, 249-
250
General practice surveys: Great Britain,
112, 113, 114, 119; Norway, 112, 113,
115, 119; North America, 112-115;
Nova Scotia, 113; French Canada,
113, 114; Martha's Vineyard, 114-120,
249-251
Group work, preventive, 193-195

Head Start Program, 187

Health-seeking behavior, 92, 127
Helping Hand, 183, 185, 186, 200-201
Hollingshead occupational categories,
106, 243
Homemaker Service, 183, 198-199
Home visits, 220
Households: by rate of predicaments,
156-161; by size and type, 243, 246
Human predicaments. *See* Predica-
ments
Human services network, 173, 180, 182-
189

Income. *See* Economic problems
Indian population, 20, 66

Jail: as predicament, 104; rates of sen-
tencing to, 255-258
Justice, system of. *See* Courts
Juvenile delinquency: recognition
process in, 92-93; as predicament,
104; rates of, 255-258

Kluckhohn-Strodtbeck values instrument, 247

Law. *See* Courts
Lawyers, in system of justice, 34-35
Leadership, community, 73-75
Legislation, role of citizens, 36
Locals, 31-32

Males: psychiatric treatment of, 124,
127, 129-131, 250, 252, 254; social
class and predicaments, 143-146, 148;
parapsychiatric experiences, 152-
153, 255, 256, 257, 259, 260
Marijuana, and court, 33
Marital choices, 27
Marital dissolution, 104, 255-258
Marital status: and disorder, 135, 136,
253, 255-258; of islanders, 242-243,
245
Martha's Vineyard Community Services, Inc. *See* Community Services
Martha's Vineyard Mental Health Center. *See* Mental Health Center